HOW GOVERNMENT EXPERTS SELF-SABOTAGE

THE LANGUAGE OF THE REBUFFED

HOW GOVERNMENT EXPERTS SELF-SABOTAGE

THE LANGUAGE OF THE REBUFFED

CHRISTIANE GERBLINGER

Australian
National
University

ANU PRESS

Australian
National
University

ANU PRESS

Published by ANU Press
The Australian National University
Canberra ACT 2600, Australia
Email: anupress@anu.edu.au

Available to download for free at press.anu.edu.au

ISBN (print): 9781760465414
ISBN (online): 9781760465421

WorldCat (print): 1348276255
WorldCat (online): 1348275956

DOI: 10.22459/HGESS.2022

Printed by Lightning Source
ingramcontent.com/publishers-page/environmental-responsibility

Cover design and layout by ANU Press

This book is published under the aegis of the Public Policy Editorial Board
of ANU Press.

Contents

Abbreviations

ABC	Australian Broadcasting Corporation
AEMO	Australian Energy Market Operator
ALP	Australian Labor Party
APS	Australian Public Service
CIA	Central Intelligence Agency
DEE	Department of Environment and Energy
DIO	Defence Intelligence Organisation
DLO	Departmental Liaison Officer
FOI	freedom of information
GST	goods and services tax
HIP	Home Insulation Program
IAEA	International Atomic Energy Agency
InCiSE Index	International Civil Service Effectiveness Index
ONA	Office of National Assessments
PJCAAD	Parliamentary Joint Committee on ASIO, ASIS and DSD
PM&C	Department of the Prime Minister and Cabinet
PMO	Prime Minister's Office
QTB	Question Time Brief
SA	South Australia
UK	United Kingdom
UN	United Nations
UNMOVIC	United Nations Monitoring, Verification and Inspection Commission

UNSC	United Nations Security Council
UNSCOM	United Nations Special Commission
US	United States
WMD	weapons of mass destruction

Acknowledgements

For their time, close engagement and encouragement, I am indebted to Joan Leach, Sujatha Raman and John Uhr.

I would not have been able to write this book without the generous support of the Sir Roland Wilson Foundation, a scholarship fund set up in partnership with the Australian Public Service to study and develop public policy in Australia and overseas. I am particularly grateful to the foundation's board and its staff.

During my time in the Netherlands, I was pleased to spend several weeks at the Nederlandse School voor Openbaar Bestuur (Netherlands School of Public Administration) and am particularly grateful to Paul Frissen and Eline van Schaik for their interest and help.

I would also like to thank my Dutch interviewees in The Hague for their valuable time and participation: Michèle Blom, Michel Groothuizen, Peter Hennephof and Frans Leeuw. In Australia, I am grateful to Ken Henry and Paul McCullough for their thoughtful insights and for so readily offering their time.

I am also thankful to many others for their help: Michael Brennan, Gerard Castles, Jenet Connell, Carol Croce, Ted Crook, Frances Cruickshank, Michael di Francesco, Grant Douglas, Peter Grabosky, Angelia Grant, John Halligan, Lin Hatfield Dodds, Bea Hogan, Rob Hoppe, Maja Horst, Justine Molony, Richard Mulgan, Beryl Radin, Brian Rappert, Ian Shepherd, Paul 't Hart, Martijn van der Steen and Stavros Zouridis.

Finally, thank you to the fantastic Andrew Kennedy, chair of the Public Policy Editorial Board of ANU Press, for seeing this manuscript through to completion.

Acknowledgement must also be made to the following, in which parts of this work first appeared:

Chapter 2 ('Strategies of Impersonality: Constructing a Framework for the Rebuffed') draws on material from an earlier article, 'Peep Show: A Framework for Watching How Evidence Is Communicated inside Policy Organisations', published in *Evidence & Policy: A Journal of Research, Debate and Practice* on 14 February 2022, and reproduced with permission of the Licensor through PLSclear.

Chapter 4 ('Excess of Objectivity: Australian Intelligence Assessments of Iraq's Weapons of Mass Destruction') draws on material from an earlier article, 'Waiting for Advice That Is Beyond Doubt: Uncertainty as Australia's Reason to Join the Invasion of Iraq', published in volume 37, no. 1 (2022) of *Intelligence and National Security*, pp. 109–25.

A much abbreviated overview of this book's findings also appeared on 27 April 2021 as a post called 'Are Experts Complicit in Making Their Advice Easy for Politicians to Ignore?' on the *LSE Impact Blog*.

List of Tables

Preface

This book is about how a particular group of experts communicates its knowledge. These experts did not come to my attention by way of a single sensational event. Indeed, while fascinating, they mostly fly under the radar of public consciousness. I did not chance on them by fortuitous accident, nor did I discover them through diligent preliminary research. I already knew them because I had worked with them for more than 15 years.

During my time with the Australian Public Service, I worked on national security issues, particularly those related to intelligence; I served as a policy adviser across a range of portfolios, such as counter-proliferation, energy, health and rural policy; and I wrote a seemingly endless stream of speeches for political and policy actors in an economic portfolio. In one way or another, many of these policy settings nudge the case studies examined in this book, yet I did not work on any of them myself. As such, I cannot claim to offer direct ethnographic insights. Spending a significant portion of my working life immersed in the language and culture of this special type of knowledge production meant, however, that I was able to weed out secondary material that could lend external validation to my own experiences inside the administration. But, more than that, my experiences, observations and conversations with a sizeable number of colleagues gave me confidence that being rebuffed was not an isolated incident and that the language of policy advisers was a kind of practised, hemmed-in expression of expertise.

When researching and drafting this book, it quickly became apparent that there was more than one type of language that ended in rebuffal; there were several. I have identified three types here, but there are probably more, in these and other policy settings, each of them tailored to their circumstances. Future researchers are likely to find a trove of typologies from across international public policy and administrative fields. Beyond my group of experts, there may be other areas of expertise that also communicate in ways that end in some form of rejection. Climate change science, the promotion of genetically modified food, vaccine advocacy, skin cancer education and anti-gun campaigning come to mind as immediate candidates. *Are they, like the rebuffed expert policy advisers in this book, also implicated in their own rejection?* There will be other, less obvious and therefore probably more interesting areas to uncover for researchers across several different academic disciplines, particularly those interested in knowledge production and communication, such as science and technology studies, policy and governance studies, behavioural science, anthropology, sociolinguistics and organisational sociology.

As I finalised this book halfway through 2021, the world was still traversing a global pandemic. Many of the successes associated with stemming the spread of Covid-19 may well have been due to receptive governments listening to cogent experts. But I suggest that any post-pandemic world— if such can be said to lie ahead—is likely to feature similar challenges to those described here. I therefore challenge experts themselves—whether academic or professional—to find instances of 'rebuffal' in their own areas of work. These readers can take the rebuffed and use them to reflect on others' practices or, indeed, their own. But research and professional (self-) reflection imply that observing the rebuffed is more or less the domain of, well, experts. I do not think this is where the rebuffed should stay. I want them to be watched, chided and encouraged by those who are ultimately affected by their language: 'everyday' readers or the public. Despite political rhetoric about including the public in policymaking, publics are mostly sidelined or ignored when final decisions are made. But publics do try to become involved, such as through submissions to parliament or policy reviews, or simply by writing letters to their government representatives. For example, I was told a few years ago that, during a nine-month period, one portfolio received nearly 18,000 separate items of correspondence, which predominantly included letters from the public. Another portfolio, which regularly publishes its own research, received more than 1 million unique online page views for one of its pieces, while another annual publication can receive more than 4 million views. These numbers point to the existence of intense interest in matters of governance well beyond the media, business and the academy.

In an environment that values them in word but not necessarily in deed, it should not be difficult for interested publics to understand the advice that goes to governments as the ostensible base (or not) of policy decisions. This book is not a manual for how to make it easier. It is, as Foucault puts it, 'a challenge directed to what is' (1991: 84). In challenging what is—no matter who is in power—it also seeks to elevate the critical contribution that courageous policy advisers could make towards helping publics determine what is in their interest. If it succeeds in doing so, it will be up to those who agree to take the next steps.

1

Introduction

Locating the phenomenon of rebuffed advice

After official policy advice to governments is publicly released, governments are often accused of ignoring or rejecting their experts. Commonly represented as politicisation, this depiction is superficial. Digging deeper, is there something about the official advice itself that makes it easy to ignore? This book asks: does the expert advice of policy officials feature characteristics that invite its government audience to overlook or misread it? To answer this, I critically examine official policy advice and find the language of the rebuffed: expert advisers reluctant to disclose what they know to accommodate political circumstances.

Perhaps one of the more infamous international cases of advice thus rebuffed is the United Kingdom's mid-1990s bovine spongiform encephalopathy (BSE) crisis, in which Ministry of Agriculture, Fisheries and Food advice to slaughter affected animals was not adequately disclosed by civil service advisers (Jasanoff 1997) and was ignored by their minister (Millstone and van Zwanenberg 2001). In a case involving a district government in Indonesia in 2003, advice related to ecological preservation was ignored because government actors—perhaps not always unreasonably—'believe that they understand the solutions better than the researcher' (Dharmawan et al. 2017: 409). In the United States in 2018, the White House ignored expert advice from the Department of Health and Human Services that separations of children and parents at the border would do psychological harm (Colby 2018) and violate migrants' civil and human rights (Shuchart 2018).

In Australia—a Westminster-style jurisdiction from which this book draws its cases—the phenomenon appears to be growing in frequency. Here, we have seen the commissioning of two major reviews of the tax system (in 2008 and 2015), with both largely swept under the carpet and cast as failures (Benson 2018b; Hodgson 2015, respectively). In 2009, advice about the risks surrounding the so-called Home Insulation Program was allegedly ignored, with the program terminated when it led to the deaths of four young installers (Padula 2017; McGhee and McKinnon 2018). The subsequent government called a royal commission into the program, with the new prime minister then ignoring the advice of his government solicitors not to break Cabinet confidentiality by forcing the previous government to release related Cabinet papers (McGhee and McKinnon 2018). In 2018, the Australian Government also rebuffed advice by one of its security agencies to return refugees to the island detention centres from which they had been medically evacuated on completion of treatment on the Australian mainland so it could continue to claim the refugees posed a security threat (Middleton 2019). In 2019, advice recommending allocation of sports funding to regional Australian communities was ignored in favour of the responsible minister's favoured electorates (ANAO 2020). This is by no means an exhaustive list, but each example is symptomatic of the phenomenon of rebuffal.

This book's focus is on where the effectiveness of such advice comes to be established: during expert policy advisers' construction and communication of advice, and its reception and use by government ministers. Stepping through these junctures, I suggest, demonstrates the argumentation of policy advisers is almost exclusively information-focused, intentionally incomplete or so neutral as to evade stable meaning. While this is at least outwardly due to advisers' commitment to notions of objectivity and political responsiveness, it also arises from knowing they could be rebuffed, because they fear clarity will damn them or because they recoil from exercising judgement in the face of risk or uncertainty—all of which is cloaked in the language of evidence to maintain an appearance of responsive expertise. This is not to say that all evidence is powerless, but a language of evidence is incomplete and cannot persuade all by itself. It also casts in rather a different light the regular refrain of evidence-based, evidence-informed or evidence-inspired policy among public policy circles.

It is difficult to imagine that civil servants have not noticed this is how their advice is constructed and used. Indeed, Boswell and Corbett (2015) describe a cynicism and even stoicism among policy elites that suggest an intense awareness of, and frustration with, the way policy is made. Yet, the status quo largely prevails, which implies that maintaining this style of advising makes them participants in their own rebuffal. With this, they have essentially institutionalised the provision of unproductive advice. One might go so far as to suggest they are complicit in their own marginalisation, as if advice were being written with an underlying invitation to 'rebuff me if you need to'. This does not simply contribute to the erosion of their integrity as policy experts, it also weakens policy advice as a tool with which to legitimately govern democracy. That is, if public institutions, whose role it is to furnish governments with thorough, unmistakable and relevant information, are not doing so, there is no record and, thus, no accountability for tracing how political decisions are made. The result is effectively the same as concealment—that is, despite proceeding in relatively plain view, advice is articulated in a language that tries its best to blend into the background. Advice of a sort is being given, 'facts' are being provided and evaluative and accountability measures are being observed, but meaning and views are invisible and cannot be critically interpreted. What one ends up with is policy advice as a political token or plaything, symbolising facts and evidence but uninterpretable by most—and, therefore, paradoxically, infinitely interpretable.

My central argument—that the language of such advice evades stable meaning and diminishes the democratic right of citizens to scrutinise the work of government—is on the grandiose side, certainly. If we want to determine whether expert advisers are holding back their knowledge, we need to be able to see the policy stories behind some of the examples above. But gaining a detailed understanding of the daily workings of organisations, particularly how their employees communicate their knowledge to each other and their superiors, can be a 'problematic enterprise' (Alvesson 2003: 13). This is perhaps especially the case in relation to policy advisers inside civil services. As Wagenaar suggests, 'we know surprisingly little about what the work of public administrators entails' (2004: 643). Rhodes concurs, observing they 'have been studied rarely' (2005: 5). Wagenaar continues that, on the one hand, critical appraisals are 'remarkably silent on the actual activities of administrators', while on the other, relevant textbooks 'largely ignore the sociology of administrative work' (2004: 643).

To be sure, there are mountains of scholarly work on policymaking and there are, indeed, some studies that provide insights into how policy advisers in service to governments communicate in some of their day-to-day dealings (Heclo and Wildavsky 1974; Mackie 2015; Stevens 2011). There is also research, largely in the interpretive tradition, that has examined the communications of policy advisers, but this broadly occurs at a theoretical level (Schmidt 2008), where policy and political communication are grouped and not viewed as separate entities (Hajer 1993), or to demonstrate how policy analysts (that is, analysts in the field of policy studies) should argue when making their case (Fischer 2003). When the impact of expert advice on government decision-making is considered, the focus is generally on scientific advisers (Boswell 2009; Cairney and Oliver 2017; Moore 2017; Wynne 1989). Overall, scholarly writing on policy tends to be quite targeted, such as on policy advising during the digital governance era (Marando and Craft 2017) or the public profiles of senior civil servants (Grube 2014a, 2015), or on the degrees to which evidence can or should be incorporated into policy (Head and Di Francesco 2019; Howlett and Wellstead 2011; Nair and Howlett 2017; Sanderson 2009).

All in all, gaining a detailed understanding of how official policy workers routinely communicate their knowledge to governments has largely been an under-researched area, at least in the English-speaking world (De Vries et al. 2010; Eriksson 2016; Hoppe and Jeliazkova 2006). This relative absence of study is due partly to the difficulty of accessing government policy advisers (Williams 2010), and to the fact that most of their advice to governments remains confidential. But it also stems from the fact that most of their advice to governments is being increasingly withdrawn from public accessibility, with Goldfarb (2009: 58) arguing 'the government has claimed more privacy for its actions but has provided the citizenry with less'. While Goldfarb writes in the US context, a similar situation can be observed in Australia, where requests for government information are on the rise and compliance with those requests by government departments is down (Australian Government 2019: 14).

Of course, the officials of public administrations and public or civil services serving executive governments are regularly reviewed or on view—for example, in royal commissions and parliamentary inquiries, during audits or parliamentary hearings where they account for outputs like policy advice. Yet most of these appearances can be characterised more by confining information than by its clear presentation. Although some inquiry processes have yielded insights into culture, becoming more cognisant of the way policy advice to governments is argued by policy workers at the coalface, as it were, does not appear to be an easily achievable task. Indeed, it is practically a given that government advisers advise impenetrably. But the popular narrative of impulsive governments ignoring the well-reasoned expertise of their policy workers only scratches the surface. Much more is at work here, because the language of official policy advisers enables certain affordances, serving as a kind of springboard from which to launch political manoeuvres. That is, it leaves political actors free to not just ignore but also reinterpret the offerings of their policy advisers as greenlighting any and all policy directions because those offerings are expressed in ways that render meaning malleable.

Given the central position of public accountability in democratic governments, one might reason that understanding how policy advisers to such governments go about the business of communicating their policy expertise should not be an arduous or prohibitive process. Further, in an ever more contestable policy environment in which citizens themselves are assigned only restricted roles in the decision-making process, they should be able to observe better than they do now how expert policy knowledge is produced and argued on their behalf. They should be able to know why and how some advice succeeds in convincing its political audience. They might also reasonably ask why and how it does not, particularly when one of its aims is to present the best available evidence. Indeed, instances of policy advice failing to convince may be particularly germane to those very citizens whose interests are thought to be at least nominally represented in that advice. If citizens cannot do any of these things, control of the government is not in the hands of the governed (Gruber 1987: 1). Further, if policy advice is being constructed in ways that curb this control, advisers risk appearing complicit in neglecting the democratic needs of citizens.

When public institutions furnish governments with such advice, interested publics are effectively excluded from gaining accurate impressions of how decisions are made on their behalf. Following Dewey, much as others have in staking out claims for more open, cooperative forms of deliberation (Forester 2012; Minteer 2005; Sanderson 2009; Wagenaar 2004), I argue that only in being able to judge and assess policy rationales can they assemble a picture of what is in their interest. Yet, far from helping assemble that picture, the language of the rebuffed seems designed to break it up.

Case studies and book structure

This book examines three Australian case studies, which are drawn from three streams of written knowledge production across the Australian Public Service (APS): the economy, energy and the environment, and national security. They have been chosen due to their originally confidential nature but eventual public availability by means of freedom of information (FOI) requests and a parliamentary inquiry. Examining advice destined predominantly for ministers' eyes makes it possible to observe, as closely as publicly possible and with some qualifications in mind, how policy advisers communicate when executing one of their core roles: supporting the government of the day to deliver its policy agendas and priorities. The first case study—on policy advice regarding the taxation of investment properties given in the leadup to an election—is discussed as a kind of abridged blueprint to help us construct a framework with which to interrogate the language of the rebuffed and the conditions under which it is produced. Two further and more exhaustive case studies drawn from distinctly different policy areas across the past two decades are then juxtaposed using this framework: advice about a 2016 statewide electricity blackout event blamed on renewable energy and Australia's intelligence assessments in the leadup to the 2003 Iraq war. Each will form one chapter, with chapters on the blackout and Iraq making up a major component of this book, and each is divided into smaller sections dealing with aspects of my framework.

A brief note on the selection of these cases is in order. Although the simple fact of their availability (the first two by FOI, the third by parliamentary review) played a role in their selection, my ultimate choices were based on the fact they brought with them the visibility of policy advice and political reaction. This was essential given it would be difficult, if not impossible, to be rebuffed without first offering something. By seeing both offer and retort, it is possible to distinguish a performative pattern in which advice has the repeated perlocutionary effect of either irritating or polarising its political audience. Seeing both offer and retort, therefore, makes it possible to identify that advice has been rebuffed, rather than having simply been considered but set aside. Moreover, to understand how advice is rebuffed as an act in which advisers participate, I chose advice that grappled with uncomfortable knowledge to observe how policy advisers communicated when they anticipated the likelihood of a negative political reaction. This, I hope to show by way of my three case studies, is the environment in which rebuffed government policy advice is generated. To test my findings, Chapter 5 discusses cases of politically accepted advice as the language of the 'unrebuffed'.

Chapter 2 briefly details my first case study on the Australian Treasury's advice about income tax deductions facilitated by investing in property (known as 'negative gearing'). Provided to the government in 2016, this advice followed an early election announcement by the opposition Australian Labor Party (ALP) of a policy to restrict how homeowning property investors could minimise their income tax burden. The conservative Coalition government called this the most 'destructive policy ever proposed', which would lead to 'mum and dad investors' being forced out of the housing investment market. Emphasising the financial mayhem this would wreak, the government also projected the ALP's policy change would reap a mere $600 million over four years. Two years later, in 2018, an FOI request by a news outlet seeking Treasury's 2016 advice on the issue found the agency had confirmed the ALP's claims that its proposed reforms would 'increase revenue in the long run between $3.4 and $3.9 billion a year' and 'the limit on negative gearing for established property would not differentiate between more or less wealthy investors'. At first glance, Treasury's advice was ignored. By carefully avoiding the political context and practising 'strategies of impersonality' (Porter 1995: 229), policy advisers constructed their advice in a way that would protect them from key political contexts. The political retort to this advice was the treasurer entrenching the government's existing policy further.

Given the gap in research on the confidential communications of public policy advisers, I construct a new framework from this short case study with which to trace the conditions under which policy advisers construct and communicate their advice, and how government ministers receive and use that advice. Briefly, this framework will unpeel three layers that encase policy advice: the rhetoric of its text, the organisational aspects of its micro-context and the international comparisons suggested by its macro-context—each of them revealing an aspect of policy language. For example, by closely analysing the text itself, I will observe the rhetorical construction of advice and its relationship to time and timing, context, framing and self-perception. The micro-context focuses on the institutional, legislative, bureaucratic and cultural effects and burdens on advisers' language, drawing much of its supporting literature from organisational and administrative studies. The macro-context connects to a much larger sphere of ideas around bureaucracy, objectivity, rationality and evidence, both in Australia and internationally. By interrogating case studies with the help of my tripartite framework, I hope to demonstrate that policy language is more than words on a page; it is a complex arrangement of tracks from which one can deduce the settings under which this expert community weakens its own credibility.

The second case study, detailed in Chapter 3, chronicles advice released under FOI by the departments of the Prime Minister and Cabinet and Environment and Energy after a statewide power blackout in South Australia in late 2016. To accommodate misleading government rhetoric about wind energy as a *bête noire* and cause of the blackout, this advice sidestepped any mention of renewable energy and climate change, thereby expunging discord and uncertainty (Rayner 2012) and giving the appearance of certainty and solid evidence. It also gave the impression of being both objective and responsive to the government by frequently issuing damage status updates, but little else. My framework here makes possible some critical discoveries. For example, one finds a widespread anticipatory compliance—a dynamic that, because government actors did not ask policy experts about deeper arguments and rationales, saw policy experts not offer them or discuss them among themselves (at least on paper). Policy advisers became entirely transactional, functioning as vendors of rudimentary information, perhaps because the only advice they could provide objectively and responsively was on the status of storm damage. Official advice was intentionally ambiguous, deliberately one-dimensional and unknowing even while political hyperbole was at its most strident; it spoke a language of 'knowing what not to know' (Taussig 1999: 2).

Chapter 4 discusses my third case study, which considers Australian intelligence assessments of Iraq's weapons of mass destruction (WMD) between 2002 and 2003. The assessments by Australia's then Office of National Assessments (ONA) and Defence Intelligence Organisation (DIO) represent political responsiveness and detached neutrality when they are pursued separately. Within the text, the DIO presented as highly objective in its repeated acknowledgements of uncertainty and gaps in the available evidence, and revealed a lack of consensus, offering an almost textbook study of how to present evidence impartially. John Howard, Australia's prime minister at the time, turned this element of doubt into strength in that it helped him demerit mounting arguments that absolute proof was needed before invading Iraq. The ONA, on the other hand, became increasingly responsive by falling into line with the dominant political discourse. Even while neither was used by the government and both were later blamed as failures of intelligence, their inconsistency and 'excess of objectivity' (Sarewitz 2004: 388) channelled an uncertainty that contributed to a highly effective political strategy.

My penultimate chapter will discuss some contemporaneous Australian examples of unrebuffed policy advice: amendments to Australian citizenship, marriage equality and the legal basis for military action in Iraq. Here, I consider whether the policy language conveyed features associated with successful advisers, such as openness to adaptation, a culture of curiosity and comfort with uncertainty (Luetjens and 't Hart 2019: 28). Is this the language of the unrebuffed? Or were additional, or entirely different, factors at play here? These examples, which follow a document-led approach, are juxtaposed with two short comparisons using a different methodology to test my findings. Following Rhodes's (2018) suggestion to take up 'bricolage' as part of a menu of tools when undertaking qualitative research, I will briefly consider interviews I conducted with Australian policy advisers reflecting on the introduction of a consumption tax in the late 1990s, as well as Dutch policy actors who worked on prison reforms throughout much of the 2000s. These show us another style of policy advising with which to test my hypothesis. A conclusion will consider how both the public and the public interest are excluded by the type of policy advice examined in this book. Envisioned by pragmatist John Dewey (1946: 208, 218) as denoting either oligarchy or soliloquy, such advice helps normalise policy advisory environments in which civil servants neglect the democratic need of the governed to understand why they are governed in particular ways and not others.

The language of policy advice

Let us now consider why I have chosen language as the locus from which to study rebuffed policy advice. Policy language is not easy to pin down. Like the rhetoric of politics and expertise, the language of policy advisers seeks legitimation by being agreed to. In a political context, the rhetoric of government leaders is said to be both central to 'the practice of modern government itself' and integral to 'the way we are governed' (Grube 2013: 3), while 'establishing oneself as an expert entails a judgment from an audience that is contingent on a rhetorical effort' (Hartelius 2008: 3). Although the rhetorics of politics and of expertise contrive to be noticed, the language of policy advice appears to aspire to authority through dullness. Rather than provoking inspiration or engagement, its flatness seems to discourage this. This does not mean policy language is less premeditated than political rhetoric, nor that it contains only univocal content. As Majone (1989: 1) has suggested, policy is 'made of language' and its contents can be understood as expressions of organisational realities (Alvesson and Kärreman 2000), such as institutional and subcultural constraints, expectations and circumstances.

Underpinning this view is an understanding of language as 'more than reflect[ing] what we take to be reality' (Fischer and Gottweis 2012: 8)— not simply as 'assertions about the world of "things"' (Shapiro 1981: 26), but also as a particular kind of argumentation determined by one's world view. How policy advice is argued and argued about is at the crux of any endeavour to examine its influence—or lack thereof. The idea that language is a construction that has much to tell us about how its users view the world also sheds light, in the institutional settings I will observe, on how its users think their political audience would like to view the world. As Michael Shapiro continues: 'Insofar as we do not invent language or meanings in our typical speech, we end up buying into a model of political relations in almost everything we say without making a prior, deliberative evaluation of the purchasing decision' (1981: 231).

Following Shapiro, Frank Fischer (2003: 43) concludes that, in the world of policy, 'given that the languages of politics inscribe the meanings of a policy problem, public policy is not expressed in words, it is literally "constructed" through the language(s) in which it is described'.

David Farmer's (1995: 19) work on the language of public administration offers the view that

> we are condemned to see the world through the eyeglasses of a language. We cannot escape from the lens of language. We can see the world only in terms of some conceptual system, some perspective. Public administration is no different in this respect.

There are thus powerfully influential, premade grooves along which the language of policy advisers within public administrations comes to be conceived of, delivered and heard. In addition to the grooves and frames provided by politics, policy language is also shaped by the educational backgrounds of its speakers and by the organisational enculturation (Srivastava and Goldberg 2017) that takes place while working inside government and policy institutions. These may not be as separate as they sound. When policy analysts or advisers come to public policy employment, they are often equipped with tertiary qualifications from the social sciences and will usually already speak at least a rudimentary version of the language of evidence or rationality (Dryzek 1993; Fischer 2003; McCloskey 1994).[1] When they enter the work environment, the language that is spoken and rewarded there takes great pains to express itself as neutrally and free of value or emotion as possible, underpinned by the vernacular of social science methodologies (Porter 1995; Stone 1997), favouring the epistemological status of statements that sound like science over those that sound like value judgements (Farmer 1995). This depiction makes policy workers sound like robots. They are not, and we will see some instances to the contrary. However, the pervasive influence of precepts and organisational ethos on policy knowledge and construction should not be underestimated.

Commentary and scholarship on the ingrained rigidity of bureaucratic or policy language are hardly new—think of George Orwell's 'Politics and the English Language' (1946), Herbert Marcuse's *One-Dimensional Man* (1964) or Murray Edelman's *Political Language* (1977). Such work centres largely on the way bureaucratese impoverishes language. A better place from which to understand the language of rebuffed and 'rebuffable' policy advisers is Deborah Stone's *Policy Paradox*, which criticises policy advice that 'cherishes argument by fact and logic, and canonizes the scientific method of discovery. It drives a search for neutral facts, unbiased techniques, and disinterested conclusions' (Stone 1997: 304).

Stone argues that, even though 'language does matter',

> most proponents of rational decision models either ignore or deny it. Theorists of rationality tend to believe that … framing effects of language are a distortion of rational thinking, and that a purely rational decision is based on objective consequences of actions, somehow purified of the poetic impact of words. (Stone 1997: 17, 248, 249)

This way of conceiving of policy—as a rational endeavour producing neutral information—is at odds with the world of politics, which is idiosyncratic and unpredictable, and 'a type of policy analysis that does

---

1   Advertisements announcing senior positions at the Australian Treasury, for instance, typically call for applicants with tertiary qualifications in economics, law, business, finance, commerce, public policy, political science and/or mathematics (see 'Current Vacancies', available from: careers.tspace. gov.au/cw/en/listing/).

not make room for the centrality of ambiguity in politics can be of little use in the real world' (Stone 1997: 157). As such, the purported presentation of evidence clothed in the language of neutral facts is likely to have very little effect. Indeed, due to the centrality of ambiguity and the social nature of manufacturing information in the real world, 'there can be no neutral facts' (Stone 1997: 308). Expecting policy advice that clings to the trappings of neutrality to successfully compete with such a multiplicity of interpretations and contingencies is therefore doomed to fail when it insists on inoculating 'facts' from the social construction of language—and politics.

Giandomenico Majone (1989: 21) charts the development of policy advice as marked by 'decisionism', which projects

> the image of technical, nonpartisan problem solvers who map out the alternatives open to the policymaker and evaluate their consequences by means of mathematical models or other objective techniques of analysis. The analyst's job is only to determine the best means to achieve given goals. He must be neutral about ends, since discussion of goals and values is necessarily subjective and unscientific. Analysis that aspires to be objective and scientific can deal only with factual statements.

This image, Majone suggests, is misguided because policy analysts or advisers should be

> producer[s] of policy arguments, more similar to a lawyer—a specialist in legal arguments—than to an engineer or a scientist. His basic skills are not algorithmical but argumentative: the ability to probe assumption critically, to produce and evaluate evidence, to keep many threads in hand, to draw an argument from many disparate sources, to communicate effectively. He recognizes that to say anything of importance in public policy requires value judgements, which must be explained and justified. (Majone 1989: 21–22)

However, the reality is that, as 'firm believer[s] in the virtues of the scientific method' (Majone 1989: 36), policy advisers will generally not produce arguments in the manner suggested. This adherence to scientism is a mistake, in Majone's (1989: 37) estimation, because '[i]n policy analysis, as in science and in everyday reasoning, few arguments are purely rational or purely persuasive. A careful blend of reason and persuasion is usually more effective than exclusive reliance on one or the other.'

Majone's 'reason and persuasion' might also be understood in terms of Sheila Jasanoff and Hilton Simmet's (2017: 763) 'facts' and 'values'— as two parts of a whole that invites broadly accepted truths. While Majone is clear about his preferred disposition for policy analysts, he acknowledges that most are still stuck in a rationalist, decisionist model of producing and articulating advice, which we will see lives on in the reform pronouncements to be considered shortly.

More than 20 years later, far from seeing the integration of reason and persuasion, or facts and values, Frank Fischer and Herbert Gottweis (2012: 3) find the 'traditional approaches—often technocratic in nature'—to constructing policy advice have not only prevailed, but have also visibly 'proven inadequate or have failed'. In their telling, technocratic approaches have continued to dominate as inputs to government decision-making, with the Global Financial Crisis in 2008 and the Fukushima nuclear disaster in 2011 among the more recent high-profile cases (Fischer and Gottweis 2012: 4). The language of policy advice thus represents an interesting dilemma. On the one hand, its mode of expressing itself— neutral, technocratic, factual—continues to be practised and is therefore likely to still be viewed as relatively authoritative. Perhaps it once was; perhaps it still is sometimes. The rhetoric of bureaucratic policy reformers in Australia certainly implies this, as we shall see.

On the other hand, there is a sense that its credibility, along with that of expertise more generally, is under siege (Nichols 2017; Thompson 2016). In shorthand, this state is usually expressed as post-truth, which casts experts as fragile or ignored. This reading would certainly account for the fact the policy experts observed in this book are rebuffed—the swell of populist politics in the halls of government across many democracies has seen to that. At first glance, this seems a valid judgement. Yet, I argue there has been no discernible change in the way policy advisers express themselves, and it is precisely the way they have always expressed themselves that has led to their complex and self-administered rebuffal. In other words, the traditional approach of expecting the language of policy advice to be somehow more influential than other, louder voices without incorporating facts and values, reason and persuasion will only hasten its own irrelevance. The image of the once-powerful policy adviser now fallen on hard times signals neither a transformation in the way policy advice is now regarded nor a lamentable death of expertise. Instead, in the worlds of my case studies, it signals the rigidity of the policy advisory system and its institutions, as well as advisers' inability or unwillingness to exercise judgement when faced with difficult or uncertain facts, favouring a retreat behind apparently neutral evidence.

When policy advisers retreat from exercising judgement and cling to the reassuring language of evidence, their approach is not merely inadequate, it ventures into the unethical. In his study on prudential public leadership, John Uhr (2015: 4) argues:

> Public administration emerges in the space between the people and their chosen political representatives, with democratic constitutions making space for systems of public administration as mediators between politicians and the people—mediators trusted to use their administrative powers to protect the public interest.

Because they are mediators balancing the two constituent parts of democracy, public officials 'work in environments of trust', where trust 'is a good test of credibility' and 'a powerful source of ethics' (Uhr 2015: 187). This kind of trust

> really means *public* trust, requiring officials to justify the public benefits of careful balancing of degrees of loyalty (often expected by the political executive) and independence (often expected in some degree by the legislature) consistent with the constitutional norms of the governance system. (Uhr 2015: 187)

To be seen to act ethically is to balance the two, but, to be able to do that, officials need to use 'their best judgment' (Uhr 2015: 187). It will become clear that this kind of judgement is not present in my case studies—not necessarily because policy advisers do not possess it but because their balancing act is tilting more towards loyalty to the political executive and away from independence and the public interest. Governments, for their part, have shown themselves willing to let officials' lopsidedness work in their favour.

Primary materials and methodology

So, what kind of expert advice do my policy advisers construct? While the APS often commissions advice by outside experts, it usually generates its own expertise for the purposes of briefing ministers. Indeed, the public service in many ways represents a microcosm of 'applied' expertise in its policy advising function (that is, it advises on anything from funding arrangements for pharmaceuticals to subsidising biofuels, to selling uranium to India). Political advisers aside, no other kind of expert has more assured and continuous access to the Australian Government than the policy advisers of the APS. Indeed, Australia's *Public Service Act* calls secretaries of departments the 'principal policy adviser(s)' to their ministers (Federal Register of Legislation 1999)—the implication being secretaries provide the most important, highest-value advice to their single intended audience: their minister. But the reality is not as neat. Government ministers are a promiscuous audience; they talk to all sorts of people—some of them experts, as well as their own political advisers. Not only do they receive a lot of advice and opinions, they, like their international counterparts, also operate in an environment of daily public pressures and political motivations. When policy advisers give government ministers expert advice, they are competing against all these inputs. To be sure, dynamic conditions like these have likely also had an influence on the phenomenon of rebuffed policy language, but this absolves advisers neither from having contributed to their own predicament nor from acting now to change it.

As in similar parliamentary systems of government, Australia's civil servants are expected to provide expert policy advice to their ministers in a way that is objective, frank, honest and based on the best available evidence. In a contestable marketplace, however, policy advisers must also be responsive to the needs of government ministers. To be anything less risks irrelevance. Two somewhat incompatible ideals, objectivity and responsiveness, suggest advice be formulated both scientifically (excluding nothing relevant) and with an eye to political requirements. Practising one without the other courts charges of intransigence or politicisation, respectively. Despite their inherent contradiction, they must therefore be performed concurrently. Yet, in practice, this concurrence means advice cannot be truly frank or based on all the relevant facts. Working hard to accommodate both its legislated obligations and the government of the day, this language calls to mind the image of using a microscope to scan the horizon. The APS performs this contortion daily and has incorporated it into its culture.

Earlier, I referred briefly to the difficulty of obtaining insights into the discursive world of policy advisers. I mentioned this was partly due to the closed nature of government policy environments (Williams 2010) and to the confidentiality surrounding government advice and deliberations. It also reflects a wider withdrawal of availability, with requests for government information on the rise and compliance with those requests by government departments down (OAIC 2019: 14). An inquirer might get around this by examining publicly available material: those two reviews of the taxation system, for example, or annual budget statements. Although this would be a worthwhile endeavour, it does not get us much closer to understanding how knowledge is communicated and argued among policy advisers and to government ministers in their natural habitat, as it were, or how advice comes to be dismissed. Although we on the outside looking in may never know what was spoken inside administrations about policy choices, there is another way of seeing certain written advice—for instance, by accessing FOI requests and review processes.

Brian Rappert makes a strong case against resting too much of one's argument on such material by arguing that 'FOI responses are characterized by limitations and vagaries that mark a highly managed form of disclosure' (2012b: 44). As such, 'trying to extract a stable reading is … problematic' (Rappert 2012b: 47). He suggests the risks associated with assigning such stability to words on a page include assuming conscious strategy (Rappert 2012b: 46), taking material out of context and attributing meaning where there may be very little (p. 47). This is because

> the incompleteness of the empirical data available stifles determining what took place. While the FOI-released material obtained [in Rappert's analysis] provides glimpses into otherwise closed-off bureaucratic deliberations, the fact that these are only partial glimpses undermined the attempt to settle on their standing and import. While many documents were made available, it is clear … that others were not. (Rappert 2012b: 54)

Recognising these limitations raise 'doubts about how social analysis can take place in situations of partial information', Rappert (2012b: 54) proposes some remedies: one is to interpret the 'back region' (the FOI releases) by placing 'more analytical investment in statements made in front regions' (p. 47), such as official public statements. Another is for analysts to become aware they are themselves

> employing many of the same argumentative techniques as those under study, such as brushing over ambiguities in the use of words, focusing on certain statements over others, making questionable presumptions to assigning meaning and offering definite claims in conditions of partial knowledge. (Rappert 2012b: 56)

In examining the language of written advice contained in my case studies, I will also tread carefully, particularly in terms of assigning excessive stability to meaning and intent. Yet, as will be shown, it is possible to perceive both to a certain degree by qualitative textual analysis, provided certain key inputs are included. Interviews, one might suggest, should be one of those inputs. Although it has been said interviews provide 'an authenticity that can only come from the main characters involved in the story' (Rhodes 2005: 20), it has not been possible to speak with the relevant policy actors featured in my case studies given many were identified in the FOI material and continue to work for government. However, despite a lack of firsthand interviews, it is still possible to gain a deep understanding of how they communicate their expertise. As Linda J. Seligmann and Brian P. Estes propose:

> It helps to talk to people, but then one must make connections among conversations, between conversations, and put a finger on networks, practices, policies, belief systems, fears, imaginaries, and ideologies that motivate the underpinnings of these conversations. (2020: 188–89)

Perhaps more critical than interviews, therefore, is delving into the layers between which organisations produce and communicate knowledge.

My framework attempts to make those connections by interrogating factors that influence language choice, such as timing, culture, legislated requirements and other pressures and expectations. These factors will clarify the underpinnings of the language selections of policy advisers in each of the case studies. Insight into those factors will be acquired from a variety of inputs: organisational and parliamentary reviews and inquiries, organisational mission statements and APS capabilities guidance, national and international comparisons with similar institutions and policies, autobiographies, speeches and other statements by relevant actors in the 'front regions'. Sifting through FOI releases can be laborious, particularly when they are long and have been significantly redacted, leaving only seemingly boring minutiae. But doing so can yield significant results, as we shall see, even in cases of overwhelming detail. As Walby and Larsen (2011: 39) point out, FOI provides an 'entrance into a little known realm of texts that are crucial to understand how government organizations operate' and researchers who overlook it 'are missing out' (p. 32). Joining this back region to the front can, at times, be painstaking and does require time, as well as a bit of nous, but my framework doubles as a guide for those seeking to uncover hidden processes by engaging in this kind of forensic rhetorical analysis.

To test my analysis of rebuffed policy language, I also examine advice that was accepted, and here I succeeded in accessing policy actors who were prepared to be interviewed and cited. This counterpoint demonstrates that there are policy advisers capable of reasoning not on behalf of a transient political context, but more durably and in the public interest. Instead of overturning my hypothesis, however, it simply highlights that the themes and behaviours observed in my case studies are the rule, not the exception.

Those following Australian politics closely will notice my main case studies are drawn from periods of conservative rule. This is not intentional. For example, I attempted to locate material rebuffed by Labor governments, such as the attempt by the Labor government under Julia Gillard to swap asylum-seekers with Malaysia, which was ruled illegal by Australia's High Court in 2011. While some material existed in the public domain, there was not enough of it to build a sufficiently comprehensive picture in which one could connect policy communication and political reaction. Further, many government departments do not make such material widely available to the public, despite it having already been released under FOI. I could, of course, have applied for my own FOI, but I wanted to be able to access data without becoming known and potentially construed as adversarial. In other words, I wanted to be able to observe from a distance at which I could still be viewed as neutral, rather than as an actor. Where possible and relevant, I have included advice to Labor governments, such as in the material exposed by the 2014 Royal Commission into the Home Insulation Program. Although this did not establish rejected advice per se, it considered at some length the culture from which ambiguous policy communication emerges. As such, it will be referred to where relevant.

Do the rebuffed know they are a phenomenon?

This is all very well, but have civil services or some of the bodies that monitor their performance ever articulated concerns about the effectiveness and uses of their advice? After all, if they do not see a problem, why diagnose one? The answer is not straightforward. On the one hand, trust in governments continues to be low (Edelman 2019: 5). On the other, the latest International Civil Service Effectiveness (InCiSE) Index finds that, even among some of the countries deemed distrustful of governments in the *2019 Edelman Trust Barometer* (Edelman 2019), the policymaking capabilities of civil servants are considered effective. For example, InCiSE estimates the top-five effective civil services are those of the United Kingdom (whose general population Edelman deems distrustful of government), New Zealand (unassessed by Edelman), Canada (neutral), Finland (unassessed) and Australia (distrustful). Drilling down further into policymaking, which it views as 'a central role of a civil service' whose 'quality of evidence and appraisal are central to the success of policy' (Blavatnik School of Government 2019: 52), the InCiSE Index assigns top honours to Finland, followed by Denmark, the United Kingdom, Canada, New Zealand, Sweden and Australia. None of these judgements suggests one needs to probe the capabilities of highly placed civil services, much less assign responsibility for a crisis.

But how reliable are such judgements? To rank countries' quality of policy advice, InCiSE relies on just two metrics taken from one source, the Bertelsmann Stiftung Sustainable Government Indicators (SGI): 'How influential are non-governmental academic experts for government decision-making? Does the government office/prime minister's office have the expertise to evaluate ministerial draft bills substantively?' (Blavatnik School of Government 2019: 53).

To answer these questions, the Bertelsmann Stiftung (2016: 22) arranges for each country to be assessed by 'two country experts (political scientists and economists) as well as a regional coordinator' using 'the SGI notebook'. Despite representing only one, somewhat arbitrary, strand of evidence of civil policy advisers' professional capabilities—and InCiSE (Blavatnik School of Government 2019: 16) acknowledges its limitations—the top-ranked countries are eager to publicise their status.[2]

Nonetheless, even while these types of rankings offer a simple appeal, I suggest their use masks self-doubt and insecurity about capability and credibility. Australia's public service, for example, has undergone three

---

2   See, for example, Dunton (2019): 'The UK civil service is often described as the best in the world, but now it's official: the latest global ranking of public administration effectiveness has seen Whitehall rise from fourth place two years ago to top spot today.' And David Thodey's (2019: 9) APS review: 'Overall, international comparisons paint a positive picture of the APS.'

major review processes that included a focus on policy capability and advice since 2010 (Moran 2010; Shergold 2015; Thodey 2019). Certainly, this could suggest an institution keen on continuous improvement, but it could just as easily imply fear of decline, irrelevance or loss of trust. Indeed, these are not mutually exclusive. So, despite the evidence—however patchy—that the policy-advising capabilities of this and other countries' civil services are above average, what can be observed in practice? When ongoing reform processes seem to hint at a less than rosy picture, it is reasonable to question the true state of the effectiveness of civil service policy advice. In this vein, it is useful to look at the literature on civil service capabilities and reforms to appreciate that concerns about ineffectiveness and loss of trust are not only related but also perennial and transnational.

For example, the United States (number 11 in the overall InCiSE Index) had already undergone several waves of reform when Carol Weiss, writing in 1980, estimated that, even without any 'particular crisis', several trends could put bureaucratic reform back on the public agenda. These included 'declining public confidence', 'declining faith in bureaucratic expertise' and 'high-complexity high-uncertainty missions' (Weiss 1980: 13–15). The last trend in particular would see bureaucrats being forced to step outside their comfort zone and 'improvise'. Yet, Weiss (1980: 15) argued, 'without a satisfactory body of expertise', those uneasily improvising bureaucrats would be forced to 'engage in strategies of trial and error—with erratic results'. Her conclusion was that, in 'this environment, the need for improvements in bureaucratic performance becomes a matter of increasing salience' (Weiss 1980: 18).

Writing in 2004, Christopher Hood and Martin Lodge also examined the United States, as well as the United Kingdom (number one) and Germany (number 20). In each jurisdiction, they found dissatisfaction with 'capacity in various roles' and 'new concerns about effective "craftsmanship" and "leadership" in public management' (Hood and Lodge 2004: 313–14), as well as the challenges of radical changes still placing 'new demands on older bureaucratic competencies' (p. 329). Describing Canada (number three) in 2009, Michael Howlett suggested 'the level of policy analytical capacity found in many governments … is low, potentially contributing to both a failure of evidence-based policy-making as well as effectively dealing with many complex contemporary policy challenges' (2009: 153).

In Australia, David Adams sees the rush to reform as 'a response to the knowledge failures of the creed of expertise' that should prompt a reconception of 'the capacity of our public administration ideas and instruments' (2004: 41). Patrick Sullivan considers 'there is little evidence that the necessary conceptual and organisational tools are available to the subordinate reaches of the bureaucracy charged with putting policy into effect' (2008: 130). More recently, Helen Dickinson et al. describe their impression—gained during research conducted on an Australian state government agency—that

> public servants manifest a lack of agency in the process of change, and a sense that they are unable to forge the sorts of changes that they want or believe are needed. Although we detected a clear and collective sense of what the future would look like, we did not detect similar conviction from public servants that they would be active players in reform. Rather we detected a concern that public services would become what others demand or allow. (Dickinson et al. 2015: 27)

Even across time and space, the overall sense of each of these excerpts is one of inadequately equipped actors forever swamped by new complexities beyond their control.

There is another important perspective on this—that of the 'audience' of policy advice. Within the time frame presented by the case studies in this book, from 2002 to 2016, several politicians have also commented on the policy-advising capabilities of the APS. For example, John Howard (2013b: 740), prime minister between 1996 and 2007, observed that 'Treasury produced few really inspiring policy ideas during our time in government'. This, of course, could be due to what journalist Paul Kelly has described as a reluctance among the public service more generally to offer conflicting advice. On Howard's decision to join the invasion of Iraq, Kelly highlights

> an astonishing and complete unity of opinion in Canberra. This is an insight into both strategy and governance. Ministers made clear they did not want contesting advice and the public service offered no advice on the merits of the war or Australia's commitment. (2010: 260)

This gives an impression of government simultaneously expecting and discouraging stimulating advice.

During the royal commission into risks and failures associated with the Home Insulation Program, Kevin Rudd (prime minister from 2007 to 2010) insisted that, 'far from being appraised about any safety concerns ... departmental advice and reporting was consistently, uniformly positive' (Rudd 2014). His environment minister, Peter Garrett (2014), told the same inquiry the 'briefs I received did not alert me to any significant issues', while Garrett's political adviser, Matt Levey (2014), went further when he explained: 'We had a repeated series of events where we didn't believe we've [sic] been given adequate information or that the department was not performing at all satisfactorily and the Minister expressed extreme frustration on a number of occasions.'

Here, the encouraged interpretation appears to be one of either difficult information being withheld to cause no offence or underperformance.

A rather different example comes from Tony Abbott (prime minister from 2013 to 2015), who explicitly criticised the APS when he declared that '[o]ne of this government's failings is that it too often takes advice from the "experts" who got us into difficulties in the first place' and, more specifically, that it was 'wrong in principle to let Treasury's accounting rules determine what's in our national interest' (Abbott 2018b). This suggests Abbott believes governments are weak if they get their advice from its technocrats, whose expertise he holds responsible for adverse outcomes. Australia's prime minister until May 2022, Scott Morrison, appears to conflate policy advice and policy implementation:

> I want to see the public service focus on ... implementation, doing ... let me explain to you what I mean by implementation. It is the job of the public service to advise you of the challenges that may present to a Government in implementing its agenda. That is the advisory role of the public service. (Morrison 2019)

In this view, policy advice is all about execution and focuses only on the government's agenda. Although this is not wrong, it leaves no room for ideas, variance or uninvited opinion. Overall, these extracts offer political impressions of the public service as either inept or restrained.

While there is little of it available publicly, criticism from inside the APS occasionally voices concern about a lack of agency and narrow-mindedness, such as in a speech by its then head Martin Parkinson:

> [F]rom where I sit, too many departments, and too many individual public servants … do not open themselves up to ideas outside of their existing knowledge base. This is a failure of leadership. [And] this is a failure of their own personal leadership. When we neglect to reach far and wide for ideas we open ourselves up to a lethal combination of arrogance and ignorance. (Parkinson 2016)

The most recent review of the APS was announced in May 2018. Its impetus centred partly on civil servants' 'struggles to provide successive governments with integrated advice and support—informed by a deep understanding of the needs of the Australian people—to best tackle complex problems' (Thodey 2019: 14). Its expectations of the APS's 'ability to rise to complex challenges' while 'bringing all its expertise, perspectives and resources to bear' (Thodey 2019: 16) suggest an unspoken deficit given the reform context and, coupled with its stated aspiration to become 'a trusted APS' (p. 6), an anxiety about the complementarity of ineffectiveness and distrust.

However, despite raising what appear to be significant, complex problems, the review's aspirations tend to singularise potential improvements. For example, its vision for 'a system geared to consistently provide robust advice to government' is one that ensures 'silos do not undermine the quality of advice to governments' (Thodey 2019: 42). Terry Moran, one of Parkinson's predecessors and himself chair of the 2010 APS reform paper *Ahead of the Game*, gave a speech in early 2019 that articulated in far more robust language what is needed for true reform in areas related to the provision of policy advice:

> We must return to a public service able to provide frank advice to Ministers while securing continuity in our system of Government. This must involve … a significant investment in its capability … Security for the most senior public servants such that they may safely offer tough, independent professional advice in the face of stakeholder blandishments, whims and aggravation at the Ministerial level, must be reintroduced. (Moran 2019)

The difference between the tone of this now autonomous player in the broader policy field and that of the current reform process is stark. But therein lies the rub. Even a comprehensive review of the civil service, no matter how independent it claims to be, must still submit its report to the government of the day. This means its language and recommendations will tend to stop short of the frank and fearless advice required for targeted and lasting improvements. A case in point is Moran's own 2010 review, which, like its more recent successor, raised the importance of public service advice being of 'the highest quality to remain influential' (Moran 2010) without pointing to any of the issues he went on to identify in 2019. Indeed, Moran—arguably, one of the APS leaders most willing to confront the standard of advice—nonetheless typifies the reverence for, and expectation of, 'objective advice' as somehow more capable of competing with other, often louder voices. For example, while his 2010 proposals for reform acknowledged that the APS 'operates in a contested market for policy ideas where business and community groups advocate their views strongly', he implied that 'forward and outward-looking, objective advice' could cut through all those views (Moran 2010: 12). To be sure, policy advice ought to be more objective than its partisan 'competitors'. Yet, the assumption that arguments are inherently more persuasive when they claim objectivity in a more neutral voice than those competitors is not only problematic; it also valorises 'information' and eschews submitting a judgement (Daston and Galison 1992: 83).

The quality of advice and the factors that undermine its effectiveness are clearly extremely sensitive issues. As things stand, however, defined remedies are lacking. Nonetheless, there appears to be an awareness of the need for reform to rescue effectiveness and trust or, as Pallett puts it in relation to UK civil service reform, 'to evolve and alter their practices in order to retain legitimacy and credibility' (2015: 784). While various reform processes have isolated several important ways to do this, such as greater staff diversity and citizen engagement, I argue that the way policy advisers communicate their arguments to governments must be urgently addressed. Without this, it will not be possible for them to fulfil many of the expectations on them, which typically include a combination of providing 'stability and surety', promoting citizens' wellbeing, supporting 'successive governments in navigating future challenges', 'tackling entrenched disadvantage' and defending national 'security and economic interests in a less stable world' (Thodey 2019: 4). Language is a main ingredient in reaching each of these goals, yet current practice will not achieve them while it avoids staring into the abyss of the language of policy advice.

Contribution and rationale

To provoke attentiveness to the circumstances in which policy advisers contribute to curbing citizens' ability to scrutinise government work, this book inquires into the undercurrents that create the incidence of being rebuffed. By examining the language of Australian policy advisers, it seeks to contribute to broader thinking about how government officials produce and communicate their specific stream of expert knowledge, and how this compares with expert advisers in other fields and countries. With this, it will address a significant lack of comprehensive analysis of not only the state of this specific type of advice, but also how it fails to persuade and effectively damages its expert credibility. This absence of analysis is evident even in the study of argumentation by and about policy actors, where much of the research focus has been on 'persuasive dialogue and negotiation' and how 'mutually acceptable decisions' are reached (Fischer and Gottweis 2012: 9). In other words, the focus has largely been on relative success and compromise, rather than on ineffectiveness.

The methodology suggested by my framework dissects this phenomenon from the inside out—that is, by unpicking three layers from the 'back' and 'front regions' (Rappert 2012b: 47), which could, at their most basic, be described as words, institution and world. It observes the practices by which written advice itself comes to be drafted and finds a language that carefully avoids political context while being almost exclusively driven by it. My framework's treatment of the micro-context then reveals the institutional struggle with uncertainty or disagreement, which culminates in the production of sufficiently truthful evidence. The macro-context shows how advisers' construction of objectivity provides expert validation for governments' preferred world view, and anchors this in international comparisons. Viewed separately, each layer of my tripartite framework reveals the hidden dimensions of official advice. Viewed as a whole, it uncovers the entrenched manner in which policy advisers stand in the way of facilitating public accountability.

This book's rationale is to elevate the critical contribution policy advisers could make to helping publics determine what is in their interest. As such, those whose professional duty it is to help shape and communicate policy must actively consider their language as vital to public deliberation. However, as my discussion has made clear, relying on the efforts of public policy reformers, however well intentioned, to provide truly difficult insights into the emergence of their language as an impediment to democratic public reasoning is not likely to bear fruit. Indeed, it is difficult to do so while governments are more likely to benefit from the status quo. Nevertheless, the need to be more open about shortcomings and impediments to improvement is no less pressing.

2

Strategies of Impersonality: Constructing a Framework for the Rebuffed

Introduction

To bring the notion of rebuffed policy language to life, a relatively recent Australian example will be discussed as a type of blueprint. This example came to my attention just as I began to formulate my hypothesis that the language of the policy rebuffed is constructed in ways that accommodate political manoeuvres. It captured all the characteristics I sought, such as causing significant media attention that pointed to politicisation, and the availability of primary material with which to gauge policy advice and political reaction. Using this example as my blueprint, I constructed a framework capable of drawing out key aspects of policy language in other examples. Each layer of my framework discusses the machinations of becoming rebuffed, including how advisers participate in their own rebuffal and the types of political affordances they enable. Further, it will be shown that even the most innocuous background briefing—deemed harmless enough to be at least partially released to the public—can shed important light on the practices of this policy-advising community. In the example at hand, those practices can be characterised as attempts at objectivity or 'strategies of impersonality' (Porter 1995: 229) with which policy advisers protect themselves from key political contexts. Finally, demonstrating how my framework works in practice will set out some preparatory markers for interrogating my two more extensive Australian case studies.

My blueprint takes us back to 2016—a federal election year. While Australia's ruling conservative Coalition was reasonably confident of winning the election on 2 July, the contest was heating up when polls began to record a slight downturn for the government and an upswing for the opposition Australian Labor Party (ALP).[1] In the months leading up to the election, ALP leader Bill Shorten gave a speech outlining his party's intention to reform negative gearing, which is a tax break

> where losses made on investments such as real estate can be deducted from taxable income derived from other sources. When an investor borrows money to buy an investment property and rents the property out and the rental income is less than the expenses relating to the property, then this loss can be deducted from other taxable income. (Blunden 2016: 342)

In Australia, negative gearing has generally been cherished by sympathetic governments and the property sector as 'propping up the Australian economy' (Pawson 2018: 132) and as an 'almost inviolable taxation right' (Blunden 2016: 342). Its benefits are generally rationalised as 'increases in the supply of housing [that] will place downward pressure on rental prices', which then 'trickle down to low-income groups' looking to rent and to 'first-home buyers' (Pawson 2018: 135). However, its impact has also been said to disproportionately accrue to 'higher income earners', with '50 per cent of the benefit going to the top 20 per cent of households by income' (Blunden 2016: 342). Most economists see negative gearing as unjustifiable, in need of reform and leading to greater inequality (Blunden 2016: 346). Even the Australian Treasury has argued that, while the 'tax system is unlikely to be an effective instrument to move housing prices toward a particular desired level', when it does affect house prices, 'it can also affect fairness, for example, if [it] makes it difficult for disadvantaged groups to afford housing' (Henry 2009). Shorten's proposal to 'level the playing field for first home buyers competing with investors' and 'put the Australian dream of home ownership back within the reach of middle and working class families' invoked this type of thinking and challenged the political status quo. As well as pledging greater fairness for entry into the housing market, he also claimed that Labor's reform would 'improve the budget bottom line by $32.1 billion over ten years' (ALP 2016).

---

1   See Wikimedia Commons (2015).

The next day, then treasurer Scott Morrison hit back in the *Sunday Telegraph*, claiming the ALP's proposed change to negative gearing would not only raise very little revenue, it 'could also have some very nasty consequences for everyday mum and dad investors just trying to get ahead'. Specifically, Morrison charged that Labor's change would raise just $600 million over four years and 'runs the risk that … modest mums and dads will be forced out' (Morrison 2016)—presumably, out of the housing investment market. Malcolm Turnbull, prime minister at the time, went further by calling the ALP's proposal 'the most ill-conceived, potentially destructive policy ever proposed by any opposition' (Peatling 2016). These are tough, definitive words. Are they informed by equally definitive advice?

To find out, one must fast-forward to January 2018, when the government's principal economic adviser, the Australian Treasury,[2] made headlines after its appeal to withhold advice raised under an FOI request by the Australian Broadcasting Corporation (ABC) was rejected. Following a two-year battle, Treasury had been ordered to release the documents, which pertained to briefings to the treasurer about the ALP's proposed changes to negative gearing in 2016. The story was big because the treasurer had not only ignored his department's advice but had also apparently contradicted it. Moreover, Treasury's advice ostensibly authenticated the ALP's policy proposals. As Christina Boswell (2009: 8) puts it, this type of expert knowledge 'can lend authority to particular policy positions … substantiate [a] party's policy preferences, and undermine those of rival[s]'. Instead of lending authority to the government, Treasury had essentially handed it to the opposition. The appearance of this may be why it was reluctant to hand over its advice.

The treasurer's comments should here be viewed alongside two important passages in Treasury's advice:

---

2   The Treasury is 'a central policy agency … expected to anticipate and analyse policy issues with a whole-of-economy perspective, understand government and stakeholder circumstances, and respond rapidly to changing events and directions. Treasury provides sound economic analysis and authoritative policy advice on issues such as: the economy, budget, taxation, financial sector, foreign investment, structural policy, superannuation, small business, housing affordability and international economic policy' (The Treasury n.d.).

> On Labor's negative gearing policy, [s. 47G redaction][3] found that removing negative gearing will increase revenue in the long run between $3.4 and $3.9 billion a year, depending on the increase in new housing construction flowing from the new housing exemption. (The Treasury 2018)

In what appears to be a response to a request to fact check the treasurer's newspaper opinion piece ahead of publication, Treasury noted:

> We presume 'Labor's proposal therefore runs the risk that more wealthy investors will continue to enjoy the same tax incentive they get now, while more modest mums and dads will have to look elsewhere.' refers to structuring opportunities, as the limit on negative gearing for established property would not differentiate between more or less wealthy investors? (The Treasury 2018)

In the first passage cited here, Treasury's amount of revenue raised seems to align more closely with Labor's figure of $32.1 billion over 10 years; Treasury puts it potentially even higher, at $3.4 to $3.9 billion a year 'in the long run' (a typically woolly expression suggesting that, if one were to sleep for 10 years, one would very likely wake up to this change). In contrast, the treasurer's figure comes in at $1.5 billion over 10 years. There could be at least two reasons for this. First, Treasury's expert advice could not help Morrison make the point he wanted, so he got his advice elsewhere. And second, Treasury's proviso around an increase in new housing construction was interrogated by the treasurer and his own ministerial advisers[4] to a point where Treasury may have had to concede that, yes, it was *possible* revenue could only amount to $600 million over four years. Beyond these rudimentary explanations lies the larger issue of how figures and numbers are used. As Stone notes: 'The resolution numbers offer is nothing more than a human decision about how to "count as". Numbers, in fact, work exactly like metaphors … Every number is a political claim about "where to draw the line"' (1997: 165, 167).

---

3   Section 47G of the *FOI Act* allows business-related text to be exempt if its disclosure would reveal 'information concerning a person in respect of his or her business or professional affairs or concerning the business, commercial or financial affairs of an organisation or undertaking' (Commonwealth Consolidated Acts 1982). In practical terms, the redaction here probably simply conceals the name of the unit or person who made these calculations and/or wrote the briefing advice.

4   Ministerial advisers work in the offices of ministers and deal with policy and political issues. While they can be drawn from departments (that is, the public service), this is generally isolated to roles that require extensive policy knowledge. Often, they are political appointments and, as such, serve as partisan advisers who operate 'in a fluid, largely unregulated universe' (Ng 2017: 117).

Viewed this way, numbers are plastic, and the treasurer may have used Treasury's numbers and advice as nothing more than inspiration for an entirely different idea.

In the second passage, the treasurer's opinion piece seemed to ignore Treasury's question about structuring opportunities entirely, going on to strengthen his original words: 'Labor's proposal therefore runs the risk that more wealthy investors will continue to enjoy the same tax incentive benefits they get now, while more modest mums and dads will be forced out' (Morrison 2016).

So, why did Treasury attempt to stop the release of its advice? According to journalist Peter Martin (2018), it was because, '[f]ar from disowning the memo, the Treasury has spent much of the past two years arguing that its contents reflected its genuinely-held opinion'. But is it accurate to accept Treasury's advice as contradictory? Its stated rationale for objecting to the release of the documents was that it would impair its ability to provide frank and fearless advice to the treasurer. In reporting the story, the ABC noted:

> Senior bureaucrats threatened to stop giving honest advice to the Federal Treasurer if negative gearing documents were not kept secret from the ABC … They argued that disclosure of the information would prejudice Treasury's 'ability to provide candid and confidential advice to ministers in the future'. Public servants often argue that if their full and frank advice to politicians about policies is released, this will damage the relationship with ministers, and releasing documents is therefore against the public interest. (McKinnon and Conifer 2018)

While Treasury's advice attempted to explain the implications of the ALP's policy, this would have occurred in response to a request by Morrison's ministerial office to do so following the opposition leader's speech. Although Treasury's explanation was probably not exactly what he was hoping to hear, he had likely also entertained the possibility that the ALP's costings were not necessarily wrong. It is stretching reality to imply that, by simply responding to a request to model Labor's proposed changes, the advice is candid and somehow at odds with the treasurer. Indeed, it seems to have had no impact on the treasurer—apart from entrenching his existing position further.

By February 2018, one month after the release of the documents, the ABC had caught up with Morrison to seek his thoughts on the quality of his expert advisers. It reported that, in 'dismissing Treasury's expert advice on negative gearing', he 'drew upon his "own experience and understanding"'. Moreover:

> 'I didn't agree with them,' Mr Morrison said on Tuesday. 'I take advice from my officials but I'll make my own decisions based on my experience and based on consulting widely.' Mr Morrison pointed to his experience as a 'research economist in the property sector'. (Conifer 2018)

Morrison's statement suggests three competitors vying for his attention: Treasury, his principal expert advisers (although note he calls them simply 'officials'); his life and career experience in the property sector; and consultations with other people presumably claiming to have knowledge or expertise, such as property lobbyists or advocates. A promiscuous audience, indeed, but it is not unreasonable to seek advice from many sources when making policy decisions with potentially far-reaching impacts. Nonetheless, here, expert advice not only failed to establish itself, but also led to the treasurer hardening his own position. Indeed, the subsequent annual budget 'largely preserved the ongoing presence of investment opportunities within Australia's housing market, including no changes to negative gearing', to 'preserve the investing interests of homeowners' and facilitate 'the ongoing growth of the housing market' (Pawson 2018: 137).

Even in an election environment in which the appetite for change can be magnified, policy advice contributed to the status quo becoming further entrenched. This is not a unique situation, of course, but the role of official advice has not been scrutinised in this scenario. My three-layered framework will probe how it contributed.

The text

The first layer examines the text itself, which will help to contextualise its language amid the two layers that follow. My examination here considers language in terms that observe its rhetorical construction, which is critical to recognising implicit meanings. Jonathan Charteris-Black (2011: 312), for example, emphasises the significance of 'becoming aware of linguistic choices' because it leads to an awareness 'of the political choices that they imply and their underlying ethical assumptions'. Understanding the language of the rebuffed thus entails thinking about how words, structure and style are constituted to guide one towards a better awareness of the social, cultural and political conditions that surround the enactment of policy advising. It is important to add that I am here less interested in the technicalities of rhetoric, and more in the circumstances and reasons for a particular type of rhetoric. As Herbert Gottweis reminds us of the Aristotelian tradition, in grasping the dimensions of how policymaking does or does not become persuasive, one should also

> try to better understand the intermediation of pathos, ethos, and logos, or, in other words, the intersecting of argumentation, feelings, and status of speakers. What thus comes into view is the complex scenography of policy making, its argumentative performativity and location in time and space. (2006: 477)

There is, then, much to be gained from noticing some of the elements that intersect across the text: the circumstances under which it came to be produced, who it was for, when it was made and how long it took. Each can reveal choice and a kind of *Weltanschauung*. Looking at the texts in this way raises several important points of inquiry.

One of these is *kairos*—that is, time as a meaningful point in a process (Smith 1969: 6) and as a guide to help 'determine and explain what happened' (p. 13). The opposition leader's speech looks to have been provided to the media on 12 February—one day before delivery. On reading it, the treasurer's office may have requested Treasury advice early on 12 February with the aim of assisting with the drafting of Morrison's opinion piece to counter the opposition. This means Treasury may have had less than 24 hours to prepare their briefing. Although this may not be ideal, it is not unusual. For instance, while it is difficult to provide a comprehensive briefing that includes modelling in such a short time, the policy-advising environment is largely reactive—that is, advice is often formulated in response to urgent requests with little room for reflection (APSC 2018b). In other words, this is a known and unsurprising reality for contemporary policymakers. Moreover, calls for reform to negative gearing are not new (see ACOSS 2015; Daley and Wood 2016; Henry 2009), meaning a government department like the Treasury should be sufficiently prepared to provide such a briefing even within a short turnaround, particularly in an election year. So, while urgency and reactiveness are not necessarily conducive to ideal policy advice, they are not unexpected. Further, illuminating how changes to well-established components of Australia's tax system like negative gearing might work in practice should not take Treasury by surprise. One should therefore examine how rebuffed advice connects to temporal circumstances and how that may impact on its language.

Within the text itself, does the advice reflect an awareness of the context in which it is being constructed? This is related to time in the sense that the advice was requested in response to the opposition's proposal and the fact it occurred during an election year. But it also connects to awareness of the government's traditional position on this policy, and of the treasurer's own point of view. Further, what context surrounds negative gearing itself? Negative gearing in Australia carries some political baggage—most notably, perhaps, then ALP treasurer Paul Keating's attempt to abolish it in 1985 only to reinstate it in 1987 after pressure from lobby groups (Blunden 2016; Jericho 2014). Treasury policy advisers might themselves recall the still recent recommendations to reform negative gearing in their own 2009 tax review, *Australia's Future Tax System*. Perhaps most pronounced within all this is the strong support for negative gearing among the property industry. Indeed, as a Treasury official quoted in Keith Jacobs (2015: 701) put it:

> The Treasury has, to some extent, internalised the arguments put forward by the housing industry against meddling with negative gearing. The memory of what is known as the 'Keating experience'—the sustained campaign following Treasurer Paul Keating [sic] decision to amend negative gearing—is still fresh in their minds. Housing can be viewed as 'the third rail' … of Australian housing politics and an issue that is viewed by politicians as too difficult to reform.

Although it has been noted that policy elites are often eager to embrace tax reform (Eccleston 2007), Treasury may have been hesitant in this instance. Whatever the case, negative gearing in Australia has a politically implicated past, which was still being brought into play in 2016 by an ALP opposition keen to reveal a conservative government in the pocket of the property sector and its wealthy electorates. Time and context, therefore, provide important insights in terms of how the environment in which advice is constructed bears on how policy advisers frame their expertise.

Another important point of inquiry relates to the audience. For example, does Treasury's advice indicate a sense that it is trying to persuade or influence an audience—one that is likely to listen to others? Does it indicate its own point of view to its audience, or does it hide behind a frame of innocuous information? Although the audience for written policy advice is usually implied, can its presence be discerned in the text of this case study? It can be tricky to locate the audience in written text, but it is not impossible. As Joan Leach notes:

> We can see in texts ways of positioning readers, or 'creating' audiences. Take, for example, the scientific paper that might appear in the journal *Nature*. The text and its context position readers in very particular ways as an 'audience'. The specialised language, the conventions of citation, the structure of the text with ordered sections, and the relationship between diagrams and the text, all select a certain audience of readers, as well as position them in certain ways … So, while the audience does not always reside in the text in any obvious fashion, the text rhetorically positions its audience in ways that can be discerned through analysis. (2000: 8)

Treasury's text, with its clipped structure and semi-technical terminology, suggests an assumption that its audience shares Treasury's vernacular. It is dispassionate, which implies a studied neutrality, but it also poses its response about structuring opportunities as a question. Treasury's question—'We presume [you are referring] to structuring opportunities, as the limit on negative gearing for established property would not differentiate between more or less wealthy investors?'—may simply be a way of confirming whether its presumption is right. Yet, there is an oxymoronic tension here: on the one hand, the question mark indicates Treasury needs reassurance of what the treasurer and his office want; on the other, pointing out what is probably obvious to Treasury—that a limit on negative gearing cannot discern the relative wealth of investors—in the form of a rhetorical, perhaps patronising, question could suggest arrogance. With this tension, the text positions Treasury's audience as both powerful and potentially ignorant. This says more about the writers than their audience and suggests they are uncertain about their own status in relation to this audience. In other words, although they may feel they possess epistemic authority among themselves, this authority becomes more tentative when faced with its primary audience.

The inherent dynamics of this type of rebuffed advice—that is, the submission of 'neutral information' to a demanding and clearly unconvinced political audience—suggest there is much to be discovered by contemplating how these advisers' tentatively framed authority might have affected their audience's perception of them. In a discussion of how expert credibility on policy issues is perceived by the public, Erick Lachapelle et al. find that 'individuals evaluate expert credibility based on the way in which experts frame issues' and 'issue framing might in fact shape perceptions of source credibility' (2014: 674, 676). A negative or deficit version of this may hold true for government ministers receiving the expert advice under consideration here—that is, the framing contrived by policy advisers shapes ministerial perceptions of their advisers' lack of credibility. To be sure, 'individuals tend to rely more on their own prior values, beliefs, and opinions than on expert cues' (Lachapelle et al. 2014: 676), and we saw this to be the case in Morrison's public statement that he relied on his own experience rather than on Treasury's advice. But on top of that, Morrison's eventual public rejection of Treasury's advice reflected his evaluation of their epistemic authority—an evaluation that may not have been formed based solely on the framing of just this advice but on how countless pieces of other advice had been framed in his time as a government minister. Using Jasanoff's (2007: 249) terminology, Treasury's advice did not meet Morrison's expectations of 'what credible claims should look like and how they ought to be articulated, represented, and defended' and thus 'about how knowledge should be made authoritative'. Deficit framing like this complicates the work of policy advisers on at least two levels: one, their authority vis-a-vis their target audience is weakened, which makes rebuffing them rather easy; and two, if necessary, ministers can choose to sow doubts about their advisers' credibility rather than fully explain how they arrived at their decisions.

What can the 'front region' (Rappert 2012b: 47) reveal about how the treasurer consumed and publicly construed this advice? More specifically, based on how it was used and publicly recast, can one make a judgement about how it might have been heard? For instance, Treasury's advice questioned the statement that 'mums and dads' would be disadvantaged by Labor's policy by highlighting that wealthy investors could structure their taxes and assets in ways ordinary 'mums and dads' usually cannot. By giving emphasis to that point, Treasury may have influenced the treasurer's decision to replace the words 'more modest mums and dads will *have to look elsewhere*' with 'more modest mums and dads will *be forced out*' (my emphasis). The treasurer and his office may have realised that, based on this advice, they could not logically make the point that mums and dads would be disadvantaged *and* able to invest elsewhere. This detail clearly prompted him to aim for maximum impact by altogether forcing them 'out'—a more extreme image of destitution. Here, one can observe something different to rejecting or stretching the accuracy of the advice. That is, one can see Treasury offering details that made the treasurer notice something, only to discard it entirely to execute the point he seemed intent on making all along. Treasury's expert advice effectively provided an affordance—that is, it provided the medium through which the treasurer boosted his already held position.

Being rebuffed suggests a two-way dynamic. Put simply, the first is action (the policy advice being provided); the other is reaction (the political response). In the negative-gearing case, the treasurer's rebuffal could be viewed as disagreement, even arguing back (Hughes and Lavery 2008: 237); indeed, Morrison said as much when he proclaimed, 'I didn't agree with them'. To judge whether advice has been rebuffed, therefore, it is important to assess how the advice put forward by policy advisers goes on to be used by ministers, in the front regions. Judging reactions connects back to framing in the sense that a frame of 'neutral information', such as Treasury's, may be neither influential nor capable of competing with others, thus effectively inviting an indifferent or unfavourable reaction. But judging reactions also shows more than weak advice being rebuffed. As Toby Bolsen et al. (2014: 2) argue in relation to effective political communication, 'a framing effect occurs when a communication changes a person's attitude toward an object (e.g., policy)'. From a rhetorical perspective, too, discourse aimed at an audience can change 'reality through the mediation of thought and action', engaging the audience in such a way as to cause it to become a 'mediator of change' (Bitzer 1968: 4). In this case study, however, one may hold the opposite to be true. That is, even though Treasury's advice neither persuaded nor nudged its audience towards change or even a neutral (re)appraisal of the issue, it strengthened that audience's already firmly held beliefs and prompted an emphatic denunciation of any change. However, while it seems clear it was not deemed sufficiently authoritative by the treasurer, Treasury's advice was nonetheless influential in a complex, even surreptitious way in that it appears to have helped him to amplify the status quo. It achieved this not despite its weakness, but because of it. This layer of my framework suggests this weakness is part of an institutional reflex.

Although one cannot know exactly how a minister's reaction is formed without being there with them, comparing the front regions with the policy advice under consideration does afford insights of the kind proposed above. It is also important to note that reactions are usually not formed in a neatly stepped process whereby advice is given to ministers, who then duly consider and respond to it in isolation. Many other factors can influence the formation of reaction, not all of them knowable. It is all but certain, however, that ministers are surrounded by their ministerial, or political, advisers. In Australia, these kinds of advisers are bound by a code of conduct, which expects them to facilitate 'direct and effective communication between their Minister's department and their Minister' (Farrell 2022). As such, ministerial advisers play a kind of intermediary role between advice given and advice (not) taken. Writing in the New Zealand context, Chris Eichbaum and Richard Shaw (2008: 356) have suggested these ministerial advisers can 'provide skepticism in circumstances where that is necessary' and thereby provide a layer of contestability in advisory situations. This means they may inject an additional dynamic into the formation of reactions and should, when possible, also be included in my analysis.

Within this first layer, there are four key focal points from which to view the policy text and four follow-on questions one should ask to help gain a better understanding of the language of rebuffed policy advisers (Table 2.1).

Table 2.1 Text framework

	Focus	Question
1.	*Kairos*	What effect does time have on the advice?
2.	Context	How does context potentially affect language — and does language affect context?
3.	Awareness of self and audience	How does the advice conceive of itself, how is it framed and what does its audience do with it?
4.	Response	What is the political reaction to the advice and how is it formed?

The micro-context

The language of policy advisers, of which Treasury's negative-gearing advice is an example, connects to an additional layer, in which institutional constraints and expectations play a major, even inhibiting, role.

In Australia, the language and framing of policy advice such as Treasury's go directly to the obligations stipulated by the *Public Service Act*, as well as to FOI legislation. I will consider each in turn. The *Public Service Act 1999* requires that '[t]he APS is apolitical and provides the Government with advice that is frank, honest, timely and based on the best available evidence'. Moreover, the APS is to be 'objective' (Federal Register of Legislation 1999: Part 3, s. 10) and 'responsive' (APSC n.d.)—a complex combination that seems to necessitate a contorted, frequently ineffective language. I will consider this in more detail in due course. Before I investigate how those requirements have played out on the language of policy advice, a brief history of how the Australian context has dealt with ideas of objectivity and evidence in terms of policy advice to governments is in order.

Expectations of objectivity and advice being evidence-based were not always as explicit as they are now. When the APS was established in 1901, its emphasis was on efficiency, management, structure and remuneration (Minns 2004) rather than on how its advice should be conceived. However, by the time of the 1976 Royal Commission on Australian Government Administration, the ideal of objective advice had come to be codified as 'one of the most important functions of a departmental head' (Coombs 1976). The 2007 election of Kevin Rudd as prime minister saw Australian public servants given the clear role of objective evidence providers. Rudd echoed UK prime minister Tony Blair's emphasis on the use of evidence in policymaking, which was as much a statement of publicising Rudd's reforming credentials and articulating difference with the government he had overthrown as an appeal to his administration to help him be seen to be governing with 'facts, not fads' (Rudd 2008).

From thereon in, evidence and objectivity seem to have become an unchallenged part of the APS's advice-giving identity. Two years after Rudd's election, then Productivity Commission chairman Gary Banks published an essay—by then already thrice delivered as a speech—entitled 'Evidence-Based Policy-Making: What Is It? How Do We Get It?'. Still in the early stages of the government's overt fondness for evidence-based policy, the audience and readers were nonetheless told: 'I don't think I have to convince anyone here of the value of an evidence-based approach to public policy' (Banks 2009: 3). Yet, exactly what was involved in being objective and evidence-based was not entirely clear, perhaps because ideals are not easily concretised. By March 2010, Rudd's secretary at the Department of the Prime Minister and Cabinet (PM&C), Terry

Moran, delivered *Ahead of the Game: Blueprint for the Reform of Australian Government Administration*, which argued the APS's role was to 'provide advice that considers all evidence and provides impartial considerations free from vested interests'. It also noted that '[p]olicy issues are increasingly complex and interrelated, which heightens the need to provide forward and outward-looking, objective advice' (Moran 2010: 12). In 2015, former secretary of PM&C Peter Shergold delivered *Learning from Failure: Why Large Government Policy Initiatives Have Gone So Badly Wrong in the Past and How the Chances of Success in the Future Can Be Improved*, which concluded that good policy advice 'needs to be analytically rigorous, carefully balanced and unbiased in its assessment of evidence', seeking to be 'as objective as possible' (Shergold 2015: 16, 18). None provided detail about what exactly such objective evidence might include and how it might be done; its mere mention seemed powerful enough.

This is not to say that civil administrators striving to craft advice based on evidence are foolish. It is clearly better to make policy recommendations to governments based on an attempt at evidence than to make them up on a hunch. Indeed, the appeal of the concept is underscored by the enthusiasm with which Australian administrators demonstrate their observance of it. However, I wish to draw attention to what appears to be an uncritical acceptance of communicating in a way that sounds like evidence without necessarily being evidence. This is apparent in some of the statements by Australia's public service leadership encountered earlier, as well as its implied—but not always real—presence in the orientation of policy advice more broadly. As David Adams observes:

> [W]hen I ask people … what are the types of knowledge that are relevant to policy considerations in your program/department and how is such knowledge constructed … [it] tends to generate more blank looks or perhaps vague statements about the importance of 'evidenced-based [sic] policy making'. (2004: 29)

Although one might reasonably expect otherwise, this unquestioned acceptance is present even '[i]n the evidence-based policy literature', where 'the idea of "evidence" itself is typically understood to be so commonsense and clear an idea to need neither exemplification nor clarification' (Watts 2014: 38).

The overall presence of objectivity and evidence in public administration, then, is a given. When they produce advice, policy advisers are engaged in a 'cultural practice' (Farmer 1995: 186), which directs how they construct and perceive their knowledge. This can mean that going through the motions of policy advising signifies the act of constructing evidence-based policy because evidence has been cast as an inextricable component of policy advice. In other words, even when evidence is not actually used in policy advice, its presence is assumed and hovers around the culture and its language, standing in for argument or knowledge. As Adams continues:

> Now it could well be that the eclectic nature of the responses are [sic] not simply because of my esoteric line of inquiry but because we don't have a knowledge orientation to our work in public administration and public policy—despite the rhetoric. Even more seriously it could be that we don't know what knowledge looks like because it has become self-referential—that is, the way we work and the tools we use largely define what is good and proper in policy work. (2004: 29)

So, within the micro-context, one sees the language of Australian policy advisers enmeshed and even stymied in legislated structures and tools cocreated by them and their political 'masters'. On the one hand, this language is expected to be robust, frank and fearless; on the other, its adherence to the tenets of objectivity leaves it sounding like evidence but far from frank—not to mention ostensibly fearful of being 'outed' by FOI requests (which will be discussed shortly). This is not to suggest that bureaucrats are robotic in their provision of policy advice. As Brian Head notes, at their best, 'policy decisions emerge from politics, judgement and debate, rather than being deduced from empirical analysis. Policy debate and analysis involves an interplay between facts, norms and desired actions, in which evidence is diverse and contestable' (2013: 398).

At its best, there is little doubt that successful policy advice has communicated knowledge in ways that proceeded from engagement and debate while acknowledging contestability and embracing judgement. My chapter on the language of the unrebuffed will offer examples of this nature. Yet, the trend I observe in my case studies on the rebuffed leads me to ask whether a culture of objectivity and evidence, which seems to steer much of the language of policy advice and whose professional energy frequently centres on political responsiveness, is causing advisers to surrender their ability to probe, argue and make a judgement.

Palmer et al. (2019: 244) discuss the relationship between advice-givers and governments in terms of 'boundary bridging' and 'co-production', where invoking 'the intrinsic substance of supposedly objective facts—whether to support or oppose [a] particular policy proposal—is unhelpful' (p. 249). It is unproductive, in other words, to reinforce 'the perception of science and politics as mutually exclusive spheres' (Palmer et al. 2019: 246) and better to acknowledge that 'expert advisory processes' are 'influenced by more transient and situated factors, including the prevailing political climate within which advisory interactions take place, the specific characteristics of the policy problem(s) discussed, and the balance of interests amongst relevant stakeholders and publics' (p. 249).

To cite one of the chief scientific advisers interviewed by Palmer et al. (2019: 249), such work 'consists of … actually explaining the scientific position, understanding it, but *working with the grain*' (emphasis in original). Working with the grain in this way could be said to 'constitute the purposeful hybridisation of science and politics', where 'good advice' is produced through 'a collaborative, iterative approach to the process of formulating advice' and engaging 'closely with decision makers on a sustained, face-to-face basis—in both cases building processes of mediation and translation into the substance of their advisory work' (Palmer et al. 2019: 250).

While maintaining a posture of both objectivity and political responsiveness seems to suggest Australian policy advisers embrace such hybridisation, it is difficult to gauge how they are 'working with the grain'. For example, if we accept that my examples of rebuffed advice represent instances of working with the grain, should some of the key assumptions about the relationship between knowledge and policy be recalibrated? That is, if advisers' and decision-makers' 'collaborative, iterative approach to the process of formulating advice' still resulted in that advice being rebuffed, working with the grain in the Australian context is not so much a bridge across which objectivity and responsiveness are actively integrated to arrive at workable arguments as a case of one overwhelming the other. If my examples do not represent instances of working with the grain, should Australian advisers focus more squarely on political relevance and embrace the notion of policy advice as a hybrid activity? I will return to this in my conclusion.

Another factor that appears to influence the language of policy advice is FOI legislation, which exists in tension with what is required under the *Public Service Act*. Recall Treasury's retort, as it was reported, that 'disclosure of the information would prejudice Treasury's "ability to provide candid and confidential advice to ministers in the future"'. This seems to imply the requirement for transparency exerts an inhibiting and unwanted influence on how forthright language can be. The Office of the Australian Information Commissioner, which administers the *Freedom of Information Act 1982* (*FOI Act*) in Australia, rejects this reasoning as misplaced in most circumstances, noting:

> [A] common factor considered to weigh against disclosure of internal working documents was that disclosure would inhibit frank and candid advice from public servants in the future … Public servants are expected to operate within a framework that encourages open access to information and recognises Government information as a national resource to be managed for public purposes … In particular, the FOI Act recognises that Australia's democracy is strengthened when the public is empowered to participate in Government processes and scrutinise Government activities … In this setting, transparency of the work of public servants should be the accepted operating environment and fears about a lessening of frank and candid advice correspondingly diminished … While frankness and candour claims may still be contemplated when considering deliberative material and weighing the public interest, they should be approached cautiously … Generally, the circumstances will be special and specific. (OAIC 2016)

In other words, democracy is supported when public servants make clarity and candour the rule rather than the exception. Yet, Treasury's argument in the negative-gearing case appears to be that candour can only be achieved when it is not possible for the public to see their advice. This argument represents one of two schools of thought on how much impact these requirements and expectations have on the language of policy advisers. The first, typified by Treasury, views FOI laws as an impediment to providing candid advice. Here, one should cite Shergold, whose 2015 report, *Learning from Failure*, concluded the *FOI Act* should be amended to support greater confidentiality around 'advice and opinion provided to support the deliberative processes of government policy formulation' (Shergold 2015: 15). At the time of their release, Shergold's comments were welcomed by a swathe of high-ranking APS officials, such as the

Australian Public Service Commissioner and others.[5] The most recent APS review echoed these sentiments, noting 'members of the review's reference group, including former ministers and senior public servants, highlighted their own experiences of FOI legislation inhibiting the provision of frank and fearless advice to government on deliberative matters, especially in writing' (Thodey 2019: 121).

It concluded:

> Ensuring that APS advice and opinion provided to support the deliberative processes of government policy formulation remain confidential will give public servants the confidence to provide frank and fearless advice, and ministers and the Cabinet the best advice to make fully informed decisions. (Thodey 2019: 121)

It seems there is no room for the public in this tight relationship. The second school of thought views candid advice as a touchstone for transparent and inclusive governments, such as former senior public servant Bill Blick, who, in 2016, noted that calls for greater confidentiality were 'self-serving comments from the usual suspects' that 'might have more credibility if supported by some frank and fearless evidence' (quoted in Towell 2016). Looking at the language offerings of Australia's public servants while working as a prime ministerial speechwriter, James Button (2013: 168) routinely saw advice that had 'no confidence in its own truth', which he considered as expressing 'a kind of powerlessness'. This suggests that, far from practising candour in most situations, the language of policy advisers is deeply entrenched in a kind of self-inhibiting form of expression that— with or without the perceived influence of FOI requirements—belies a lack of confidence in what its expert advice should be and do. Treasury fighting the FOI release therefore also provides an important insight into how it views its own identity, its role and its responsibilities. When viewed in tandem with its actual advice, what does Treasury's claim that disclosure would prejudice its 'ability to provide candid and confidential advice' say about how it views its own abilities? Moreover, what does this say about its understanding of candour, objectivity and evidence? Does the requirement to be responsive conflict with communicating clearly?

---

5   They included then PM&C secretary Martin Parkinson, then Department of Industry, Innovation and Science secretary Glenys Beauchamp and then Treasury secretary John Fraser (Belot 2016).

The micro-context should also include a discussion of the reputation and organisational identity of the institution giving the advice. In Treasury's case, its reputation rests on being one of the two oldest Australian government departments, having operated since 1901. It is usually deemed to be powerful, with 'a strong track record of delivering to government' and 'successive governments … request[ing] it to take a lead role on a broad range of issues, some of which are arguably beyond the traditional remit of a national treasury' (APSC 2013b). However, while its 'reputation is a cornerstone on which its ongoing influence is founded',

> [t]here is a widespread view among stakeholders … that Treasury is closed to external experience and that practical implications are not always given sufficient consideration in forming policy advice. This widely held perception has the potential to undermine Treasury's reputation and so will be important to address further to protect the department's reputation and influence. (APSC 2013b)

The 'front regions' with which I will augment my discussion include publicly available material on capabilities and performance, such as the two reviews cited above, as well as annual reports and other statements. For example, after 'missing its budget revenue forecasts for most of the decade', Treasury came under fire from Australian National University academic Bob Gregory, who said forecasting should be taken away from the department given it had 'continued to apply the same approach of "reversion to a 30 year trend … despite the fact that the experience of the last ten years doesn't fit that model, and despite the fact that we can't explain what is going on"' (quoted in Potter 2017). Similarly, the Grattan Institute's John Daley charged that

> Treasury is using the same assumption for the last 40 years as if the world hasn't changed … We have been doing this for quite a long time and the answers have been the same, the projections are not matching reality. Why hasn't Treasury changed its approach yet? (FINSIA Staff 2017)

On this issue, even Treasury's own earlier internal review tentatively noted:

> [T]here is a natural bias in forecasting to assume that the past will be a reliable guide to the future. This is not a bad assumption most of the time but will bias forecasts in periods like the present when we are dealing with not one but a range of unusual forces. (Tease 2016)

These types of statements help assemble a more complete impression of the reputation and, more specifically, the organisational identity and culture of this policy adviser. In the case of Treasury, one might conclude it is an institution whose perceived dominance will slip without recourse to a more expansive, open-minded approach to constructing policy knowledge.

In summary, this second layer looks at the institutional—that is, administrative, legislative, organisational and cultural—effects and burdens on policy language. With the foregoing discussion in mind, the focus and questions arising from this layer are shown in Table 2.2.

Table 2.2 Micro-context framework

	Focus	Question
1.	Expectations	What are the expectations — legislated and/or institutional — of the adviser?
2.	Culture	Does culture influence the language of the policy adviser?
3.	Effect on knowledge	How might this bear on how policy expertise is constructed and communicated?

The macro-context

As the term suggests, the macro-context represents the widest of the three layers. I have panned out from examining the text itself to observing the culture within which it is constructed. I will now consider how rebuffed Australian policy advice compares with the rest of the world. For example, what comes to light when one considers the characteristics of my Australian case studies alongside international scholarly work on policy advice and language? Can international policy norms or appraisals regarding policy advice identify whether the examined advice is unique or astonishingly similar to global counterparts? How do my case studies compare with similar international policy examples? I will briefly take each question in turn to lay out some signposts for how my two more substantial case studies will proceed.

A diverse span of scholarship from the social sciences to science policy studies has noticed the constraints imposed by concepts like evidence and objectivity. Many have argued that what has come to be regarded as objectivity is—perhaps paradoxically—incompatible with public reasoning. Economist Deirdre McCloskey, for instance, asks:

> If some good economists espouse positivism the question arises how economics would be different without it. That remains to be seen, though one thing is clear: economics without positivism would be more, not less, rigorous and scientific, because it would have to face up to more arguments. (1994: 23)

Science historian Theodore Porter (1995: 8) claims, rather damningly, that '[o]bjectivity lends authority to officials who have very little of their own'. Objectivity can thus be worn as a defence against being seen as biased or arbitrary. Being 'objective' is therefore connected not only to immunising oneself against criticism, but also to publicly projecting professional authority. Such 'strategies of impersonality' 'must be understood partly as defences against such suspicions [and] generally take the form of objectivity claims. Objectivity means knowledge that does not depend too much on the particular individuals who author it' (Porter 1995: 229).

Objectivity, in this sense, takes the heat off; it works to pre-empt potential charges of bias, lack of expertise or lack of authority. Ironically, its anonymity has also created an ethos in which policy advisers can leave out any arguments or judgements—perhaps for fear of seeming subjective.

But despite some of its undesirable spillover effects, it is difficult to see how government advisers can offer their knowledge in diverse and contestable policy situations without a standard like objectivity. To round off my scholarly trio, political scientist Aaron Wildavsky (1979: 7) observes: 'Without agreement on a starting place, there is no end to debate.' Objectivity provides common ground—an agreement from which to proceed towards reaching decisions. Without that initial agreement, Wildavsky (1979: 7) continues: 'Theories harden into dogma, and assertion replaces evidence. Policies then are judged not by their merits but by the motives of their proposers.' This is a prescient statement, yet the language of rebuffed policy advisers may have managed to effect a rather similar endpoint despite sounding like objective evidence. As the phenomenon was described in my introduction, the Australian advice under consideration here may symbolise facts and evidence—something akin to Wildavsky's 'starting place'—but its content provides the policy basis for facilitating assertion-driven outcomes.

The works cited here may be wideranging, but the emphasis in each on how a device like objectivity can shape and even bend epistemic authority is consistent. Sandra Harding (1992: 568–69) adds nuance to these considered reflections by calling this conception of objectivity the 'neutrality ideal', which 'certifies as value-neutral, normal, natural, and therefore not political at all the existing scientific policies and practices through which powerful groups can gain the information and explanations that they need to advance their priorities'. While references to objectivity in the legislation, rules and guidelines that encase the advice under consideration promise truth or at least truthfulness, Harding (1992: 569) calls this out as depoliticising and substantiating the already held intentions of those in power, with scientists—or policy advisers, in our case—playing the role of enabling 'company men'. To strengthen the notion of objectivity, Harding calls for 'a strong objectivity' (1992: 569), which maximises the possibility of objectivity by reaching outside 'institutions, practices, and conceptual schemes' to 'gain a causal, critical view of them' (p. 581). Different points of view—or 'standpoint epistemologies', as Harding (1992: 569) calls them—must therefore be included in any attempt to be strongly objective. This kind of reaching outside institutions and practices is patently absent in the examples under review, as we shall see. While each reflection on objectivity will weave its way through my case studies, it is Harding's that will inform some early proposals in my conclusion.

Can international policy norms regarding the quality of language and advice point to something distinctive in the Australian context? In the United Kingdom, for example, a House of Commons report on official language found much to criticise in the 'unlovely language' of politicians and civil servants (House of Commons Public Administration Select Committee 2009: 6). Arguing that 'good government requires good language, while bad language is a sign of poor government' (House of Commons Public Administration Select Committee 2009: 19), the committee's chairman proposed that 'cases of bad official language should be treated as "maladministration", as for any other type of poor administration' (p. 20). These sentiments show just how seriously the accessibility of government and public-sector language has been taken in the United Kingdom. Subsequent initiatives, however, appear to have been discontinued after only short periods of operation. It is easy to discern here echoes of Australia's frequent but short-lived attempts at reform. Does this shared diffidence emerge from jurisdictional similarities?

Perhaps not. New Zealand—another Westminster-style jurisdiction—has placed advice-giving at the core of its operations rather more enduringly, as well as more substantially. Its Policy Project's 'policy quality framework' describes the characteristics of good advice as encapsulating:

Purpose and story: engages the decision-maker and tells the full story

Inputs: is informed by evidence and insights and is analytically sound

Context: is put into context, links to the desired future state and exposes risks, opportunities and implications

Best option: balances what is desirable, can be delivered and is cost effective. (DPMC 2017)

Under this framework, quality advice should also include a focus on 'the decision maker's intent' and should be 'frank, honest and apolitical about the best way to achieve that' (DPMC 2017). Although these are good words and are not dissimilar to Australian aspirations, New Zealand Government policy agencies are required to use the framework and report their results in their annual reports (DPMC 2022). This means their quality, effectiveness and status can be accessed and gauged by anyone.

For its part, Australia's Public Service Commission, which generally sets the direction for performance and training, is not ignorant of the need for attending to clearer communication—for example, it provides communication-related training and encourages staff appraisal against criteria that include 'communicating with influence' (APSC 2012b). Yet, the focus here tends mostly to be on plain English rather than on the construction or courage of policy advice. Having said that, one serious attempt has been made at evaluating the policy advice of the APS, in 1995, when the Australian Department of Finance joined with The Australian National University to explore bureaucrats' inputs into government decision-making. This included evaluating policy advice in the form of policy management reviews, a colloquium and a publication, *Evaluating Policy Advice: Learning from Commonwealth Experience*, with contributions from academics and senior public servants (Uhr and Mackay 1996).

In 2000, Michael Di Francesco assessed these policy management reviews, concluding that 'bureaucratic politics' had actively avoided linking the quality of advice to public accountability by refusing to assume responsibility for policy outcomes (as outcomes were thought to be a political responsibility). Instead, bureaucrats focused on 'arrangements for achieving more effective control of the processes underpinning production of advice' (Di Francesco 2000: 36). Process was therefore viewed as within policy advisers' control, while linking accountability to policy outcomes meant policy advisers could not be blamed, even though their advice is clearly part of the outcomes mix. When it came to making such reviews public:

> sanitised 'public' versions of [policy management reviews] will inevitably exclude much of the classified evidence of either good or bad advisory processes [and] there is every likelihood that the advising programs or the discrete policy tasks to be evaluated will be carefully selected so as not to reflect too badly on a department's performance. (Di Francesco 2000: 46)

Apart from this 'evaluation experiment in Australian government' (Di Francesco 2000: 36), and the 2001 'Developing Policy Advice' report by the Australian National Audit Office assessing three departments' advice output as 'adequate' when measured against 'standards established by the departments themselves' (ANAO 2001: 12, 17), there have been no other concerted efforts to evaluate the effects of policy advice in the Australian context. Even though numerous reviews have delved into other aspects of administration (such as capability reviews,[6] which will be consulted in due course, and an 'efficiency through contestability programme'),[7] it seems likely Australia will not follow New Zealand's rather more transparent, less risk-averse approach. Diffidence may therefore not be a characteristic problem of Westminster-style jurisdictions, given the New Zealand example.

The foregoing discussion, as well as my introduction, seem to indicate that, despite undergoing various review processes, Australian policy norms are not generally subject to deep or sustained appraisal, while the execution of policy advising itself may be perceived as a safely separate output that has nothing to do with political outcomes. What about international comparisons in similar policy situations? The practice of negative gearing is not universal; only New Zealand and Germany have similar provisions, while Canada, the United States and Sweden have limited versions of it (Martin et al. 2017: 42). This does not mean one should expect to find predictable parallels and contrasts between Australian and other countries when looking at negative gearing. For example, as Chris Martin et al. suggest:

---

6   See APSC (2021).
7   See Department of Finance (2015).

> Australia and Germany's treatment of negative gearing and capital gains tax underlie quite different housing market outcomes: speculative inflation in Australia; relatively steady house prices in Germany. The United Kingdom taxes landlords more heavily than most other countries, yet has a faster growing [private rental sector] than most countries included in our survey. (2017: 71)

But I am specifically concerned not with policies themselves, as consequential as they may be to the way advisers articulate their advice, but with a particular way of constructing policy evidence and how that creates an affordance. It could therefore be more instructive to compare how international policy counterparts have sought to express similar, totemic issues within the context of tax reform more generally, given what is ultimately suggested by the political fight over negative gearing is whether to change or maintain the status quo, and which of the two is more likely to attract voters in an election year. What interests me here, therefore, is how policy advisers choose to communicate their expertise in the face of that fight. I will briefly examine four countries' attempts to enact various reforms in a contested taxation space: Ireland, New Zealand, Norway and Japan.

In his comparison of tax reform in Ireland and New Zealand, Johan Christensen argues the policy advice approach of tax policy bureaucrats—advisers, just like those in my Treasury case—'had a major impact on tax policymaking' (2013: 563). In New Zealand, whose neoliberal tax reforms under the left-leaning Labour government of the 1980s were world-leading, Christensen found a civil service that

> produced tax policy bureaucrats that identified as economists, had extensive economic expertise, were highly receptive to the neoliberal ideas from the economics discipline, and took an activist approach to policy advice. Through the formulation and advocacy of reform ideas, officials influenced the policy preferences of politicians and led tax policy change in a neoliberal direction. (2013: 566)

During the same time in Ireland, where governments moved between centre-right and centre-left:

> The persistence of a generalist civil service with closed recruitment policies created a tax policy bureaucracy that identified as civil servants, had little economic expertise, was oblivious to micro-economic ideas about taxation, and took a passive approach to

policy advice. These features allowed tax policymaking to be completely dominated by the ideas and concerns of politicians. (Christensen 2013: 566)

In relation to this short Australian case study, Treasury (2019c) recruits, and identifies as, economists and has previously been associated with influencing both Labor and Liberal governments (Gittins 2015), which aligns it more closely to New Zealand in Christensen's analysis. Yet, my more contemporary example demonstrates the Australian Treasury appears to have assumed a passive, non-advocacy approach to policy advice dominated by politicians, like Ireland's generalist civil service.

In Norway, Rune Ervik and Tord Skogedal Lindén (2015: 394) consider government reforms to pensions in the face of declining revenue and find a Ministry of Finance that 'held a dominant position over the politicians … regarding both the description of the problem and possible policy solutions'. This leads the authors to conclude that 'Norwegian policy actors have had great success in conducting comprehensive retrenchment reform without long-lasting protests' (Ervik and Lindén 2015: 406). Richard Eccleston's observations of Japan's attempts to introduce and then increase a value-added tax (VAT) in the 1970s, 1980s and 1990s chart the dominance and later decline of the Ministry of Finance (MoF) in setting the economic policy agenda. Yet, despite its earlier 'bureaucratic independence and expertise' (Eccleston 2007: 117), the ministry's initial attempts to introduce a VAT in 1979 failed. Ten years later, due to various factors that included the 'MoF's central role in agenda setting and commitment to the introduction of a national consumption tax', Japan introduced a 3 per cent VAT. By the time it was raised to 5 per cent in 1997, however, the 'reputation of the MoF was tarnished and its bureaucratic influence limited still further by the widely held perception that the agency had mismanaged the recession economy and fiscal reform' (Eccleston 2007: 130).

One may never know whether tax reform would have happened in these examples without the involvement of policy bureaucrats. Yet, it seems clear there were two types of policy advisers in these circumstances: those who dominated or actively argued for certain policy choices and those who took a passive stance or held a rather ineffectual position. Judging by the briefing under consideration, not to mention the subsequent unfavourable reaction to it, the Australian Treasury would seem to fit into the latter category, despite claiming to be 'the Government's pre-eminent economic adviser' (The Treasury 2019b: 1). But is it fair to compare one small piece of policy advice from the 'back regions' with publicly available retrospectives of major reform initiatives? I propose it is—provided it is judged using a framework, such as mine, that considers its meaning from multiple perspectives or layers.

As noted above, at the time the text under consideration was constructed, Treasury had several decades of experience in the establishment and development of negative gearing, including facilitating the attempt to both abolish it in 1985 and reinstate it in 1987; examining it at length in its own 2009 tax review; and even, as it was claimed, internalising 'arguments put forward by the housing industry against meddling with negative gearing' (Jacobs 2015: 701). Just like its international comparisons here, it is highly likely Treasury has solid, expertise-driven views. Just like the other tax reforms referred to above, negative gearing has a politically charged past. And just like all those other attempts at reform, this small piece of advice offered an opportunity to be influential. Perhaps some of the redacted text in this back region attempted this. Judging by the tone and style of the remaining, unredacted text, however, one might hazard a guess that it did not. Further, I argue that the unredacted text demonstrates habitual practices of a kind that will be observed repeatedly in this book.

Given the rather substantial history of negative gearing inside Treasury itself, it would not be wrong-headed to assume that many of Treasury's policy advisers favour at least some degree of reform to the way investment properties are geared. Even in the face of political resistance, it is not impossible to find alternative ways of making one's expert view cut through. For example, when New Zealand's Treasury failed to persuade ministers to cut personal income tax rates following the usual advisory routine, it 'started looking for a different format' (Christensen 2013: 576) by taking the debate outside government circles and into a conference that included nongovernmental actors. Taking the heat out of the argument by moving it into the public arena where its pros and cons could be discussed and then normalised eventually led to convincing 'key ministers that reform of the tax system was integral to growth' (Christensen 2013: 577). It was possible for policy bureaucrats to help political actors make difficult policy decisions, even though they had not originally found them electorally palatable. In my example, Treasury appears to have abstained from seizing the opportunity to provide a more incisive briefing and its advice for the treasurer serves as a broader illustration of advisers' reluctance to exercise judgement in the face of complex political circumstances.

As a final point in the macro-context, rebuffed advice does not exist in isolation to other advice. Rather, there are important interplays between this policy advice on negative gearing and advice on other policy issues at the time. For example, shortly after Treasury's negative-gearing advice and Morrison's rebuffing of it became public, former prime minister Tony Abbott commented on the impact of 'the *rate* of immigration at a time of stagnant wages, clogged infrastructure, soaring house prices and, in Melbourne at least, ethnic gangs that are testing the resolve of police' (Abbott 2018a; author's emphasis). His colleagues, treasurer Scott Morrison, finance minister Mathias Cormann and trade minister Steven Ciobo (Hunter 2018), as well as the Housing Industry Association (Baxendale 2018) and Infrastructure Australia (Benson 2018a), repudiated the claims, citing expert policy advice that immigration, especially skilled migration, was undeniably beneficial to the nation. Even ultraconservative home affairs minister Peter Dutton followed suit, proposing there was 'an economic benefit to bringing people in who are skilled, who will work and pay taxes and contribute to society' (Hunter 2018), despite having earlier in the year claimed that

> people are scared to go out to restaurants of a night time because they're followed home by these gangs, home invasions and cars are stolen and we just need to call it for what it is. Of course it's African gang violence. (Dutton 2018)

There are powerful, often populist, narratives and players with whom policy advisers must vie for ministerial attention. I am not blind to the fact that even the most convincingly argued advice cannot always cut through this type of noise. But one can see that, when it comes to looking at immigration purely through the lens of economic benefits, expert policy advice is valorised, particularly when its emphasis is on skilled migration—people who, presumably, will pay tax and own property on arrival in Australia. Other elements linked either to negative gearing (for example, equality of opportunity to enter the housing market) or to immigration (for example, humanitarian settlement or social cohesion), however, may not be afforded the same diligence.

Comparing advice that is rebuffed (on negative gearing) and advice that is not (on skilled migration) tells us something about political narratives. In the case of negative gearing, that narrative may convey something like 'we want growth in the property sector to continue but we won't let Labor take "mum and dad" voters away from us, which is why we like immigration when there's an economic benefit, as long as we reserve the right to target certain groups if it helps us highlight aspects of our persona that appeal to various audiences'. As Adam Masters and John Uhr (2017: 21) argue: 'Public leaders use whatever evidence they think works with their audiences.' For the purposes at hand, I propose that examining the language of unrebuffed advice will lead to some conclusions about whether and how it is different to the language of the rebuffed.

The macro-context thus prompts the focus and questions in Table 2.3.

Table 2.3 Macro-context framework

	Focus	Question
1.	Engagement with objectivity and evidence	Is the spectre of 'objectivity' present in policy advice? How does the advice engage with or construe the notion of evidence?
2.	International comparisons and contexts	What do international comparisons tell us about Australia's rebuffed advice? Are contexts and circumstances similar or is Australia unique?
3.	Language of contemporaneous, unrebuffed advice	Can some conclusions be reached about rebuffed advice by viewing it alongside advice sourced from around the same time that was accepted?

Each of the preceding questions will be asked of my case studies. However, the last (number three above) will be considered in a separate chapter on the language of the unrebuffed to test my findings. Finally, all these questions should guide any interested future researcher's inquiry rather than control it. Similarly, the works cited here and the examination of negative gearing itself represent an indication of what I will do in the comprehensive case studies that follow, and what could be done more generally by others when scrutinising the language of policy advice. These questions will therefore help to construct a map of the neighbourhood towards which I am headed. In subsequent chapters, I will dig a lot further and land on some conclusions. In them, I will follow the framework constructed here, but—due to different topics, circumstances and access to both primary and secondary materials—each will unfold slightly differently and point to different tropes in how rebuffed advice is communicated and what it affects.

In closing, I have drawn together all my preceding questions with which to interrogate the language of the rebuffed to provide an overall, and more surveyable, analytic framework (Table 2.4).

Table 2.4 Complete rebuffed framework

	Focus	Question
1.	*Kairos*	What effect does time have on the advice?
2.	Context	How does context potentially affect language — and does language affect context?
3.	Awareness of self and audience	How does the advice conceive of itself, how is it framed and what does its audience do with it?
4.	Response	What is the political reaction to the advice and how is it formed?
5.	Expectations	What are the expectations — legislated and/or institutional — of the adviser?
6.	Culture	Does culture influence the language of the policy adviser?
7.	Effect on knowledge	How might this bear on how policy expertise is constructed and communicated?
8.	Engagement with objectivity and evidence	Is the spectre of 'objectivity' present in policy advice? How does the advice engage with or construe the notion of evidence?
9.	International comparisons and contexts	What do international comparisons tell us about Australia's rebuffed advice? Are contexts and circumstances similar or is Australia unique?
10.	Language of contemporaneous, unrebuffed advice	Can some conclusions be reached about rebuffed advice by viewing it alongside advice sourced from around the same time that was accepted?

3

Knowing What Not to Know: Advice on South Australia's Blackout and the Role of Renewable Energy

Introduction

The first of my two in-depth case studies is about renewable energy and describes a statewide power blackout that occurred in late 2016. This case was chosen because, at first glance, it appeared to be an example of policy officials being ignored by their government. Yet, when I interrogated related FOI material with the help of my framework, I found this depiction was based on just one short, early statement by one official. By keeping the whole release in scope and aligning it with political actions and reactions at the time, I was able to observe how one instance of acknowledging uncomfortable knowledge was quickly silenced by other official voices uneasy about challenging the dominant political narrative. The other voices—who largely provided factual, somewhat tedious updates—tended to be overlooked at the time yet proved to be far more illuminating, particularly in relation to organisational culture and behaviours. To find the choreography of rebuffed policy advice beyond one simple interpretation of ignored advisers, in other words, it was important to cover as much of the available material as possible.

This case study, then, follows a statewide electricity blackout in South Australia (SA) in 2016. Malcolm Turnbull, prime minister at the time, exploited and maintained the initial doubt about the cause of this blackout, which he achieved by casting 'intermittent renewables' as the culprit and extolling energy security as a reassuring source of certainty.[1] Framing renewables as a threat to energy security and certainty helped Turnbull flesh out his government's policy preference for maintaining the energy status quo, which, in Australia, means baseload power through burning coal and gas. The two departments constructing advice on the blackout, the federal departments of Environment and Energy (DEE) and of the Prime Minister and Cabinet (PM&C), seemed very quickly to become aware that reporting all known facts about the blackout could disrupt the government's narrative and therefore excluded any information from their briefings that had the potential to do so. As we will see, policy advisers were clearly rebuffed only initially, with rather more complex rebuffals occurring later. In the discussion to follow, we will observe a language of policy advice characterised mainly by what is left out—a language of 'knowing what not to know' (Taussig 1999: 2).

Before drawing out the conceptual aspects of this chapter, I will introduce the details of this case study. At 4.18 pm on 28 September 2016, severe storms in SA knocked out major electricity transmission lines and plunged most of the state (with a population of about 1.7 million at the time) into blackout. Within hours, DEE and PM&C began emailing each other information that included status reports and media releases from the Australian Energy Market Operator (AEMO), as well as updates from various teleconferences between officials and the offices of the prime minister and the energy minister. We know this because policy think tank The Australia Institute lodged an FOI request with PM&C for material related to the blackout event. PM&C made some of this—partly redacted—material available on its website on 24 January 2017.[2] DEE also received an FOI request related to this event, which it

---

1   The day after the blackout, Turnbull (2016b) told journalists 'these intermittent renewables do pose real challenges … energy security should always be the key priority'.

2   See pmc.gov.au/sites/default/files/foi-log/FOI-2016-178.pdf, from which all cited departmental material is taken. The Australia Institute's request was for 'all correspondence created by the Department (including briefings, reports and advice) sent from the Department to any Minister or Minister's office between 18 September and 18 October 2016 which related to: the blackout event in South Australia on 28 September 2016; state level renewable energy targets; the impact of renewable electricity generation on electricity prices; "energy security", "reliability", "grid stability"; frequency; or the South Australian blackout event 28 September' (see PM&C n.d.).

posted on its website on 2 February 2017.[3] In DEE's case, FOI material is not automatically disclosed on its website. Rather, one must contact the department to request access, which is granted once for 20 minutes, and material cannot be saved or printed. I will also refer to this material, which I surveyed for the allotted period, but most of my focus is on the material published by PM&C. Suffice to say, for now, DEE's material is similar to PM&C's.

As the grid and market operator, AEMO issued a media release at 5.32 pm on 28 September stating that South Australia's electricity market had disconnected from the neighbouring state of Victoria and caused an outage. It explained that it was 'working closely with transmission network service provider ElectraNet to identify and understand the severity of the fault, as well as determine a power restoration time' and that its understanding was 'that this issue has not caused any supply interruptions in Victoria' (AEMO 2016a). This represents all the publicly available information at this time, provided by those with firsthand knowledge. Just two hours later, federal energy minister Josh Frydenberg appeared on the national current affairs program *7.30* to offer his description of events, raising questions about 'the virtue of the increasing amount of renewables' in terms of 'the stability of the system' (Cooper 2016).

Later that evening, AEMO issued a second media release, reiterating much of its first release and adding that, although power was slowly returning to the state, restoration times could vary given the severity of the storm (AEMO 2016b). The following morning, AEMO issued a third media release, stating:

> Initial investigations have identified the root cause of the event is likely to be the multiple loss of 275 kilovolt (kV) power lines during severe storm activity in the state.
>
> These transmission lines form part of the backbone of South Australia's power system and support supply and generation north of Adelaide. The reason why a cascading failure of the remainder of the South Australia network occurred is still to be identified and is subject to further investigation. (AEMO 2016c)

On the same day, at an event in Tasmania, Turnbull spoke to journalists about the blackout. In a lengthy response to a question linking the storm to South Australia's renewable energy target, Turnbull set forth his views

---

3   See DEE (n.d.).

about 'extremely aggressive, extremely unrealistic' targets driven by the ideology of his political opponents currently occupying state governments, including in South Australia. He closed his response by noting that, to meet the 'real challenges' posed by 'these intermittent renewables', the focus for governments should be on energy security, which he labelled 'the key priority'. Targeting 'lower emissions is very important', he subsequently added, 'but it must be consistent with energy security' (Turnbull 2016b). Meanwhile, Deputy Prime Minister Barnaby Joyce told a radio program that wind power 'doesn't work when there's no wind, it doesn't work when there's excessive wind, and it obviously wasn't working too well last night because they had a blackout' (Burke 2016). By 30 September, just two days after the blackout event, Turnbull had fully consolidated his message about energy security and the threat of aggressive state renewables targets. From this point, he and his government ministers repeated that message and also explicitly linked renewables with unreliability and expense.

Discussion of departmental advice

The material made available because of The Australia Institute's FOI request includes email exchanges commencing at 7.17 pm on 28 September and concluding at 9.20 am on 13 October 2016, as well as copies of parliamentary Question Time Briefs (QTBs)[4] dated 4 October, 7 October and 17 October 2016. From this, we can observe a flow of information that is dominated by descriptions of the level of storm-related damage and repairs. Initial advice briefly cautioned against speculating about causes and requested clear advice to avoid spreading misinformation. The impression is of a neutral situation report momentarily adopting an explanatory tone that is relinquished to assume the style of the descriptive, and more innocuous, situation report. The released material culminates in the announcement of an 'independent review to develop a national blueprint to maintain energy security and reliability in the National Electricity Market', to be headed by Australia's chief scientist.

To comprehensively trace how policy actors communicate and adjust their advice to forestall negative political reactions, FOI material will here be examined across four phases:

---

4   In Australia, QTBs or Possible Parliamentary Questions (PPQs) are short, informational and largely defensive briefs prepared by departmental officers for ministers on issues of potential interest on which questions are likely to be asked without notice by members during parliamentary question time.

1. 28–30 September: This phase consists of situational updates, including from the AEMO, and public statements, primarily by the prime minister.

2. 1–7 October: This includes the release of the AEMO's initial report on the blackout and the announcement of the chief scientist's review.

3. 11–13 October: This captures the leadup to a major speech by the prime minister to the minerals industry.

4. QTBs: Parliamentary responses proposed by PM&C (each entirely redacted apart from descriptive background information), linked to contemporaneous parliamentary statements by the prime minister.

To ascertain how policy advice moves with and even accommodates political manoeuvres, each phase will also be compared with corresponding government communication from the 'front regions' (Rappert 2012b: 47). The subsequent discussion will then connect my observations across text, micro-context and macro-context as suggested by my previous chapter.

Phase 1: 28–30 September

This first phase appears to include mostly forwarded updates compiled by others, such as the AEMO and the National Electricity Market Emergency Management Forum, which is convened by the AEMO when electricity emergencies occur. These 'forwards' are not surprising, given federal officials were at this point effectively transferring information from first responders to government and, as such, raising specific policy matters or obligations would likely have been premature. Email traffic moved mainly between senior officials from DEE and PM&C, as well as PM&C's duty officer attached to its crisis management area. Between the first email at 7.17 pm and just before 8.30 pm on 28 September, information pertains primarily to what happened ('a blackout, most likely triggered by strong winds which have brought down transmission lines') and the Commonwealth's role in such situations ('given the impact is localised in South Australia, we are maintaining a watching brief').

It was during this time that energy minister Frydenberg appeared on *7.30*. When asked by the show's interviewer whether South Australia's reliance on wind power had put pressure on the electricity system, Frydenberg responded:

> Well, renewables are being used in increasing amounts across the country and South Australia, as you say, has 41% of its power generation coming from renewables.
>
> Primarily solar but—sorry, primarily wind, but also solar. Now, that does raise questions for the stability of the system, not just for supply because when the wind is not blowing and the sun is not shining, electricity is not being generated.
>
> But also for the stability of the system because of the frequency that is generated as opposed to base-load power which has historically been more coal and more gas.
>
> So questions are raised by the virtue of the increasing amount of renewables. But it has to be underlined that this was a weather event which led to this occurrence. (Cooper 2016)

At 8.28 pm, PM&C's duty officer sent a brief update. This seems to be a different update to those making the rounds at this point, as it, unlike the others, has been redacted under Section 47c of the *FOI Act*, which relates to 'deliberative matter' regarding 'opinion, advice or recommendation' (Commonwealth Consolidated Acts 1982). It is curious that, amid the straightforward descriptions and updates in this phase, a missive from the duty officer, whose main function to that point was to forward basic information, has been withheld. It is possible the reference, coming just one hour after Frydenberg's television appearance, was made to it. Given the formal appearance of the email, which seems to begin with the addressee's first name or title and ends with a full signature block (absent in previous emails), it is possible this email served as an update to a senior PM&C official—perhaps the secretary—to convey that the current state of play appeared to have moved on to wind intermittency as a cause.

Minutes later, at 8.31 pm, but possibly as part of a separate email stream, a senior PM&C official emailed colleagues to ask for more detailed information than that provided earlier:

> Helpful if we can have some information on the cause and why the system responds as it did, [sic]
>
> I listened to the Premier who repeatedly indicated the outage is not generation related, but Some [sic] are suggesting related to renewables.
>
> I'm concerned that if the reason is because the system shut down to protect itself and it is not a supply issue we do not repeat misinformation.

To this, a senior official from DEE responded 'we'll get back to you on this question' before moving on to further descriptive updates. I will return to this shortly and in detail.

At 7.20 the next morning, the same DEE official forwarded a status report from a teleconference that included the offices of the prime minister and the energy minister, as well as DEE officials. She added that a note like hers was also sent to the Prime Minister's Office (PMO). What follows is a 2.5-page preliminary summary describing the continuing uncertainty surrounding this event. Four short passages appearing halfway through the document are worth quoting here:

> It is important not to speculate on how this happened. There are processes in place which support a proper investigation by the Australian Energy Market Operator …

> It is too early to be definitive about the cause, but we do know that a massive storm passing over South Australia knocked out four major transmission lines …

> Based on preliminary information the cause of yesterday's blackout was a cascading event …

> AEMO's advice is that the generation mix (ie renewable and fossil fuel) was not to blame for yesterday's events—it was the loss of 1000 MW of power in such a short space of time as transmission lines fell over.

The summary also mentions 'the agreed system restart procedures', which normally 'involve gas fired power', 'for unknown reasons … were not available'. This failure is never referred to in the ensuing political debate. For now, I will simply note that the FOI material does not show officials discussing causes in their own emails or debating the AEMO's advice about the blamelessness of the generation mix. Apart from the previous evening's email seeking clarification to avoid miscommunication, officials did not again raise possible causes in any of the unredacted material.

Throughout the day, further updates derived from National Electricity Market Emergency Management Forum teleconferences were forwarded, each describing the damage and progress. Later that afternoon, at 3.01 on 29 September, a senior adviser from PM&C's climate, energy and resources section circulated a draft of 'proposed whole of government talking points on the South Australian power outage', adding they 'have been tested with DEE and they are comfortable'. Government talking points are like QTBs in that they provide material to elected government members on matters of the day and are used largely to maintain a unified message. Importantly, they are intended for public communication. In this case, the email containing the 'SA power outage talking points' is classified 'Protected', which is located midway on the spectrum of Australia's classification system (from 'Official' to 'Top Secret') (Attorney-General's Department 2018). Left unredacted is descriptive background information about damage and weather.

About this time, on 29 and 30 September, Prime Minister Malcolm Turnbull gave three statements that may have borrowed from those talking points: a 'doorstop' interview in Tasmania on 29 September, a radio interview and another doorstop interview as part of a book launch (both on 30 September). We have already seen the 29 September event had the prime minister linking renewable energy to uncertainty ('these intermittent renewables do pose real challenges'), prioritising energy security as the way to combat that uncertainty ('energy security should always be the key priority'), blaming the states' high renewables targets on ideology ('let's end the ideology, focus on clear renewable targets') and establishing an order of priority ('we've got to recognise that energy security is the key priority and targeting lower emissions is very important but it must be consistent with energy security') (Turnbull 2016b).

The radio interview on 30 September traversed terrorism, Russian aggression and bushfires before settling on the situation in South Australia. In it, the prime minister consolidated his securitising rhetoric and introduced issues of reliability and affordability:

> You could be vulnerable—you will be vulnerable, if governments approach these energy policy issues in an ideological way … what [Premier of Victoria Daniel Andrews] is doing is creating distortions in the market … without regard to maintaining security … I'm very keen on renewable energy, but we've got to remember that yes we've got to reduce our emissions—that's very important—but we have to maintain our energy security and reliability and we have to maintain affordability … Yes, cut emissions. Yes, renewables are good, we love them, terrific. But the number one priority is, keep the lights on. Keep the lights on, that's the responsibility of government. (Turnbull 2016a)

During the doorstop interview on 30 September, Turnbull reiterated his comments about the left-wing ideology of high renewable energy targets, calling on states to get behind the more moderate federal target of 23.5 per cent by 2020. In response to a question specifically about whether renewables played any part in South Australia's power outage, he stated:

> I've been quite consistent in recognising that the power outage in South Australia, the blackout was caused by a massive storm disrupting, knocking over important transmission assets and that's quite clear. Having said that, this does bring to the forefront energy security issues and it is particularly pertinent in South Australia where they have got a very large dependence on an intermittent renewable, that is to say wind ... the reality check that we've had with South Australia, we've got to make sure you keep the lights on. Keep the lights on—that's the duty of governments. Also cut emissions, maintain affordable levels of energy supply, all of that has to be done together. (Turnbull 2016a)

Because officials' proposed talking points are redacted, we will probably never know to what degree they align with Turnbull's statements. It is still possible to speculate whether the government—particularly the prime minister—rebuffed officials' proposed material.

There are probably only two explanations for redacting these talking points. The first is that officials provided points that broadly aligned with Turnbull's comments, meaning they linked the blackout to renewables. This is unlikely given none of the pieces of supplied material bears this out and Turnbull did not explicitly link the two (preferring, instead, to place the two assertions—that the blackout was caused by storms and that South Australia's dependence on renewables was significant—alongside each other rather than substantiating a concrete connection). The second, more likely, explanation is that officials' talking points echoed advice about the ongoing uncertainty of the situation as well as its causes. The AEMO's 29 September advice that 'the generation mix (ie renewable or fossil fuel) was not to blame' was at this point no more than 24 hours old and may still be contained within those talking points. However, we know from the AEMO's 5 October 2016 preliminary report that, as at 6.25 pm on Thursday, 29 September 2016, it still 'had insufficient information about the original cause of the Black System that led to market suspension' (AEMO 2016d: 20). As such, it is possible the talking points drafted by policy advisers had shifted towards even more conditional language.

One might conclude the redacted talking points portrayed a far more ambiguous reality than the prime minister's public statements. This and the 29 September email advising that the generation mix was not to blame represent the first rebuffal under consideration.

Phase 2: 1–7 October

This phase begins on 1 October and sees more descriptions of damage and repairs, continuing in this vein until 5 October, when the AEMO's preliminary report is published. Two separate emails refer to the report: one at 10.29 am on 5 October, offering a brief overview; the other at 10.33 am on the same day, also giving an overview and a record of a National Energy Market teleconference discussing the report. Again, as was the habit, the emails provide straightforward outlines in a descriptive style that is not misplaced here given the report's purpose to provide 'preliminary information [and] observations based on data provided to date' (AEMO 2016d: 2). The report itself describes the event dispassionately and without reference to causes:

> The weather resulted in multiple transmission system faults … Generation initially rode through the faults, but at 16:18, following an extensive number of faults in a short period, 315 MW of wind generation disconnected … The uncontrolled reduction in generation resulted in increased flow in the main Victorian interconnector (Heywood) to make up the deficit. This resulted in the Heywood interconnector overloading. To avoid damage to the interconnector, the automatic-protection mechanism activated, tripping the interconnector. In this event, this resulted in the remaining customer load and electricity generation in SA being lost. (AEMO 2016d: 2)

Both emails are silent on what this might mean, particularly in the contemporary political context, or how to proceed given the report's preliminary inconclusiveness.

While wind is singled out[5] in terms of disconnection following faults, the report does not make explicit or implicit pronouncements regarding causes. Yet at this time, two different political narratives compete over the

---

5   South Australia's energy generation at the time was 883 MW from wind, 330 MW from thermal and 613 MW imported from the neighbouring state of Victoria (AEMO 2016d: 8). Given the high proportion of wind generation—representing almost half the total before the event and just less than one-sixth of the loss during the event—the singling out of wind is not surprising.

meaning of the report. As reported by *ABC News* on 5 October 2016, South Australian premier Jay Weatherill claimed the report confirmed the blackout was 'not a renewable energy event'. It also reported Weatherill as saying: 'The Prime Minister was "politicking" at a time of emergency by blaming renewable energy, and accused Malcolm Turnbull of using the emergency to "lecture South Australians about the dangers of renewable energy"' (Henderson and Sutton 2016).

On 7 October, during a radio interview in Adelaide (South Australia's capital), the prime minister stated with regard to the report:

> Let's be quite clear what the assessment concluded. Because of South Australia's very heavy reliance on wind power, which is an intermittent renewable, you know, it only generates electricity when the wind's blowing. The State has become more and more dependent for baseload power on Victoria, on actually Victoria burning brown coal by the way, which is the dirtiest form of fossil fuel generation—it generates the most CO_2 per megawatt. So what happened, as you know and it was quite clear, the storm knocked out transmission lines to the north of Adelaide which was connected to a large number of wind farms. That then caused more demand to be imposed on the interconnector with Victoria. That overloaded the interconnector, which turned off, switched off, and of course then you had the blackout. And that is basically what happened. So the real question is, one of the many questions, and this [is] what the energy ministers will be talking about today, is was that over reliance on intermittent renewables, did that cause in turn and [sic] over reliance for base load power on generation in Victoria and hence on those interconnectors. (Turnbull 2016d)

Later in the interview, Turnbull returned to the theme of energy security, affordable energy and lowering emissions: 'We've got to have all three. They're all of importance but the fundamental one is keep the lights on' (Turnbull 2016d).

Each rendition—Weatherill's and Turnbull's—offered certainty, with each imbuing the report with far greater certainty and conclusiveness than it presented. Both inferred conclusions that are not present in the report—that is, that wind energy either was or was not to blame. Table 3.1 aligns the main points from AEMO's report and the prime minister's depiction of it. While matching the report from statements one to five, it is clear the report does not bear out the conclusion made in the prime minister's sixth statement. Any generation source could disconnect following extreme weather but, because South Australia's generation mix included such a large proportion of wind, one could still blame it over other sources without being incorrect. This was a matter of choosing where to place emphasis. As this was a preliminary report, AEMO did not take the generation source into explicit account and, as such, the prime minister overinterpreted what was said without outright lying. He also, however, chose to ignore the report's inconclusiveness. This represents the second rebuffal.

Table 3.1 Comparison of AEMO report and the prime minister's outline of the report

	AEMO	Prime Minister
1	Storm	Storm
2	Faults cause 315 MW of wind generation to disconnect	Large number of wind farms knocked out
3	Increased flow to interconnector	Increased demand on interconnector
4	Interconnector overloads and trips	Interconnector overloads and is switched off
5	Blackout	Blackout
6	The root cause is subject to further analysis	The real question is overreliance on intermittent renewables

Source: AEMO (2016d: 6).

On the same day, 7 October, a special meeting of the Council of Australian Governments (COAG)[6] announced an independent review into energy security and reliability to be chaired by Australia's chief scientist, Dr Alan Finkel. I will discuss this when I turn to QTBs in Phase 4.

Phase 3: 11–13 October

There is no material between 7 and 11 October. Phase 3 therefore begins on 11 October with an email to PM&C from its Departmental Liaison Officer (DLO), who is situated within the PMO as a kind of go-between, relaying a request from the PMO for 'a quick fact check':

---

6   COAG is a federal, state and territory intergovernmental forum that meets to consider 'matters of national significance or matters that need co-ordinated action by all Australian governments' (see 'Australia's Federal Relations Architecture', available from: www.coag.gov.au/about-coag).

Is it still the case that following smelters/foundries are without power? [*And do we know what this is costing the SA economy per day?*]

Prominent Hill

Nystar [sic]

Arrium

Olympic Dam

The following day, the same official who on 28 September had asked for accurate information about the cause of the blackout, emailed a response to the DLO. She advised that all sites had had some power for 'at least a week, but have been constrained because there had been only one line going into the area'. She then provided information from ElectraNet, an electricity transmission company operating in South Australia, that 'additional load was made available to industrial customers yesterday' and included a statement from BHP regarding its South Australian Olympic Dam mine. Regarding economic costs, she included recent media reports on how much the outage was costing Arrium and Nyrstar.

Although not overtly presented as such in these emails, it is clear this fact check forms part of the content used in a prime ministerial speech to a dinner with the Australian minerals industry at Parliament House in Canberra that evening. In it, Malcolm Turnbull paid tribute to the innovation and risk-taking contribution the resources sector had made to the Australian economy, and what the government had done to maintain a policy agenda conducive to such endeavours. Rounding off a list of achievements, he moved on to the government's commitment to 'ambitious but achievable climate targets—emissions 5 per cent below 2000 levels by 2020'. Although 'we are on track for our 2020 targets', there is 'more to do':

> [W]e understand what we need to achieve. We need to achieve energy security. You've got to keep the lights on. You've got to keep the wheels of industry turning … Now, the issue about energy security is coming to a very sharp focus following the recent state-wide blackout in South Australia. It was a dramatic reminder of the importance of maintaining a reliable and affordable energy supply. The crisis in South Australia was a wake-up call for every jurisdiction in Australia to settle on a single renewable energy target but we have seen what has happened when state jurisdictions decide to set heroic targets. (Turnbull 2016f)

Turnbull then returned briefly to his familiar themes of energy security, affordability and meeting international obligations—all of which, he argued, needed to be disengaged from political ideology. What followed were statements at least partly derived from PM&C's fact check:

> Four of South Australia's largest economic contributors were without power for 15 days costing the economy tens, if not hundreds, of millions of dollars.

> According to reports in the media, Arrium steel works is just coming back on-line and they have estimated that the blackout has reportedly cost them $30 million.

> At Port Pirie, Nyrstar's lead smelter will take two weeks to repair at a cost of up to $7 million.

> Olympic Dam was forced to cease operations. To their credit, BHP Billiton's immediate focus in the aftermath was on securing and restoring sufficient power to supply the Roxby Downs township and on avoiding sustained damage to equipment and infrastructure.

> And at Prominent Hill, OZ Minerals is still without power, costing the company millions of dollars per day.

> After talking to some of the businesses and indeed farmers who lost so much, it's obvious that we have to have a clearer focus on those three objectives—energy security, energy affordability and meeting your international obligations. (Turnbull 2016f)

These assertions were clearly intended to play to Turnbull's audience, which is a reasonable goal for any speech. They also framed the blackout and its assumed cause as significant costs to the economy. This frame implies that, even in all fairness—even if one were favourably inclined towards renewables—the cold, hard reality is that lowering emissions cannot come at the cost of the nation's economic wellbeing. Taken further, high renewable energy targets will undermine our economy, which relies on our resources in the ground.

Several observations are worth making in relation to this passage and Phase 3. Speech drafts are usually, at least initially, written by departments for their ministers. Once they arrive in a minister's office, drafts tend to be changed, particularly when they concern contentious or politicised issues. The PMO's 'quick fact check' suggests the material to be checked was new—that is, it was written by the office and was not part of the department's earlier draft. The department was therefore being asked to react quickly to material that was neither sourced nor written by them. This is probably why their reply was fragmentary and somewhat unauthoritative. Although we can see some use being made of PM&C's response (such as the cost to Nyrstar), most of Turnbull's statements were either exaggerated (being completely without power for 15 days, rather than with some power for less than that; and the uncheckable price tag of 'tens, if not hundreds, of millions of dollars') or sourced from elsewhere ('talking to some of the businesses and indeed farmers'). Finally, at no point—neither here nor elsewhere in these FOI releases—did anyone ask the department to check whether the blackout could logically be connected to endangering Australia's energy security.

By themselves, none of these observations amounts to the type of rebuffal observed in my examination of the treasurer's rejection of Treasury's negative-gearing advice. Taken together, however, they point to a broader condition whereby government actors do not ask policy experts about deeper arguments and rationale, and policy experts do not offer them— at least not on paper. In each case, the bureaucracy seemed to function mainly as a vendor of rudimentary information, perhaps because the only advice it could provide frankly and objectively was on the status of damage. This type of rebuffal operates almost as a kind of self-inhibiting mechanism, along similar lines to Bruce Dover's 'anticipatory compliance',[7] which results in offering nothing unwanted in case one is sidelined. I argue that, far from being an oddity, this pre-emptive, self-administered rebuffal, in which nothing of consequence is offered for fear of rejection or charges of unresponsiveness, represents an important type of rebuffing and is connected to what is legislatively and culturally expected of policy advisers. Although it constitutes the third instance of rebuffal, this nuance suggests a more complex typology than my previous rebuffals. I will return to this at length in due course.

Phase 4: Question Time Briefs

The final phase takes in a series of QTBs titled 'Energy Security and Renewable Energy', issued on 4 October, 7 October and 17 October 2016. As noted briefly above, QTBs are prepared by departments and

---

7   Dover worked as Rupert Murdoch's vice-president in China. His book *Rupert's Adventure in China* calls executives' and editors' responses to their boss's expectations 'a sort of "anticipatory compliance". One didn't need to be instructed about what to do, one simply knew what was in one's long-term interests' (quoted in Watson and Hill 2015: 13).

provide information to ministers on issues of potential interest to be used in response to questions from members during parliamentary question time. They are similar to government talking points except they are mainly intended for use in parliament as defensive responses to questions from the opposition. As such, they project possible questions and supply answers to them. They are composed as factually as possible but can also refer to a minister's previous comments on the subject, sometimes even including them as answers, which may become accepted as facts over time. The QTBs under examination here are entirely redacted under Section 47c of the *FOI Act*. This may be because energy security and renewable energy were here explicitly drawn together by the department in the QTBs' titles, which is notable given this explicit connection is not made elsewhere in the departmental material, despite the government doing so on numerous occasions. Referring to the prime minister's statements in parliament around those dates may help determine what the redacted QTBs contained and whether parts of those statements were supplied by the department.

On 10 October 2016, the first sitting day after a three-week parliamentary break during which the blackout occurred, energy minister Josh Frydenberg was asked a question by one of his colleagues. He obliged with a response about progress made by COAG and the announcement about an independent review, briefly mentioning the prime minister's refrain of energy security, reliability and affordability, and concluding with the by-now familiar condemnation of the opposition's 'reckless pursuit of an ideological approach to renewable energy targets without thinking through the implications for energy security' (Parliament of Australia 2016b: 1288). This was followed by a question from shadow energy minister Mark Butler to the prime minister. Butler asked: 'Why did the Prime Minister champion renewable energy in South Australia before the election only to use an extreme weather event to play politics after the election?' In response, Malcolm Turnbull began the 'economic cost' narrative that he went on to use in his address to the minerals industry dinner two days later:

> I do thank the honourable member for his question because in asking it he puts his finger on the very central problem that Labor faces with this issue: that they treat renewable energy as an ideological issue rather than a technological issue. The bottom line is simply this: that there are many sources of electricity. There is intermittent renewable. There is hydro. We have many forms of

fossil fuel generation. All of them have different characteristics. What we have to do is take away the ideology and the political claptrap with which the Labor Party surrounds all of their policies and focus on these objectives. What we need to do is ensure that we keep the lights on—something the honourable member's Labor colleagues in South Australia demonstrably failed to do. We have to keep the lights on. We have to ensure that there is energy security. We have to ensure that households and businesses can afford to pay for it—and his Labor colleagues in South Australia have created the most expensive wholesale electricity in Australia. That is very helpful, isn't it, I ask the honourable member— terribly helpful if you want to revive your manufacturing base … So you have got to do have [sic] energy security and energy affordability, and we have to meet our emission reduction targets as set out in the Paris treaty. So we have to do all three and we have to make sure we achieve them all together … This is a time when we must stop putting ideology into something that is essentially an engineering issue. How do we achieve those three goals? There is a way to do it. We are leading the way. (Parliament of Australia 2016b: 1291)

On 12 October, Butler returned with a similar question: 'In July 2011, the Prime Minister said that 100 per cent of stationary energy will need to come from clean sources by the middle of the century. Prime Minister, what happened to you?' (Parliament of Australia 2016c: 1706).

Turnbull responded with an overview of Australia's obligation to reduce emissions under the Paris Agreement and boasted that 'we are well on track to meet our 2020 targets—indeed, to beat our 2020 targets'. He closed with an appeal to pragmatism that expanded on the economic cost frame he floated at that evening's dinner:

The important point honourable members have got to recognise is that if you turn these technologies into matters of ideology, if you turn them into matters of some kind of secular religion— if that is not a contradiction—or if you mythologise them, then you will mislead yourself and have the result of undermining energy security and affordability or, indeed, your path to emission reduction. These are engineering and technology issues. We know what we need to achieve and what his [Butler's] state[8] has lamentably failed to achieve. We need to keep the lights on. We need energy

---

8 Mark Butler was the Member for Port Adelaide, an electorate in South Australia, at the time of the blackout and its aftermath.

> to be affordable—not the most expensive in Australia, as it is in South Australia. And we need to meet our emissions reduction target. We need to achieve those three objectives. That is what the government's policy is all about. We are doing it, but we are doing it in a clear-eyed, hard-headed, rational manner. This is not an ideological issue; it is an engineering one. And we are approaching it pragmatically and effectively. (Parliament of Australia 2016c: 1291)

The bottom line, Turnbull argued, was that energy security, reliability, affordability and emissions reductions were matters not of ideology but of technology and engineering. They must be approached 'pragmatically and effectively' and 'in a clear-eyed, hard-headed, rational manner'. This line of argument goes to the heart of the primacy he assigned to energy security over ideology, while the associated necessity of settling on a single renewable energy target is an oblique way of saying that states whose targets are high are politically grandstanding against the federal government's target, which is a 'pragmatic' 20 per cent by 2020 (at this time, Queensland's target was 50 per cent by 2030 and South Australia's was 75 per cent by 2025). Turnbull's statements may also go to the heart of the way he became prime minister, which Butler alluded to in his questions. I will return to this in my consideration of context.

For now, let us return to the QTBs themselves. It should be noted here that those who rise to speak often, such as the prime minister, tend not to have to avail themselves of the text provided in QTBs. In other words, as a frequent and practised speaker, Turnbull may not have needed his department's proposed speaking points in formulating his responses on 10 and 12 October. In any event, given the redaction of the text, there is no way of knowing and one can only speculate about the QTBs' title linking energy security and renewable energy. In the leadup to the start of each parliamentary sitting, ministerial offices send their respective departments a list of titles for new or updated QTBs. Departments then develop those titles into draft QTBs. One might therefore assume the link was made by the PMO and that PM&C provided whatever text it could to populate this QTB. Given the text we have observed in the other, unredacted material, however, no such link had been made by policy advisers. In that case, it seems more likely PM&C's QTB followed the kind of language we saw in some of the updates we have considered, which described a sequence of events and repairs. One might conclude, therefore, that—much like its earlier fact check—the department simply supplied sufficiently relevant information about the blackout situation in the blandest possible way. But why would this be redacted under Section 47c when the fact check was not?

At least four further explanations are possible. The first is that PM&C substantiated renewables as a threat to energy security. At this point, however, that represented political opinion only and had not been raised by the AEMO's preliminary examinations. This explanation would imply that PM&C consciously helped turn unsubstantiated opinion into policy-derived evidence. Although this could explain why these QTBs have been redacted—and would mean they were not rebuffed—it does not seem plausible. The language of policy advice tends, on the whole, to be anodyne largely because it works hard to avoid overstatement and the unknown. The second explanation is that PM&C may have used this opportunity to explain that renewable energy did not pose a threat to energy security as no current evidence suggested a connection. The terms in which they explained this may not have been as stark, but the overall message would have been at odds with the prime minister's public statements. This explanation would be in keeping with the material we saw in Treasury's negative-gearing briefings—that is, a department providing its minister with information he publicly rejected. The third is that PM&C attempted to connect renewable energy and energy security by arguing that security could be maintained if one committed to diversification by embracing renewables in the generation mix. This, however, would have gone against the dominant government narrative that renewables were too unreliable to guarantee secure generation. The fourth, perhaps most likely, explanation is that PM&C provided talking points about renewables and talking points about energy security—on the same page, to be sure, but under separate columns, thus avoiding having to construct an argument about how the two might be related. This would have ensured both responsiveness and objectivity, thus lending authority (Porter 1995: 8). We now have before us a variety of explanations, none of which can be entirely substantiated. Yet, the redaction of all the QTBs' talking points allows us to contemplate Phase 4 as the final rebuffal.

Mention should also be made of the AEMO's final report of its review of the blackout, published on 23 March 2017, which concluded:

> Wind turbines successfully rode through grid disturbances. It was the action of a control setting responding to multiple disturbances that led to the Black System. Changes made to

> turbine control settings shortly after the event has [sic] removed the risk of recurrence given the same number of disturbances. (AEMO 2017b: 7)

Further:

> The most well-known characteristic of wind power, variation of output with wind strength (often termed 'intermittency'), was not a material factor in the events immediately prior to the Black System. Other potential causes for the sustained power reduction have been subject to analysis by AEMO, including wind turbine disconnection due to excessive wind speed. Typically, wind turbines exhibit a protective behaviour whereby they shut down to protect themselves from excessive mechanical stress in high winds, typically 90 km/h or more. Of the 456 MW sustained power reduction by nine wind farms, approximately 35 MW of wind generation was disconnected due to excessive wind speed during the last five voltage disturbances. This was not a material contributor to the event. (AEMO 2017b: 47)

Obviously, none of this information was available during the phases under consideration. Its certainty would surely have been welcomed. What was available at the time was necessarily preliminary and uncertain, and what policy advisers formulated from it did not prevent a miscasting of events.

The final word in this section should go to the independent review by Chief Scientist Dr Alan Finkel, which is mentioned in the background of the QTBs. Although announced during the period under consideration, the Finkel Review did not report until June 2017. Commissioned to 'develop a national blueprint to maintain energy security and reliability', the review explained any potentially negative relationship between security and renewables simply in terms of generator integration and timing:

> Australia needs to increase system security and ensure future reliability in the NEM [National Energy Market]. Security and reliability have been compromised by poorly integrated variable renewable electricity generators, including wind and solar. This has coincided with the unplanned withdrawal of older coal and gas-fired generators. (Finkel 2017: 5)

On the blackout itself, Finkel notes:

> One of the factors that led to the blackout in South Australia in September 2016 was that some wind generators had a control setting that disconnected or reduced their output in response

to multiple power system disturbances. In particular, upon detecting a series of voltage dips, nine wind farms simultaneously disconnected or cut their output after exceeding a pre-set limit for the number of ride through responses in a two minute period. AEMO was not aware of their pre-set protection limits. The event highlighted that access to correct technical information about grid-connected equipment is critical for system security. (Finkel 2017: 59)

As already suggested by the AEMO's final report, the blackout was largely the result of human error and not technology. Nonetheless, the political narrative and the policy advice that accompanied it did not emphasise this human element. This is probably because blame would then have needed to shift towards organisational elements and human accountability, closing off opportunities for the government to undermine the reliability of renewables. As Charles E. Naquin and Terri R. Kurtzberg observe, 'people will have a propensity to blame an organization more for a misfortune when it was directly caused by human error than if the same misfortune had been caused by a technological error' (2004: 130).

The text

Let me briefly reiterate the four instances of rebuffal here. The first is perhaps the most obvious. Following an explicit question on the night of the storm from one of PM&C's senior officials that information on the cause would be helpful to avoid spreading misinformation, a senior DEE official the next morning forwarded a status report from a ministerial teleconference that included an update from the AEMO about the generation mix being 'not to blame'. This report was forwarded without substantive comments or discussion about a handling strategy. Later that day, draft government talking points were circulated and probably not used by the prime minister, who called the blackout a 'reality check' about the threat of renewables to energy security.

The second is slightly more nuanced in that the AEMO's report did not explicitly condemn or acquit a particular cause, instead describing a sequence of events and highlighting the report's preliminary nature. Given this early yet unavoidable ambiguity—framed as flat evidence and used by the department as a buffer, presumably to avoid giving policy advice—the prime minister (re)cast the report as leading to the 'real question' of 'over reliance on intermittent renewables'.

The third and fourth rebuffals are more complex. The prime minister's speech fact check revealed a subtle dynamic between policy advisers and ministerial offices, in which advisers tend not to proactively offer deeper arguments and government actors do not request them. Fielding only isolated questions taken from the body of a speech being redrafted by ministerial staff implies that policy advisers are not invited to contribute their broader professional insights. Further, responding with nothing unwanted seems to indicate that policy advisers engage in a kind of anticipatory compliance—that is, they supply only what has been asked for and offer nothing else, perhaps in case of rejection. Finally, the redacted QTBs suggest the possibility that policy advisers, when confronted with unsubstantiated hyperbole about energy security and unreliable renewables, intentionally framed their advice as plain descriptions of events. In other words, conceived of as merely transferring sets of information, this policy advice was deliberately one-dimensional, even unknowing. This takes on a deeper resonance when one considers it was issued against a backdrop of intense political conflict, the roots of which can be traced to the breakdown in Australia's climate change consensus, much of it driven by debate over sustaining the role of Australian coal. If one was to define this intentional unawareness, one might characterise it as a particular skill—one, as Michael Taussig (1999: 2) has put it in a different context, of 'knowing what not to know'. I will discuss this in detail and with reference to some of the literature on deliberate ignorance shortly.

In the previous chapter, I constructed a framework to help drive my examination of rebuffed advice. In considering the text of that advice, I focused on four key areas, each of which prompted a question:

1. *Kairos*: What effect does time have on the advice?
2. Context: How does context potentially affect language—and does language affect context?
3. Awareness of self and audience: How is the advice conceived of, how is it framed and what does its audience do with it?
4. Response: What is the political reaction to the advice and how is it formed?

Like the next chapter on Iraq, here, time and context are closely linked and play a role in shaping the language of both expert advice and political statements. Time is clearly linked to the urgency of the crisis—an entire state without power—and this means advisers had to tread carefully to ensure rapid and correct dissemination of information. In such circumstances, being rebuffed in the first and second phases may have been unmerited, but, given the political drama unfolding at the same time, probably unsurprising. With government ministers almost simultaneously juxtaposing the blackout with South Australia's political choices about energy supply, the political narrative swiftly unfastened itself from the preliminary evidence. When Energy Minister Frydenberg raised questions about 'the stability of the system ... by virtue of the increasing amount of renewables' that night; when Deputy Prime Minister Barnaby Joyce told ABC Radio the following morning that wind power 'obviously wasn't working too well last night because they had a blackout' (Owens 2016); and when Prime Minister Turnbull claimed on the same day that South Australia presented a 'reality check', the political narrative and the language driving it took a specific path. This is probably why, despite initially attempting to dispel misinterpretations, officials largely did not try to correct their political masters.

However, the speed with which official advice fell into place suggests there may have been additional temporal and contextual forces at play, which, I proposed above, are related to the breakdown in Australia's climate change consensus. Although that consensus has been unravelling globally for the past few years, in Australia, it also appears to be at least partly connected to the ongoing leadership crises for which Canberra has come to be known as 'the coup capital of the world' (see, for example, Bryant 2015; SBS News 2018; Perrigo 2018). An abbreviated version of this—which for my purposes concerns only Turnbull's leadership in opposition and as prime minister[9]—begins in 2009 when, as leader of the opposition Liberal–National Coalition, he proposed siding with the Labor government's proposed 'carbon pollution reduction scheme' to combat climate change. Before voting on the Bill could take place—which would have seen Turnbull cross the floor to side with the government—those conservative colleagues unwilling to back the scheme replaced him in a narrowly won leadership contest with self-described climate 'weathervane' Tony Abbott (Turnbull 2009). Abbott went on to win the 2013 election with a promise to repeal Labor's legislated carbon price. After an unpopular budget in 2014 and several other highly critiqued decisions—such as knighting

---

9   From 2007 to May 2022, Australia had seven prime ministers, four of whom were ousted before the end of their terms by their own side: Kevin Rudd in 2010 by Julia Gillard, Julia Gillard in 2013 by Kevin Rudd, Tony Abbott in 2015 by Malcolm Turnbull and Malcolm Turnbull in 2018 by Scott Morrison.

Prince Philip (Lewis 2015)—Abbott's leadership became precarious. In September 2015, after losing '30 Newspolls in a row' (Turnbull 2015), Turnbull challenged and beat Abbott in a leadership contest, 54 votes to 44 (Martin 2015). With Turnbull's reputation for progressive views on climate change, marriage equality and an Australian republic, public expectations were high (Patrick 2018), which was reflected in subsequent polling. In November 2015, 70 per cent of respondents viewed him as 'a capable leader', 63 per cent as 'understand[ing] the problems facing Australia', 59 per cent as 'good in a crisis' and 51 per cent as 'visionary'. But those expectations began to fade as Turnbull slowly revealed himself to be incapable of delivering on any of them. By March 2016, his total approval rating had drifted downwards across each of the above four characteristics (to 64, 53, 52 and 44 per cent, respectively) (Lewis 2016). On 2 July 2016, just two months before the blackout, Turnbull scraped in to win the federal election with a bare one-seat majority.

It has been suggested that, to garner sufficient votes to take the leadership from Abbott, the centrist Turnbull made a deal 'with the jackals of the right' (Daley 2018; Hartcher 2018), who, in exchange for their support, forced him to shelve his more progressive views on climate change, among others. Even so, for the duration of Turnbull's time in office, many among the right-wing factions of the party continued to thrill to Abbott's statement while prime minister that 'coal is good for humanity, coal is good for prosperity, coal is an essential part of our economic future, here in Australia, and right around the world' (Massola et al. 2014). To win and maintain power, therefore, Turnbull had somehow to diverge from his previous views and the rhetorical path[10] with which he had, until this point, been associated. The South Australian blackout, I argue, presented an opportunity through which Turnbull could strengthen his flagging leadership and maintain his party's support. Thus, while still claiming to 'love' renewables, what really mattered to Turnbull now was 'keeping the lights on' and doing so 'pragmatically and effectively' and 'in a clear-eyed, hard-headed, rational manner'. Although this new rhetorical path was ultimately not sustainable for him,[11] the uncertainty surrounding the blackout in its early days gave Turnbull sufficient rationale to credibly

---

10 For a discussion of rhetorical path dependency, see Grube (2014b).

11 After months of agitation led by former prime minister Tony Abbott over the National Energy Guarantee (a policy proposal that essentially concluded the trajectory from the South Australian blackout via the Finkel Review), Turnbull lost the support of his party in August 2018, and was succeeded by his treasurer, Scott Morrison (Fernando and Bedo 2018).

embrace energy security—procured with coal—over doubtful renewables, particularly wind. In effect, Turnbull's frame was simple: yes, I used to embrace renewables as a mitigation strategy and they still have their place in meeting our climate change targets, but seriously, who would not choose security over insecurity, certainty over uncertainty?

A brief sidenote about securitisation as a rhetorical construct is useful. Securitisation can be valuable because it lends authority, particularly in situations, such as the one under consideration, in which debate is not desirable. It has been said to work to 'silence opposition' and can give 'power holders many opportunities to exploit "threats" for domestic purposes, to claim a right to handle something with less democratic control and constraint' (Buzan et al. 1998: 29). When deployed in this way, 'security should be seen as a negative, as a failure to deal with issues as normal politics' (Buzan et al. 1998: 29). Turnbull's securitising of energy can be viewed as a rhetorical device with which he sought to portray himself as strong and capable of guarding against threatening change— not just in the climate, but also in his own party.

Turnbull's fraught political history has been captured here as no more than a sketch. There are clearly many other factors at play in his leadership crisis, and in Australia's more generally (see, for instance, Kelly 2018; Bongiorno 2018; Chang 2018). Yet, the potency of the backdrop—leadership struggles arguably connected to climate change and its mitigation partly through renewables and the decline of coal—suggests the blackout offered an opportunity born of time and context. That is, the blackout should be viewed as a moment when a crisis—the blackout itself, but more subtly also the government's internal problems and Turnbull's own—was used to convey a solution to all three problems. The blackout, in other words, was a *kairotic* moment. John E. Smith describes *kairos* as pointing to 'the significance and purpose of events and to the idea of constellations of events yielding results which would not have been possible at other times and under other circumstances' (1969: 2).

Elsewhere, he explains that the notion of *kairos* encompasses 'three distinct but related concepts':

> There is, first, the idea of the 'right time' for something to happen in contrast with 'any time'; a sense that is captured nicely in the word 'timing' … Second, *kairos* means a time of tension and conflict, a time of crisis implying that the course of events poses a problem that calls for a decision at that time, which is to say that no

generalized solution or response supposedly valid at any or every time will suffice. Third, *kairos* means that the problem or crisis has brought with it a time of opportunity … for accomplishing some purpose which could not be carried out at some other time. Implicit in all three meanings embraced by *kairos* is the concept of an *individual* time having a critical ordinal position set apart from its predecessors and successors. (Smith 2002: 52)

Borrowing from Smith's definitions, the blackout presented an opportunity for Turnbull to reframe himself as reminiscent of what he used to be but, more importantly, what he needed to be now to stay in power. That is, he reframed himself as just progressive enough but mainly as sufficiently pragmatic to maintain Australia's resource-rich status quo and, with that, the support of the government's conservative factions. For Turnbull and his party, the blackout thus became the moment at which renewables could be justifiably denounced as both too unreliable and progressive ideology gone mad. In a sense, the blackout represented both crisis and solution for Turnbull, and perhaps even symbolises his own struggle and attempted transformation. It was therefore acutely positioned at the 'right time'.

Although not confronted by the crisis in these specific terms, policy advisers in the APS would have been aware of much of this when formulating their advice. Indeed, civil servants tend to follow political developments closely and, as former long-serving Treasury secretary Ken Henry puts it, good policy advisers should be 'politically aware' (2017a: 16). This awareness is described in guidance on working with ministers as understanding 'the current political context' (APSC 2021b). Further, the 'Integrated Leadership System', which identifies the capabilities by which most of the APS is performance-managed, describes this awareness at the levels of seniority we saw among our email correspondents as the ability to draw 'on information and alternate viewpoints' and monitor 'information channels to understand new issues of importance to the government' (APSC 2018c).

Although clearly not required to participate politically, Australian public servants, then, are expected to understand the political environment to perform their functions at a high strategic level. As such, it is not unreasonable to assume that, at least among the more senior email correspondents,[12] there

---

12 The two primary correspondents from PM&C and DEE were assistant secretaries, or Senior Executive Service (SES) Band 1. There are three 'bands' across the SES below the level of secretary, which is the highest. To reach the level of SES Band 1 from a junior or graduate entry level would take several years (recognising that some may be direct recruits).

would have been good awareness of the context and its evolution over the previous few years (seven years by 2016 if one includes Turnbull's ousting as opposition leader in 2009). I am not implying that overt references to Turnbull's political troubles should have been made. There seems, however, to be an almost studied silence even on issues of concern to departments such as PM&C and DEE. For instance, with the blackout providing a platform for government disparagement of renewable energy, it may have become strategically necessary for public servants to consider and raise policy implications, such as how emissions will be lowered in the event wind energy is reduced in the generation mix. Maybe this happened—but it did not happen here, concurrently with information about the trigger event and prime ministerial commentary that put the generation mix in doubt. In other words, acknowledging 'new issues of importance to the government' seems to have been carefully avoided here.

This leads to consideration of how the advice itself was framed. After the early and decisive rebuffal of advice about the generation mix not being to blame, the sole focus of the FOI-released material seemed to be on relaying crisis information. Apart from one early question about the accuracy of blaming renewables, as well as what I have inferred from the redactions, one sees a frame that casts advice as a mere channel for transmitting accounts of reality as they are conveyed by the emergency management forum and various others. This frame, as well as the unanswered question, the speech fact check and the redactions—all suggest a kind of reticence, which is probably partly related to the complexity surrounding Turnbull and his riven party. It is almost certainly related to the widespread bureaucratic belief that FOI laws are somehow inhibiting—that is, they necessarily cause public servants to prepare innocuous written advice or deliver it orally. As we saw in the previous chapter, Shergold's *Learning from Failure* was particularly robust in its regard of FOI laws as 'a significant barrier to frank written advice', citing then APS commissioner John Lloyd's even stronger view that they are 'pernicious' (Shergold 2015: 19).

But there is something else at work here—something that takes us beyond imagining a language that does its best to fly under the radar simply by being slippery. Linsey McGoey suggests the transparency required by FOI legislation has given rise, on the part of bureaucrats, to 'resourceful strategies of non-disclosure' such as 'feigning ignorance' because it 'answers the twin demands of appearing transparent while wielding control over the very information one has an interest in concealing'. More specifically, feigned ignorance 'allows those in authority to deny knowledge of the truths which they are increasingly expected to share' (McGoey 2007: 216–17). Under these terms, one might even describe the frame at hand as one of 'feigned ignorance'. If that is correct, it depicts an uncomfortable reality that warrants closer examination.

McGoey quotes Niklas Luhmann to explain further this 'purposeful cultivation of ignorance':

> The communication of ignorance relieves authority. Whoever communicates knowledge absorbs uncertainty and must consequently take responsibility for the truth and untruth of his knowledge. Whoever communicates ignorance is excused. (McGoey 2007: 228).[13]

Maintaining uncertainty, therefore, absolves those who might otherwise be held responsible were they to transform it into something more resolute. Absconding from the transmission of deeper expertise, in other words, evades responsibility and even accountability. Further, 'appearing uncertain rather than authoritative' can hold political capital, which takes us well beyond the conviction that ambiguous language is simply an unfortunate symptom of FOI laws:

> In recent times, those carrying political or cultural power have increasingly grasped that uncertainty provides a reprieve from having to answer for the consequences of one's knowledge. Conditionality becomes a more advantageous rhetorical tool that [sic] certainty: one need not provide answers for what one could not have known. (McGoey 2007: 230)

In this sense, ignorance and ambiguity offer 'protection from blame' (McGoey 2007: 230) and, for my purposes, may also pre-empt rebuffal. Others have also noticed this tendency, such as Jacqueline Best, who considers that 'uncertainty poses a considerable challenge to experts who guide … decisions since they may be held accountable for unfortunate outcomes' (2012: 88). As a response to this challenge, experts have not eliminated ignorance but incorporated it, which, Best asserts, has become 'an institutional response' (2012: 92). Rappert notes: '[d]epending on the situation, both claiming knowledge and [claiming] ignorance may be advantageous. Ambiguity in relation to what you know is a way of resisting lines of interrogation' (2012a: 30–31).

---

13   McGoey quotes from Niklas Luhmann's 1998 essay 'The Ecology of Ignorance'.

Ambiguity and its bestowal of blameless ignorance can therefore carry political capital or, at the very least, the absence of political wrath, deeper analysis or rebuffal. It also offers a further benefit. Based on her examination of regulatory agencies and industry, McGoey proposes that '*not* managing to reach conclusions' had the desirable effect of preventing the relationship between the two groups from fracturing (2007: 232; emphasis in original). That is, uncertainty was observed as a kind of social glue that conserved a relationship, which moves us well beyond mere FOI avoidance strategies. This echoes Stone's (1997: 138) finding that ambiguity enables 'coalition and compromise'. In my study of South Australia's blackout, one might say something similar about the relationship between policy advisers and government ministers—that is, 'knowing what not to know' became a useful tool for avoiding the friction that might otherwise have arisen had advisers chosen to emphasise and repeat early advice that renewables were probably not to blame.

I suggest that policy advice during the blackout effected a lack of awareness around some of the key temporal and contextual factors driving the political narrative that renewables could not be trusted as an input to baseload power. Ignoring the political context so steadfastly, however, also meant having to ignore related policy issues that were within advisers' own domain, such as implications for emissions and clean energy targets, issues of diversification, the sustainability of the generation mix and the future of fossil fuels. By focusing solely on what could be seen on the ground, the policy advice under consideration essentially positioned itself as a kind of reportage. Simply updating ministers and their offices about events, and overlooking all other potentially problematic factors, gave the advice an appearance of certainty without anyone having to take responsibility for any of the underlying complexities. However, while bypassing uncertainty with their almost exclusive focus on status updates may have allowed policy advisers to avoid the consequences of their expertise, ambiguity was allowed to flourish. This, in turn, made it easier for ministers to stretch the narrative to wherever they wanted it. As Annick de Vries et al. (2010: 103) put it: 'the interpretation option for politicians increases when extensive uncertainty information is provided'. Rappert suggests this is a game, which he calls 'In gray you can play': 'Ambiguity cannot be underestimated as a resource. Clarity marks out trench lines for conflict. A lack of it leaves much room for maneuvering' (Rappert 2012a: 30).

If policy advisers effectively relieved themselves of their responsibility to be frank about evidence by leaving out relevant policy issues, one might say they gifted government ministers with an ambiguity that made many interpretations of reality possible. That is, furnished with official advice that withdrew from contradicting them, political actors were free to construe wind energy as unreliable, play down emissions reduction and, with it, deprioritise the Australian Government's international commitments to mitigate climate change. Each played to Turnbull's frame of pragmatism—repeatedly formulated as energy security—which transformed the uncertainty and even chaos of the situation into enablers for certainty and reliability. One might conclude that advisers vacating the policy field in favour of status reports created an empty space that an increasingly unpopular prime minister and government readily filled with definitive and reassuring language about energy security.

The texts themselves featured only two passages that lacked ambiguity: one that referred to the early finding that wind was not to blame, and the other that it was too early to reach conclusions, each of them based on initial AEMO advice buried within a lengthy departmental update. These were very clearly rejected. I hypothesised that a further three may have been unambiguous: the redacted email to a very senior PM&C official, the redacted government talking points and the redacted QTBs on energy security and renewable energy. These may have explained that seeking consistency between the type of energy security Turnbull was pursuing and renewable energy could not be logically achieved without affecting the government's commitment to climate change mitigation. Across the 15 days of email traffic, only one official challenged her departmental colleagues about the unfolding political narrative about wind energy, and she was never answered directly. We do not know whether ministers were ever provided advice that questioned or contradicted their views. Yet, given what this analysis has observed, there is almost nothing to suggest that official advice to ministers and their offices was anything other than tunnel-visioned: focused on the blackout itself and carefully blocking out anything troublesome—such as the government's internal conflicting views on climate change—that may have undercut the government's description of events or its preferencing of energy security.

In his report *Learning from Failure*, Shergold writes extensively about frank and fearless policy advice. In a report prepared as a result of the findings of the 2014 Royal Commission into the Home Insulation Program (HIP) (which chronicled public servants' failure to provide robust advice to their ministers, indirectly leading to the deaths of four young insulation installers), Shergold notes that it takes courage to give ministers robust advice, but it must be done:

> Good advice is not only responsive—but also responsible … This can mean telling ministers things that they do not wish to hear, but of which they need to be aware. Only then can we be assured that decisions are made in full knowledge of all the facts. Governments should act with eyes wide open … Giving frank and fearless advice can be difficult. It can be complicated by the desire to preserve good working relationships with ministers. There can be pressure to be 'pragmatic' and act in a way that is expedient or convenient. The community's legitimate expectation that the APS serves the public interest with integrity requires more than this. It can require steely resolve. (Shergold 2015: 18)

Shergold knows that providing this type of advice is hard, but he is also suggesting it is possible and necessary. On the other hand, the primary audience for this advice—government ministers—tends frequently to disparage the material it receives from the APS:

> Ministers themselves frequently bemoan the quality of advice that they receive. There have been recurrent complaints over the years from ministers about their departments' apparent lack of innovative ideas and inadequate standard of advice. (Shergold 2015: 15)

In other words, ministers report being unhappy with advice they perceive as lacking ideas, which implies a lack of independent thought, and clarity. The APS itself strives to achieve those goals, as emphasised in its 'Values': '[E]mployees should provide forthright and professional advice; and develop robust and innovative options, supported with persuasive argument, good analysis and strong evidence' (APSC 2021a).

Indeed, when working with ministers, the APSC also makes note of what Shergold called 'steely resolve' in their description of good advice: 'relevant, comprehensive and unaffected by fear of consequences, not withholding important facts or bad news' (APSC 2021a).

There is, then, an expectation of public servants that their advice to ministers be bold, persuasive, innovative and unafraid of leaving out significant information. Yet, ministers complain they are not getting this. From what we have observed, we might agree that they are not. Yet, I suggest this complaint rings hollow when one considers that advice like

PM&C's and DEE's must be rather convenient to ministers in that it forestalls potential embarrassment further down the road—for instance, by pointing out some important, related facts. In this sense, ministers are getting exactly what they want, at least when the issue is subject to intense political manoeuvring.

We have thus arrived at a point where expert advice may forestall, and thus not encounter, rebuffal. That is, the reaction to this advice was not negative because it proved useful in terms of providing and fact-checking information and, as we saw, because policy advisers were not asked for, nor did they offer, their views. Indeed, this transactional relationship, which ministerial advisers also help to shape, seemed efficient, familiar and coordinated. After an initial challenge, advice seemed largely choreographed by silence, in that providers and receivers were never obliged to produce more, or less, or something different. In this way, advice and the reaction to it were 'in sync'. In other words, because advice was concerned with only one thing, it proved useful (as it provided good information only about the blackout and avoided criticism by not raising anything else) and minimised rejection. In effect, ministers did not have to rebuff much of the advice because public servants arranged the advice accordingly. We might say the advisers chose tactics (for instance, self-preservation) over strategy (providing frank, comprehensive advice).

Finally, my framework asks whether advisers' language affected context—whether, in other words, policy advice helped facilitate the government's rhetoric. Judging by what we have been able to observe, the answer is yes. It is affirmative not in the sense that advice had a hand in forging the government's rhetoric, but in that it avoided trying to persuade government ministers that shifting away from renewables towards energy security was premature given the preliminary nature of investigations, not to mention incompatible with policy commitments (more on this below). Its influence on government rhetoric was therefore by way of absence. This does not mean policy advisers offered nothing. On the contrary, as the government's expert advisers, their silence on relevant matters effectively provided additional authority to the government's rhetoric. As Rappert suggests, it is wrong to assume this kind of absence simply indicates 'a void or lack' (2015: 11). Instead, one should view this absence as implying presence because 'to be empty is to be empty of something' (Rappert 2015: 7). This emptiness was the presence of left-out departmental, expert views, which gave the advice the hue of policy consistency with government rhetoric and government rhetoric the authority of policy consistency and even an evidence base.

I have noted that this absence effectively increased what de Vries et al. (2010) called the interpretation option for politicians and Rappert (2012a) elsewhere termed leaving room for manoeuvring. Yet, it should also be acknowledged that it would have been hasty for early advice about the blackout to be definitive. Certainty about causes would have been premature. As such, maintaining the inconclusiveness of the event seems to have been inevitable, at least while preliminary investigations were taking place. Indeed, inconclusiveness is not rare in public policy work. Policy actors are accustomed to uncertainty and ambiguity, and the policy environment is often, even mostly, in flux. As Marteen Hajer and David Laws note, ambiguity is 'a significant feature of policy work' (2006: 262). In their estimation, policy actors tend to try to reduce 'uncertainty and respond to the need for stability by deriving generalizable knowledge and universal principles that can be applied to achieve policy goals' (Hajer and Laws 2006: 251). Engaging ambiguity and doubt as 'a key part of good policy work', they suggest, can generate work that 'typically takes place between two poles: one pulling in the direction of clarity and the reduction of complexity, the other illuminating precisely that which we do not fully understand' (Hajer and Laws 2006: 252). This is not, however, necessarily how policy advisers deal with uncertainty in practice, despite being surrounded by it. As Alex Stevens' ethnographic research of UK policy advisers indicates, there is a

> distaste for uncertainty, complexity and contradiction within policy-making circles. It suggests that civil servants learn to avoid such problematic features when they construct policy stories. This does not mean that they deliberately avoid, neglect or misuse evidence, but they are influenced in their use of evidence by the constraints of a particular thought world, whose limits they reproduce in their turn. (2011: 247)

In this interpretation, advisers avoid having to integrate uncertainty into their advice, choosing instead to shape advice using only data that will not challenge the government's judgements and viewpoints. Although we do not have evidence to propose that policy advisers in my blackout example reproduced in their advice the type of assessments they were hearing from the government, I suggest the government's rhetoric communicated a specific world view to its advisers from which the advisers, aside from the early unanswered query about the accuracy of blaming wind power, did not stray. This, and the *kairotic* baggage of Turnbull and the Liberal Party's knotty relationship with climate change, is why advice that may have contested this world view, such as a public handling strategy that could cope with the weight of early uncertainty—which would have been possible and desirable even at the preliminary stages—did not seem to be offered. In this sense, Stevens' observations align with what we have seen in the advice under consideration.

As Martin Rein has put it, 'clarity can be costly and the only pragmatic course to follow is … the use of ambiguity' (2006: 392). This supports the notion that ambiguity can conserve relationships. But, aside from this subsidiary benefit, it is unclear whether staying out of the hasty miscasting of renewables as a threat to energy security fulfilled the expectations on policy advisers as they are set out in the *Public Service Act 1999* and the APS Values. In other words, it is not possible to conclude that this advice was remotely close to being 'comprehensive and unaffected by fear of consequences, not withholding important facts or bad news'. Even while we may recognise that it is unrealistic for advice to live up to these expectations all the time, it seems that falling short of them is becoming the rule, rather than the exception. For example, the Royal Commission into the HIP, reporting only two years before my case study played out, found several 'systemic or fundamental shortcomings' (Hanger 2014: 299) that were 'capable of repetition' without redress—chief among them 'a failure to provide candid advice to Ministers' (p. 302). Most damningly, its commissioner, Ian Hanger QC, found that after

> having read all of the documents provided to the Commission, and having heard all of the evidence given particularly by public servants, I have little doubt that had such advice been given at key junctures of the HIP, the tragedies that occurred would have been avoided, and much of the adverse publicity and outcomes obviated. If such advice was given … but ignored by the political arm of government, there was little else the public service could reasonably do. The politicians would then, as appropriate, bear the opprobrium and responsibility of ignoring good advice. But that is not what happened with the HIP. Analysing the failings of the HIP was made much more difficult by the lack of clearly articulated advice by senior officials involved. (Hanger 2014: 303)

Shergold's *Learning from Failure*, undertaken in 2015 as a consequence of Hanger's findings, outlines a vision of ideal advice, which, by being expressed mostly in the subjunctive, seems to imply a contrast with reality:

> Advice and options should be ... proactive, vigilant for opportunities and anticipating problems ... Over-responsiveness —where public servants hold back on giving critical advice in a display of undue deference to their ministers' views—can be fatal to good policy outcomes ... Advice that is contrary to ministers' expectations is justified where it is based on a solid grasp of the government's objectives and aimed at supporting their achievement in the best way possible. It must reflect departmental knowledge, obtained by thorough analysis and consultation, of the likely benefit of alternative approaches. It should be informed by a clear assessment of what can go wrong, because there is a good chance that it will. (Shergold 2015: 16)

Both Hanger and Shergold, in other words, call for advice that does not exclude issues of relevance even if they are unwanted. Despite these findings, which precede the case of renewable energy by only two and one year/s, respectively, the language I have examined is none of those things. Here, we saw advisers leaving out factual information—evidence, if you will—that may have contradicted the government's narrative. By doing so, policy advisers effectively cast their advice as conclusive, despite the preliminary nature of the situation. Perversely, ignoring the inconclusiveness of the situation only contributed to it—that is, providing just a sliver of information concerned solely with the event made it possible for others to furnish the rest of the tableau with any interpretation. This left ministers free to pursue their accounts of uncertain renewables as a threat to energy security despite the lack of available evidence.

The micro-context

Chapter 1 provided an outline of the broad expectations of the provision of advice by the public service. Recall, for instance, that the *Public Service Act* requires the public service to provide 'the Government with advice that is frank, honest, timely and based on the best available evidence' (Federal Register of Legislation 1999). The APSC rephrases this slightly as '[t]he APS is responsive to the government in providing frank, honest, comprehensive, accurate and timely advice and in implementing the Government's policies and programs' (APSC n.d.).

The word 'responsive' is important and will help us interpret the micro-context, particularly in terms of legislated and cultural expectations, as well as the reputation and self-perception of my policy advisers. I will also discuss the legislative expectation to implement 'the Government's policies and programs'. Before proceeding, let me remind readers of the questions my framework asked about the micro-context:

1. Expectations: What are the expectations—legislated and/or institutional—of the adviser?
2. Culture: How does culture influence the language of the policy adviser?
3. Effect on knowledge: How might this bear on how policy expertise is constructed and communicated?

According to Richard Mulgan, in Australia's Westminster-style regime, responsiveness 'refers to the readiness of public servants to do what government ministers want' (2008: 345). It is not a straightforward concept and 'does not necessarily involve acceding to explicit directions from ministers' (Mulgan 2008: 346). Indeed, responsive public servants 'act in accordance with what they perceive to be the wishes of their political masters … much, if not most, responsiveness takes place within departments without ministers being aware of it' (Mulgan 2008: 346).

On the other hand, being responsive

> may be a matter of looking past the minister's immediate demands and recalling other wants temporarily eclipsed in the minister's mind. On this understanding, public servants may be responsive to ministers while going against what ministers are actually pressing for at the time. (Mulgan 2008: 347)

In this sense, responsiveness supports the government's democratic legitimacy, which public servants help ministers uphold by providing frank advice. As the APSC suggests, responsiveness pertains both to the provision of that advice *and* to helping governments implement their policies. These do not always work in harmony. As Mulgan puts it: '[T]he awkward and unpalatable elements to such advice (about which one should be properly frank and fearless) are those that ministers need to know if they want to meet their chosen objectives' (2008: 347).

Public servants thereby need to demonstrate responsiveness and frank advice if they are to fulfil the expectation of helping elected governments deliver on their promised goals. What, then, were the government's stated objectives to the Australian electorate on energy, particularly in relation to climate change mitigation and security? A brief inspection of its campaign promises in the leadup to the 2016 election is warranted, specifically as expressed in its campaign launch speech. Campaign speeches are a useful illustration in that they constitute a distilled version of the party's promised policies, an invitation to be held democratically accountable and a 'final test of your ability to say … why one exists, why one ought to exist, why one has more of a right to exist than one's opponents' (Watson 2002: 312).

Regarding clean energy, climate change and the environment more generally, on 26 June 2016, Malcolm Turnbull's campaign speech declared:

> Fairness between generations means we must live within our means.
>
> And it also means we can afford to leave a cleaner environment to those children with programs like our $1 billion investment plan to improve water quality in the Great Barrier Reef catchment, our $1 billion Clean Energy Innovation Fund, our $1 billion National Landcare Program or our $2.55 billion Emissions Reduction Fund.
>
> A strong economy means we can meet and beat our international obligations to address climate change and do so without massive hikes in electricity prices as Labor would do. (Turnbull 2016a)

Perhaps this did not articulate the government's commitment clearly enough for its policy advisers. Kevin Rudd's campaign speech in the leadup to the 2007 election arguably represents a more comprehensible commitment to mitigating climate change:

> I make this commitment: If we are elected, I will immediately ratify Kyoto … If elected, I will implement a 60 per cent carbon target and establish Australia's first national emissions trading scheme … If elected, I will implement a renewable energy target of 20 per cent by 2020 so that Australia can have a solar future. I [will] establish [a] clean coal innovation fund. And today I announce that if elected I will set up a major new renewable energy fund to develop, commercialise and deploy renewable energy technologies across Australia. We need to harness our enormous potential in

> solar, wind, geothermal and wave power. This fund will support projects that take renewable energy technology from the lab to the grid. I am determined to make Australia part of the global climate change solution—not just part of the global climate change problem. (Rudd 2007)

While Turnbull may not have been as expansive as Rudd, his speech was nonetheless noticeably more inclined towards environmental concerns than his predecessor, Tony Abbott, whose 2013 campaign speech centred largely on ending commitments to address climate change:

> We'll abolish the carbon tax so power prices and gas prices will go down. We'll abolish the mining tax so investment and employment will go up … The Clean Energy Finance Corporation will cease making non-commercial loans with taxpayers' money … Trust the party that will abolish the carbon tax, not the one that inflicted it on you. (Abbott 2013)

Importantly, Abbott signalled his commitment to the mining industry, and thus to fossil fuels, in parallel with his disconnection from clean energy and reducing carbon emissions. It can thus be said the Abbott government's priorities and objectives clearly laid out the promises against which it could be held accountable. Turnbull's objectives, however, did not favour fossil fuels at the expense of the environment. Indeed, the governor-general's speech opening the forty-fifth Parliament,[14] some weeks after the election, emphasised Turnbull's commitment to the environment:

> As we sustainably use Australia's natural resources to the best advantage, my Government will meet our international environment, climate change and energy obligations.

> Climate change will continue to be a critical area of policy attention for my Government.

> Australia will meet its 2020 emissions reduction targets and the Government will review Australia's climate change framework next year to ensure it remains effective in achieving the 2030 target.

---

14   Although not constitutionally required, 'at the beginning of each new Parliament or each new session, the governor-general makes an opening speech to Parliament setting out the government's proposed legislative program' (see Parliament of Australia 2017). Text related specifically to policy commitments is submitted to the governor-general by the prime minister and his portfolio ministers ahead of the drafting of this speech.

My Government will promote a more effective gas market, improve governance arrangements for Australia's energy markets, integrate emissions reduction as a part of the energy framework, empower energy consumers and ensure the regulatory framework can accommodate the market's rapid transformation.

The attainment of these objectives will be assisted by all aspects of energy policy being combined in the one portfolio of Environment and Energy.

My Government will share stewardship of the environment with communities across Australia through the National LandCare Program and the new Solar Communities Program and a range of locally-focused environment programs including the Threatened Species Recovery Fund and the Improving Your Local Parks and Environment Program. (Parliament of Australia 2016a)

The Turnbull government's chosen objectives, therefore, were demonstrably committed to meeting its various emissions obligations while integrating emissions reduction into Australia's energy framework, ensuring it could adapt to a market that was beginning to rapidly shed conventional energy inputs in favour of renewables. Merging the energy portfolio—previously partnered with resources—with that of the environment emphasised that commitment. It would be difficult for public servant policy advisers to misconstrue the government's objectives in this field—but perhaps those commitments had moved; the political commentary at the time of the blackout certainly suggests this. Further, in 2018, it was reported that a group of up to 20 government backbenchers had now formalised a group that had been meeting for 'some years' to discuss support for coal and building new coal-fired power stations (Karp 2018b). Support for renewables was therefore clearly not unanimous among government ranks even in 2016, and we saw this discord play out in leadership contests. But it is not the function of the public service to align its advice with such commentary in its briefings to ministers, treating it as though it were new policy and replacing the government's original objectives.

As I have suggested, and as Mulgan articulated more robustly, the requirement for policy advisers is to faithfully implement the government's objectives and commitments with both frank and responsive advice. When this requirement is not fulfilled, public servants effectively withdraw from their legal expectations and the public's ability to hold governments accountable can be compromised. Mulgan lists several examples in which this occurred, among them the Australian Wheat Board saga, in which officials appeared to ignore the board's payment of kickbacks to Iraq in breach of UN sanctions (to be discussed briefly in Chapter 5); and the Children Overboard Affair, in which officials were thought to have suppressed information that asylum-seekers at sea were not throwing their children overboard, despite the then government maintaining they had. Regarding the former, Mulgan considers

> ministers had a clear political and economic incentive to allow the trade to continue so long as they could claim to have no knowledge of kickbacks to the Iraqi regime. Officials would have recognised obvious benefits to ministers in not being informed.

In relation to the latter, he notes:

> The silence of senior public servants allowed ministers to persist in not correcting the public record, to their electoral advantage, on the ground that they (the ministers) had not been officially informed that the earlier version of events was correct. (Mulgan 2008: 352)

Choosing not to inform and being silent forsakes not simply the expectation to give frank and fearless advice, but also

> the duty to inform ministers of misstatements and other possible improprieties entails more than just the normal duty to give robust and relevant advice as part of loyal (and responsive) service to ministers. This duty stems from independent considerations of democratic integrity which cut across responsiveness. (Mulgan 2008: 352)

This strongly recalls Shergold's (2015) statement about responsive and responsible advice as a legitimate public expectation. Read in this way, the deliberate silence and ambiguity deduced in the passages under consideration represent more than just a way to avoid criticism and its attendant potential for losing relevance; they are an abstention from the legislated obligation to help governments deliver their promised commitments to the community. Shergold acknowledged the difficulty in providing this kind of advice. Yet, when knowledgeable expert advisers feel compelled to adopt not knowing as a form of responsiveness, perhaps providing the kind of advice Shergold favours has become unworkable.

Can examining organisational culture help shed further light on the 'silent' rhetoric of my policy advisers? When considering the Treasury's language on negative gearing in this respect, I attempted to gain an understanding of its culture by way of so-called capability reviews, which

I describe further below. As others have observed (Mackie 2015; Stevens 2011; Williams 2010), given infrequent access to policy workers and their views, it is difficult to ascertain their culture and how they regard their roles within the policymaking system. While this author has benefited from conversations with senior public officials, there has been a general reluctance to go on the record, even anonymously. This could be partly due to the ease with which officials in various portfolios could be identified and to the potentially discomfiting nature of the topic. Nonetheless, it is still possible to form impressions with the help of other information from the back regions. I will therefore explore capability reviews of the PM&C (in 2012) and the then Department of Resources, Energy and Tourism (RET, in 2013), parts of which merged with the Department of Environment in 2016, just ahead of the blackout. The Department of Environment did not undergo a capability review, but research on the department undertaken by Australian academic Kathleen Mackie between 2010 and 2013 provides some enlightening assessments by officials about policy failure and success, through which we can gain valuable insights into organisational culture. A brief review of the 2016–17 annual reports of PM&C, DEE and the AEMO will shed some light on how each organisation viewed its performance in relation to the blackout. I close this line of inquiry with a short appraisal of a routine Senate estimates hearing in October 2016.

Capability reviews formed one of a set of recommendations proposed by then secretary of PM&C Terry Moran's 2010 'Blueprint for the Reform of Australian Government Administration'. These reviews were intended to survey 'agencies' institutional capabilities, covering strategy, leadership, workforce capability, delivery and organisational effectiveness' and 'act as accountability mechanisms' for several other of the report's recommendations, such as strengthening strategic policy and embedding APS Values (Moran 2010: 64). Although long since discontinued and now several years old, they offer a rare and reasonably contemporaneous organisational view into the departments under consideration.

The review team found PM&C staff to be 'highly committed, flexible, responsive and politically aware' (APSC 2012a: 19), but 'overwhelmed with day-to-day issues' and feeling 'unable to make effective choices on how best to spend their time, reducing their capacity to do the work that really matters' (p. 23). It was found that senior staff should be

> freed of some of their more routine tasks … to focus on the issues that really matter to the Prime Minister, the government and the nation more broadly, including by being more able to step in, if needed, when something goes wrong. Understanding what keeps prime ministers up at night is a critical consideration in all the department's operations, and senior leaders need to have the space to perform this role adequately. (APSC 2012a: 23)

This work had to be performed 'within an understanding of the government's overall objectives and values. If necessary, it should warn or prompt, and do so firmly'. This, the review team reported, was 'a deeply held value in the department' (APSC 2012a: 24). While the review team seemed to provide a helpful delineation between reactive and strategic work, the broader sense is one in which the two have merged—that is, where praxis no longer distinguishes between the two because one must constantly scan the horizon to capably react in case of calamity.

Externally, the view of PM&C was not altogether positive:

> A number of external stakeholders commented that PM&C has at times taken a competitive approach to policy development. The overwhelming view of those outside and inside PM&C is that this competitive approach has eroded trust across government and does not lead to the best outcome for the Prime Minister or the government. (APSC 2012a: 26)

Although not explicitly referred to as such, this competitiveness is reminiscent of the same review team's finding that Treasury—a central agency like PM&C—was 'closed to external experience' (APSC 2013b: 6). That is, PM&C's 'competitive approach' and subsequent erosion of trust suggest—not atypically for a central agency—it may have been perceived as elitist and possessing a tendency to go it alone, without engaging portfolio agencies or stakeholders. This view is borne out in the PM&C executive's descriptions of the department's skillset as its 'craft', which they expressed as:

> Focus on the Prime Minister—know what is important and what will become important;
>
> Intervene with discrimination—influence what matters;
>
> Lead through partnership—but do not avoid acting if things are going off track, or big change needs to be inspired or supported from the centre;

Through first-class analytic, writing and oral communication skills—excel in being able to present what the Prime Minister needs to know at the time, with the clarity and at the length that is appropriate, presenting clearly a preferred outcome, highlighting any risks, and guiding the Prime Minister in handling conflicting parties;

By choosing wisely where we spend our time to influence what matters. (APSC 2012a: 10–11)

Overall, this suggests an organisation taking its role seriously, which may spill over into a tendency to overestimate its capability and influence. These comments also imply a tension between being across everything and choosing where to achieve the highest impact. In practice, these two qualities may overlap to form an ethos of excessive attention to detail in case emerging problems necessitate instant responsiveness to the prime minister.

In the case of RET, the review team found 'most key industry bodies and central agencies generally regard the department as cooperative, engaged in policy issues and able to think analytically', but it needed to address a number of issues, such as being 'more innovative and influential in both policy development and program design' and becoming 'less risk averse, more proactive and forward looking to better anticipate challenges and risks' (APSC 2013a: 5). More specifically, with the department's evolution 'through a series of MoG [machinery of government] changes',[15] which had 'made it difficult to have a common identity or purpose', the review team observed 'a predisposition for divisions to work in silos. The department has three separate energy divisions and there is less interaction than there should be between those responsible for the supply and demand side[s] of energy' (APSC 2013a: 7).

Externally, stakeholders were concerned 'that the department has a focus on short-term issues and is too reactive' (APSC 2013a: 6). The review team judged there was 'scope for the department to improve its evidence base to better anticipate emerging issues and understand market considerations' (APSC 2013a: 18), which, according to its secretary,

---

15   MoG, or machinery of government, changes occur 'when the Government decides to change the way Commonwealth responsibilities are managed. It can involve the movement of functions, resources and people from one agency to another' (APSC 2019a). In 2016, an Australian National Audit Office report assessed that MoG changes occurred, on average, more than 10 times a year and, following the 2013 election, 14 departments were affected by such changes (including RET) (ANAO 2016).

could be achieved by growing the department's capacity to 'measure success in terms of broader policy impacts and the government agenda' and enhancing 'its capacity as a policy maker, rather than a policy taker, while avoiding claims of "industry capture"' (p. 8). While the department needed to address these and similar issues, there was also recognition of its capabilities, such as having been 'at the forefront of exploring innovative options for improving the way it supports the development of clean energy technologies' (APSC 2013a: 26).

One might conclude this department possessed good analytical capabilities but not necessarily a flair for proactive, strategic assessment. Further, there appears to be a lack of awareness that the broader policy environment and the government's priorities are linked to the department's remit, while empathy may extend only to industry. This could be partly due to staff either being sourced from industry or performing their roles for an extended time and thus subject to 'capture'. However, while policy development appeared to suffer a lack of innovation, RET was viewed as strong in its work on clean energy. Finally, a series of MoG changes were viewed as having taken their toll, perhaps particularly on those working in the department's energy divisions. As we know, following the July 2016 election, these divisions were again 'MoGd' to the Department of Environment.

This is where I pick up Mackie's work on success and failure in environment policy, for which she gained uncommon access to senior Department of Environment officials between 2010 and 2013. This period sits between the discontinuation of the department-administered HIP, which Mackie notes triggered her research, and the commencement of Hanger's royal commission into the deaths associated with the program. While Mackie's interviews with officials indicate a cohort somewhat more inclined to pronounce success than failure (with 89 nominations of success and 63 of failure) (Mackie 2015: 293), much of the material gives the impression of a culture of despondency. For instance, with government expectations for a rapid rollout of the HIP not merely high but also time-sensitive (due to the HIP's aim of stemming Global Financial Crisis–related unemployment), officials were directed to 'just get the money out the door' (Mackie 2015: 299) instead of raising risk factors. 'Fearing the worst', officials either moved jobs or 'committed "agency by omission", failing for example to attach the Risk Register in a critical April 2009 brief to Minister Garrett … and otherwise providing (as an interviewee put it) "sterile" briefings on critical safety and fraud issues' (Mackie 2015: 299).

'Agency by omission' would 'rarely be evident to the external eye, such behaviour being referred by interviewees to [sic] as "covert" or "hidden … in the DNA of the organisation". Officials tended not to discuss it with each other' (Mackie 2015: 299).

This suggests a strong, even habitual, tendency to withhold or remain silent when confronted by pressures and expectations for something different to what officials may be more inclined to offer. This echoes some of Hanger's findings about this department. The phrase 'the DNA of the organisation' implies a modus operandi that is timeworn, familiar and even conditioned. Perhaps this is an approach that developed because of contested policy areas. As Mackie puts it: 'The contested nature of environmental policy problems helps to explain why officials might proceed through veiled manoeuvres, massaging policy objectives, corralling stakeholders, and working around evidence gaps' (2015: 299).

As we have seen, proceeding through contested policy terrain in this way indicates that policy advice is either cautiously silent or transferred by stealth. Indeed, Mackie reports that the bulk of officials' effort

> was not aimed at outright wins, but rather at stemming the loss of environmental values and the potential harm of questionable policies. Such strategies made sense, in that the interviewees generally envisaged low prospects for outright policy success. Over half the interviewees represented their environment policy roles more as avoiding failure than pursuing success. (Mackie 2015: 300)

In other words, they 'approached new policy tasks cautiously, aiming for the "least-worst" outcome rather than actively thinking about success' (Mackie 2015: 300). This may not be entirely surprising. After all, the role of public administrators is to help governments implement their policies, no matter what their personal opinions may be. As such, aiming for the 'least-worst' outcome may simply be a matter of opinion. However, there is in Mackie's interviews and findings also a sense of resignation, disillusionment and even despondency, where aiming low is a widely shared aspiration. As one highly regarded official volunteered during interviews: 'I can think of only one example of a policy process where I was able to have a role that made a difference' (Mackie 2015: 301). Another admits that they 'would have to say that [climate change] was perhaps the most disappointing failure of mine. I worked on it for eight or nine years' (Mackie 2015: 302). Within such a culture, it is not difficult to imagine mindsets like these submitting promptly to their ministers' 'thought world', to borrow Stevens' phrase, simply to avoid further disappointing failures.

Information of this kind does not exist for the AEMO. Further, the AEMO is not quite the same type of organisation as the agencies thus far examined. Its material effectively served as the scientific input, as it were, to policy operators. Unlike the other agencies under review here, the AEMO is governed by the *Corporations Act 2001* and operates independently as a public–private partnership between government and industry, with the former owning 60 per cent and the latter 40 per cent. Accordingly, expectations are rather different. Under the *Corporations Act*, directors and other officers are expected to exercise care and diligence, such as making business judgements 'in good faith for a proper purpose' in 'the best interests of the corporation' (Federal Register of Legislation 2001). While obviously different to the public expectations of officials described by the *Public Service Act*, these words might be read as those expectations' commercial equivalent. Perhaps because of reports that the AEMO's claim of unfamiliarity with South Australia's preset wind generator limits rang hollow,[16] its 2016–17 annual report shows the agency eager to disclose its activities during the 2016 blackout. Calling it 'the most dramatic event of the year', the AEMO devoted more than one page to outlining its 'larger public role in the media to clearly report the facts of what happened and outline technical facets of the power system that played a role' (AEMO 2017a: 4). Regarding causes, the AEMO notes the storm's damage to the transmission system

> resulted in five faults in very quick succession on the transmission grid in the northern part of the state. Some wind generators reduced output after experiencing a number of voltage disturbances caused by these faults, as protection systems were triggered at pre-set limits. The Heywood interconnector immediately picked up the reduction in output, but this tripped when it exceeded its safety limits, causing the state to go black. (AEMO 2017a: 16)

AEMO concludes the blackout 'highlighted the requirement for better information on how new technology responds in extreme circumstances' (2017a: 16). Apart from the obvious difference that AEMO appears

---

16   This stems from the fact this issue was 'identified and addressed a decade ago in Europe, where no blackouts have been reported despite the high reliance on wind energy in some countries' (Parkinson 2017).

particularly keen to account for itself to publicly justify its actions to its stakeholders, these passages suggest a community of relatively unconstrained producers of evidence. While the dry tone suggests an element of diplomacy to avoid political minefields, this frame signifies data decidedly, even proudly, without frills. Although the cause of the blackout continues to be delicately phrased, it is neither predominantly ambiguous nor absent. However, a frame of pure evidence, as we have also seen in the case of Treasury and will encounter again in the next chapter on Iraq, can be too subtle and leave wide open spaces for reinterpretation. As we know, despite AEMO's findings, government ministers continued their narrative of uncertain renewables. Neither PM&C nor DEE made any mention of the blackout in their annual reports, which may represent instances of Rappert's 'absence' and its implied choices about what to include and what to leave out.

Finally, I should briefly note a Senate Estimates Committee[17] that took place not long after the blackout on 17 October 2016. I observed earlier that the first parliamentary question time in the House of Representatives after the event produced a range of robust questions related to political commentary and misconstrual of the event's causes. As Senate estimates represent an important mechanism for holding the executive to account, one might expect at least a short line of questioning of officials, such as who knew what when and when ministers were given that information. Only one such question was asked, by opposition Labor Senator Anthony Chisholm: 'The Prime Minister, Energy Minister and Deputy Minister all made comments linking the blackout to South Australia's use of renewable energy, in particular the intermittancy [sic] of some renewable generation. Is there any evidence to support their claims?' (Senate Standing Committees on Environment and Communications 2016).

Remarkably, DEE took this question on notice—that is, it did not respond at the time and provided a written response some weeks later. Instead of answering the senator's question, DEE referred only to AEMO's updated report of 19 October 2016:

> The report finds that five transmission line faults, which resulted in voltage disturbances on the network, led to the SA region black system.

---

17 'Estimates of government expenditure are referred to Senate committees as part of the annual budget cycle. This opportunity to examine the operations of government plays a key role in the parliamentary scrutiny of the executive' (Parliament of Australia n.d.[b]).

> The voltage disturbances caused an unexpected reduction of 445 MW of wind generation due to an automatic response from the wind farms' control systems. This is a design setting of the affected wind farms. The AEMO report indicates that nine of the 13 wind farms in operation at the time automatically suspended operation due to the size of the voltage dips. (Senate Standing Committees on Environment and Communications 2016)

This presents a clear provision of available evidence, even though it avoids directly answering the question, not to mention evading it at the time asked. By offering the evidence of a third party (admittedly the expert), it also avoids having to respond as the department originally questioned— that is, in its own voice and in relation to what this information might imply in a policy context. Similarly oblique advice is contained in DEE's FOI material. In an email dated 6 October 2016, DEE was asked to provide a response to a question by the PMO related to whether it was right, wrong or too early to be sure that, as reported in *The Australian*:

> production settings in a number of wind settings were too conservative and shut down prematurely, causing overload on the interconnector in Victoria, which then shut down, blacking out the state. [Industry insiders] are saying the protection settings in those windfarms have been changed since the blackout. (DEE n.d.)

In response to this direct question, DEE quoted from AEMO's 5 October 2016 preliminary report and did not itself answer the query.

An interesting contrast to these responses is contained in the answers supplied by Oliver Yates, then chief executive officer of the Clean Energy Finance Corporation (CEFC), a corporate Commonwealth entity and portfolio agency of DEE. At the same hearing, on 17 October, Yates was asked about sovereign risk in relation to investment in renewables by Greens Senator Peter Whish-Wilson. Yates reported that the level of sovereign risk around renewables had declined because of their decreasing dependence on government programs. Whish-Wilson followed up by asking whether the 'knee-jerk reaction after the Adelaide storms to the contribution of renewables' had 'bothered' Yates or his investors (Senate Environment and Communications Legislation Committee 2016: 93), to which Yates responded:

> I really cannot say that I think there was a general surprise in relation to how it all worked and why. We are changing our energy system. If you change your software on your iPhone I can assure

you it does not work, either, as well as it does the first time. We will see issues as we change over a system, but these issues are very easy to fix and very easy to address. When they come up we learn from them. To be blaming one thing or another does not get you anywhere. We know we need to transfer to a new software system on our phone because the other one will not work, and when you do that you have to deal with the challenges that are involved. It is just a matter of understanding what you intend to do. You intend either to get on with it or not—and you are going to have to get on with it. (Senate Environment and Communications Legislation Committee 2016: 93–94)

Perhaps alarmed at the candour of Yates's statement, government Senator Simon Birmingham quickly steered the matter away from the blackout:

It is a matter that I am sure energy officials might be better placed to comment on. But I think one of the things that makes a second link into Tasmania and some of the projects Mr Yates was speaking about appear attractive. (Senate Environment and Communications Legislation Committee 2016: 94)

Evidently, it is possible to be clear even in circumstances of relative uncertainty and political conflict. Indeed, one might read Yates's statement as an expression of what Mulgan called a duty that 'stems from independent considerations of democratic integrity', where it was important to respond in a way one considered to be ultimately helpful, even truly responsive. One can also see that this candour—quietly frank and fearless—was not welcomed by the government's representative at the hearing. Perhaps coincidentally, Yates announced his resignation from the CEFC just two days later (CEFC 2016).

To recap, I asked whether culture could help illuminate the 'silent' rhetoric of my policy advisers and found some indicators among the examined material. AEMO maintained a data-driven approach to its reporting and, in its role as the independent market operator, acted in the manner of an advisory expert procuring evidence for its government administrator client. We also encountered a confident CEFC CEO conveying some frank but politically unwelcome parting words. In PM&C, we saw a department proud of what it called its 'craft' but tending towards being over-responsive and viewed as imperious by outsiders. In combination, RET and the Department of Environment presented as analytically astute but change-weary and potentially captured by industry, as well as having developed a practice of aiming low and sterilising or hiding unwanted information. This splits the language I have examined here into two camps: that of arm's-length operators who responded in a manner closer to what Mulgan called 'independent considerations of democratic integrity' and Shergold called serving 'the public interest with integrity'; and that of public service policy advisers who seemed concerned primarily with responding to their ministers' 'immediate demands' by 'acting in a way that is expedient'.

This separation helps highlight that the two APS departments appear to have developed an organisational culture and set of behaviours, perhaps in response to the political environment, that influence how they communicate knowledge. In the context of organisations, this is not altogether surprising. Posing the question 'what effect, if any, does the organizational setting have on the production of facts', Diane Vaughan explains that organisations 'have powerful and continuous effects on how information is created, gathered, processed, exchanged, recorded, stored and used'. In so doing, organisations can limit 'knowing in some directions' and value 'some kinds of information and discounting others, depending on the goal' (Vaughan 1999: 931). My examination of the texts and the agencies' organisational cultures revealed an almost uninterrupted commitment to an exchange of information that can best be characterised as limiting knowing, particularly on the part of DEE— the principal disseminator of information. Although mostly continuous throughout the texts, this limiting is most obvious when DEE responds, after PM&C's early question about the cause of the blackout, that 'we'll get back to you on this question' yet never does so directly, preferring to bury the relevant information halfway through a two-page status report that was forwarded subsequently.

In the context of organisational culture, Gerald Zaltman has called this 'knowledge disavowal', which he describes as 'the avoidance of knowledge in order to preserve or maintain the status quo or to avoid a difficult choice or threatening situation' (1983: 173). More recently, this has been described as 'silent silencing', whereby employees silence themselves as they progressively grow into an organisation, become more implicated in the work and its culture and finally begin to share responsibility for decisions (Mathiesen 2004: 54–56); and as 'systemic silence', which sees organisational actors turning 'away from knowing' because their work culture censures dissent (Thomas 2016: 493). Organisational cultures of silence have been further broken down into three types by Linn Van Dyne et al. (2003): acquiescent silence, defensive silence and prosocial silence. They describe acquiescent silence as 'withholding relevant ideas, information, or opinions, based on resignation' and, like Zaltman, 'passive acceptance of the status quo'. In short, this type of silence 'represents those who are fundamentally disengaged' (Van Dyne et al. 2003: 1366). Defensive silence withholds information 'as a form of self-protection, based on fear', which represents 'intentional and proactive behaviour that is intended to protect the self from external threats' and involves 'awareness and consideration of alternatives, followed by a conscious decision to withhold' (Van Dyne et al. 2003: 1367). This type of silence resembles Thomas's systemic silence. Prosocial silence withholds information 'with the goal of benefiting other people or the organization' and is 'motivated by concern for others' (Van Dyne et al. 2003: 1368).

Although I do not have sufficient evidence to confidently point to any of these descriptions as definitive diagnoses of my texts and the cultures of their originating departments, they exhibit shades of them all. Just hours after the blackout but ahead of any prime ministerial statement, PM&C was concerned about misinformation, seeking primarily to protect the prime minister both reactively (from the immediate embarrassment of falsehood) and strategically (from policy missteps). As a central agency, however, PM&C is frequently the receiver of information and was here largely dependent on DEE, which was directing—and stemming—its flow. With Minister Frydenberg's national television appearance only a few hours old, DEE must have instinctively understood his comments as a possible judgement against renewables. Its concern was therefore mainly about maintaining that status quo by meeting Frydenberg's 'immediate demands', even if they were not overtly expressed. 'We'll get back to you on this question' was effectively a kind of control language, by which DEE cautioned PM&C to retreat and defer its line of inquiry. When, the next day, the prime minister publicly strengthened Frydenberg's speculation about renewables, PM&C joined DEE in its silence.

In this depiction, we see Vaughan's goal-dependent limiting of knowledge, where the departments' goal was to ensure the facts could not undermine political statements. We also see Zaltman's knowledge disavowal as a way of preserving the status quo and avoiding difficult choices, particularly on DEE's part. That is, as a department operating under an unspoken code of 'hiding'—perhaps more so following the failures surrounding the HIP and Hanger's findings—DEE's organisational culture seems to have adopted behaviours that could deal with restrictive circumstances. As Stephen Wilks has commented, 'past mistakes burn themselves into a collective consciousness and set up strong resistance to actions which appear to comprise a repetition of previous errors' (1987: 28). Thomas Mathiesen's 'silent silencing' is probably true of most organisations dominated by longer-term employees and, with a median length of APS employment of 11 somewhat homogeneous years,[18] a degree of association and identification—even institutionalisation—is not surprising. Nina K. Thomas's systemic silence because of fearing censure is something one can readily observe not by studying the language of my texts but rather by noticing, as I have, what was missing: frank, comprehensive advice about the available evidence. This was eschewed in case of censure, not just from ministers, but probably also from colleagues, as we saw in DEE's subtle response to PM&C's early noises of dissent about causes. In this way, fear of censure probably goes to employees' concerns about their reputation and opportunities for career progression. Van Dyne et al.'s prosocial silence can here be read as pre-empting censure or threat by helpfully aligning departmental advice with political commentary almost in time with that commentary. As such, prosocial silence should be viewed as a form of responsiveness.

The cultures of the two departments under consideration influenced the language of their policy advisers. They also influenced how advisers communicated their policy expertise: by disavowing it when, in the early hours of 29 September, it became obvious that AEMO's advice about the blamelessness of the generation mix was being rebuffed. Submitting so swiftly to the dominant narrative about energy security—by ignoring the messy context of renewables and focusing only on network damage— attests to the strength and incidence of resignation within the culture. Certainly, we do not know how advisers briefed ministers or each other orally, nor did we see all their written advice. They may have argued vehemently about the accuracy of claims, policy implications, government objectives, legislated obligations to be frank and even their commitment to democratic integrity. Yet, all we have been able to observe are seemingly well-worn strategies of disavowal.

---

18   The median length of APS service is 11 years, while almost three-quarters of APS employees (71.2 per cent) have worked in only one agency (APSC 2019b: 7).

The macro-context

1. Engagement with objectivity and evidence: Is the spectre of 'objectivity' present in policy advice? How does the advice engage with or construe the notion of evidence?

2. International comparisons and contexts: What do international comparisons tell us about Australia's rebuffed advice? Are contexts and circumstances similar or is Australia unique?

I have demonstrated that policy advisers stayed silent on unwanted evidence. This was likely connected to the government's *kairotic* requirements, as well as the cultures of the two policy organisations. The two cultures probably developed, each in their own way, in response to the quandary of being both responsive *and* evidence-based, attuned to ministers *and* apolitical interpreters of reality, despite none of these facets necessarily being complementary. Yet, objectivity and responsiveness must be enacted concurrently and cannot be selected depending on the occasion. This means they must together contort themselves into a kind of myopic expertise, where particular facts are recognised while others are deliberately overlooked. Knowing what not to know is an expression of this myopic expertise. As such, the production of evidence by policy advisers is necessarily highly selective.

I have discussed this type of knowing in relation to text and micro-context in terms of culture. Before turning to consider how objectivity and evidence are present in the advice under examination, let me briefly mention some of the other dynamics that can influence the construction of advice like this. One is the growing need to be timely and the pressure to be useful amid rising contestability. As Kathy McDermott puts it, 'the motivation to "please" the minister, always a powerful driver, has been reinforced by institutional drivers intended to enhance the contestability of agencies' (2008: 40). Another is meeting performance measures, both at an organisational level and individually (McDermott 2008: 40). Increasing political oversight and the move from tenure to secretaries' five-year appointments have also been cited as influences in aligning advice with government positions (Podger 2007). Constant movement between jobs, while potentially increasing experience and capabilities, can also be viewed as a barrier to developing deeper expertise. The need to maintain relevance, especially when coupled with the seemingly ever-present prospect of funding cuts (Whelan 2011), also exerts pressure

(Tingle 2015). A workforce whose diversity still has room to grow[19] may also contribute to exhibiting unidimensional views (Woolcott 2018b). Although I have suggested FOI laws should not curb the frankness of advice, there is clearly a perception among the APS leadership that they do (Parkinson 2016). This role-modelling opinion is voiced by much of the APS leadership and its influence is likely to flow across an organisation like a self-fulfilling prophecy. It is also possible, as Michael Howlett (2009) suggests in the Canadian context, that many policy advisers simply do not have the analytical capability or training to successfully carry out and communicate the type of evidence-based policymaking required of them. This is not an exhaustive list. These and perhaps many other elements hint at an operating environment and world view—whether informed by real or perceived inputs—that motivate how advice is constructed.

In answering this section's first question about the macro-context, this book seeks to understand whether and how requirements to be objective and evidence-based influence how advice is constructed. It tries to understand whether those requirements affect the language and world view of the public service. It also wants to know whether this influences policy advisers' production of facts and, with it, their expert validation of a 'reality' that (cor)responds to the government's rendering of it. Stone (1997) has argued that objectivity or 'what we think of as facts—statements about the true state of the world'—are 'produced in social processes'. Indeed, most of 'our knowledge and ideas about the world come not from direct observation but from social knowledge'. The social elements of constructing knowledge are repeated in organisations: there are 'numerous social institutions charged with finding facts', such as government agencies, and these 'institutions, or rather the people within them, make numerous choices in developing information' (Stone 1997: 308–9). Choosing and producing objectivity and evidence in policy advice, then, can be viewed as parts of an organisational process. One might even read them as being intrinsically connected—that is, organisations cannot help but engage in producing a shared version of reality.

---

19   In a *State of the Service Report*, the APSC records diversity in the APS as 59.6 per cent women (many part-time and across junior ranks), 16.2 per cent non-English-speaking backgrounds, 4.8 per cent LGBTQI+, 3.7 per cent people with disability and 3.5 per cent Indigenous (APSC 2019c: vii). See also APSC (2017, 2018d).

I cannot definitively show how this may have occurred in relation to the texts under examination with the available primary material. I have attempted to provide an insight into the organisational culture by analysing a small range of accessible sources and have introduced some early findings on how the organisational culture of two APS departments may influence the language of their policy advisers. However, finding corroborative comparisons is difficult given there are very few extensive studies of how organisations go about creating facts and a shared language, particularly policy and administrative organisations.[20] Hugh Heclo and Aaron Wildavsky's 1974 book, *The Private Government of Public Money*, is a meticulous, almost anthropological account of the work of the UK Treasury and its administrative culture, which remains largely observatory until its final pages, where it concludes that policy advice has a need 'not for unanimous agreement but for better argument' (Heclo and Wildavsky 1974: 384). There are some less exhaustive reviews of administrative cultures (for example, Salminen and Mäntysalo 2013; Sullivan 2008; Wilks 1987), but it is Vaughan's 1996 account of the *Challenger* space shuttle disaster that most comprehensively details how organisational culture arrives at accepted facts. While the organisations I have considered here are not associated with a disaster of the *Challenger*'s magnitude and the National Aeronautics and Space Administration (NASA) is not a policy department, it is Vaughan's depiction that most closely describes the formation of objectivity as 'routine and taken-for-granted aspects of organizational life that created a way of seeing that was simultaneously a way of not seeing' (1996: 394). Because of this resonance with my case study, Vaughan has been chosen as a guide in trying to establish how the language of my texts can be read as a reflection of choices about objectivity and evidence.

Vaughan describes her book as chronicling 'the formation of worldview and how it affects the interpretation of information in organizations' (1996: 409). She notes that the explanation for NASA's decision to launch the *Challenger*, despite information warning against it, 'is not only about the development of norms but about the incremental expansion of normative boundaries: how small changes … gradually became the norm … No rules were violated; there was no intent to do harm' (Vaughan 1996: 409).

---

20 Gunilla Eriksson's *Swedish Military Intelligence: Producing Knowledge* (2016) is a recent exception, albeit in an intelligence setting. It will be discussed in detail in the next chapter on Iraq intelligence assessments.

These norms, which she defines as

> cultural beliefs and conventions originating in the environment … create unreflective, routine, taken-for-granted scripts that become part of [the] individual worldview. Invisible and unacknowledged rules for behaviour, they penetrate the organization as categories of structure, thought, and action that shape choice in some directions rather than others. (Vaughan 1996: 37)

World views can shape choice in simple ways. For instance, the term 'expert' implies

> that professionalism will somehow result in a more 'objective' assessment than that of the amateur. But professional training is not a control against the imposition of particularistic worldviews on the interpretation of information. To the contrary, the consequence of professional training and experience is itself a particularistic worldview comprising certain assumptions, expectations, and experiences that become integrated with the person's sense of the world. The result is that highly trained individuals, their scientific and bureaucratic procedures giving them false confidence in their own objectivity, can have their interpretation of information framed in subtle, powerful, and often unacknowledged ways. (Vaughan 1996: 63)

Individuals may therefore already be prone to presuming they are neutral before merging with the world view of the organisation. Although the content may change, over time, these procedures repeat over and over, solidifying into

> a shared worldview that shapes future choices. It displays the forces in culture and social structure that simultaneously set limits to and present possibilities for rationality, showing how taken-for-granted assumptions, predispositions, scripts, conventions, and classification schemes figure into goal-oriented behavior in a prerational, preconscious manner that precedes and prefigures strategic choice. It conveys a stunning message about the influence of these preconscious schema on the production, exchange, and interpretation of information in organizations. (Vaughan 1996: 405)

Revisiting the case three years later, Vaughan adds that, when NASA engineers 'constructed charts that deleted the messiness of their empirical experience' (1999: 926), this systematically winnowed information and guaranteed partiality of exchange (p. 917). As information was further sifted and solidified into facts, this contributed to

> the conversion of ambiguous, contradictory, disordered, uncertain technical facts to hard, convincing, ordered knowledge and official certainty … The solidification of argument and the dropping of ambiguity that go into negotiation and document creation affect not only the audience but the creator: the author becomes committed to a rendition of the world. (Vaughan 1999: 930)

As this increasingly becomes the dominant operating mode, it is easy to see expert advisers reacting to disparate pieces of information in much the same way, as 'shaping choice in some directions rather than others'. Organisations thus become united in fact-sorting, implicitly knowing and solidifying what counts as orthodox fact and what does not. Morten Egeberg corroborates this when he states that, although the process of selection is complex, it is greatly aided by institutional culture, or administrative milieu:

> [F]ormal organization provides an administrative milieu that focuses a decision-maker's attention on *certain* problems and solutions, while others are excluded from consideration. The structure thus constrains choices, but at the same time it creates and increases *action capacity* in certain directions. The organizational context surrounding individuals thus serves to simplify decisions that might otherwise have been complex and incomprehensible. (Egeberg 1999: 159; emphasis in original)

Like Vaughan, Egeberg also considers that time plays an important factor in solidifying facts: 'Through time decision-makers can be expected to partly internalize an organization's value premises' (1999: 159). In specialised spheres, such as those of government policy advisers, this is not surprising. Organisational culture becomes embedded over time and, as Karin Knorr Cetina suggests, 'when domains of social life become separated from one another', they 'curl up upon themselves and become self-referential systems that orient more to internal and previous system states than to the outside environment' (2007: 364).

Although writing before the advent of evidence-based policy as a more codified requirement, David K. Cohen and Charles E. Lindblom capture how policy advisers as a group construct knowledge:

> [D]espite the convention that [professional social inquiry practitioners] are engaged in the pursuit of conclusive fact and proof, they are instead engaged in producing inconclusive evidence and argument. Problem complexity denies the possibility of proof

and reduces the pursuit of fact to the pursuit of those selective facts which, if appropriately developed, constitute evidence in support of relevant argument. (1980: 133)

With this observation, they call attention to 'the inevitably incomplete character of attempts at proof, the consequent reduction of such attempts to informed argument, and the highly selective search for just those facts that bear on argument as evidence for or against the argued position' (Cohen and Lindblom 1980: 133).

When one adds to these organisational processes a government's usual requirements, which in this instance were also intensely *kairotic*, the subtle direction by DEE to 'get back' about an undesirable point with no intention of doing so, PM&C's immediate sense to drop the matter of renewables to focus only on damaged equipment and the subsequent and exclusive focus on damage, one can see: Vaughan's conversion of ambiguity into solidified, official certainty; Egeberg's simplified decisions; and Cohen and Lindblom's selective search for facts in action. By being positioned as a conduit for status reports, the advice under consideration transmitted reality on the ground—standing in for evidence—and it professed its responsiveness, both by providing regular updates and by leaving out the bits ministers did not want to be told by their officials. Thus, deliberately incomplete evidence supported the official argument, lending the government's version the objectivity it needed or at least not standing in its way.

Objectivity, as Mulgan (2007) suggests, should include articulating a range of options or interpretations to avoid distortion and misrepresentation. We saw PM&C's early attempt to infuse subsequent advice with such a range by requesting clarification on the blackout's causes. Seeking guidance on handling, PM&C also shared (and left unredacted) some negative correspondence to the prime minister, which tended to construe the government's statements about the blackout as demonising renewables. Yet these attempts at even-handedness were quickly subdued. Objectivity, as we saw, was not achieved by excluding (unwanted) issues of relevance. If seeking to inform policymaking with recourse to evidence is about 'the quest for facts as a means to policy enlightenment' (Strassheim and Kettunen 2014: 261) and 'an attempt to enhance the possibility of policy success by improving the amount and type of information processed in public policy decision-making' (Howlett 2009: 157), my case study did not acquit itself well. Certainly, constant status reports gave the appearance of transmitting reality as it was on the ground in South Australia, but this is not the same as being expansive about available, sometimes inharmonious information. Yet, this misses the point about evidence in policymaking and the legislated requirement to use it. Following Foucault, Helen Sullivan suggests it is more realistic to call evidence-based policy a 'regime of truth' in the sense that truth 'is produced only by virtue of multiple forms of constraint' (2011: 502). Viewed thus, policy-based evidence is a constriction of truth. It features objectivity not so much as an absolute or ideal, but as a type of knowing what not to know, leaving only what is considered worth knowing and discarding what is not.

Can we observe this constrained way of constructing policy evidence elsewhere, especially in relation to renewable energy or broader environmental policy issues? In particular, as my framework asks, can international comparisons shed further light on the conditions for Australia's rebuffed advice? Are contexts and circumstances similar or is Australia unique? It is difficult to find international studies that deal with these exact questions, of course, but it is possible to surmise answers to these questions by reviewing related research. I have previously mentioned Stevens' work on evidence selection among UK policy advisers who avoided integrating evidence that challenged the government's viewpoint. Stevens characterises that policymaking progress as shunning uncertainty, usually by zeroing in on the informational aspects of a particular policy:

> Many policy documents transmitted between policy-making civil servants were in the form of PowerPoint 'packs', stuffed with bullet points, diagrams, short text boxes and simple graphs. None of these permitted lengthy discussion of the uncertain or imprecise nature of the knowledge they presented. (2011: 243)

Controlling uncertainty in this way not only 'strengthens the narrative of a policy document'; it 'also plays a wider role in structuring the context in which civil servants operate'. Once uncertainty was sufficiently whittled down by way of repeated modification across the department, there finally came a moment of realisation that 'if we were to worry incessantly and individually about the profound limits to our knowledge of the world we inhabit, then collective action could not emerge' (Stevens 2011: 243). Uncertainty was thus something to be overcome and it marked a line in the sand; it was progressively avoided by way of advisers' proceduralisation of it and was used as a catalyst for bringing about the point at which a decision could be made.

In addition to the guiding features of uncertainty, Stevens observed deference to the status quo—typified by his description of an exchange about unwelcome evidence between a civil servant and his boss:

> 'Well, you're young. Why don't you suggest we look again at [policy area] and see how far that takes you in your career?' So there are certain areas where officials will self-censor and they won't suggest to ministers to change policy on certain areas even though the evidence suggests it. (Stevens 2011: 245)

Although I had access only to a portion of advice by which to observe how Australian policymakers grappled with uncertainty, Stevens' remarks resonate among several instances: the request from the PMO for specific facts about heavy industry's access to power and the cost to the economy as isolated inputs to the prime minister's speech; the aborted attempt for clearer information; and the reflexive, perhaps timeworn, manner in which departments avoided creating uncertainty (by sticking to status updates) and embraced it (by allowing enough ambiguity to avoid contradicting the government's version of events).

Andy Stirling's consideration of the United Kingdom's nuclear energy policy between 2002 and 2008 is also worth mentioning. Against a backdrop of the UK Government's historical 'fixation with nuclear power ... exerting unusually heavy influence over central government policy', Stirling considers two government white papers that highlighted the 'feasibility and viability of strategies based around renewables and energy efficiency' (2014: 87). Rejecting both papers, the UK Government convened 'a third, more superficial, "review" in order to reinstate the nuclear option' (Stirling 2014: 87). Despite that paper being later overturned by a judicial review, the UK prime minister declared this 'won't affect the policy at all'. Stirling cites statements by the government's chief scientific adviser, Sir David King, during the same period: '[W]e have no alternative to nuclear power: if there were other sources of low carbon energy I would be in favour, but there aren't' (Stirling 2014: 87). When confronted with evidence of viable alternative low-carbon energy sources, King simply widened his argument by stating 'we need to do everything' and 'we need to keep the nuclear option open' (Stirling 2014: 87). This suggests that, faced with expertise that contested its favoured pathway, the UK Government needed to be legitimated by one of its senior civil servants:

As with other essentially political ends in plural societies, it is equally possible legitimately to propound (or contest) either a renewables or nuclear-based global energy vision ... what is clear, is that the overall industrial, infrastructural and operational implications of broadly contrasting visions for nuclear and renewable-based zero carbon energy infrastructures are so disparate, that real-world energy systems cannot be *optimised* simultaneously around both pathways. Despite the latitude for diversity, then, there emerges significant scope for social—and therefore political—choice.

This is where there arises a remarkable further indication of the effects of power on knowledge. For it remains the case that in many energy policy debates ... the fact of this choice is frequently not only side-lined in the 'evidence base' constituted by high-level policy documentation, it is sometimes effectively excluded. (Stirling 2014: 87; emphasis in original)

We have been able to observe this choice in my examination as well. We know that, although proceeding as a simple description of network damage and repairs, the advice under examination was not simply describing something. A conscious decision—a choice—was made to exclude other options and evidence, to avoid contradicting political choices. Of course, excluding certain evidence means responsiveness trumps contestability.

Perhaps my comparisons so far have been unfair. After all, the material on South Australia's blackout is not formal policy advice, at least not in the sense of Stirling's rather more high-profile white papers or even Stevens' descriptions of policy development. We have only a few emails sent between departments and their ministerial offices. Yet, these emails not only provide a window into how policy advisers communicate with each other and their political masters, they also represent a continuation of policy advising on renewable energy and the generation mix. Indeed, the act of policy advising is neither singular nor punctuated solely by formal written briefings; rather, there is a continuous exchange through various modes of communication. Additionally, the exchange at hand preceded the establishment of the Finkel Review, as well as the set of policies later dubbed the National Energy Guarantee, which that review inspired (see, for instance, Potter et al. 2018). It might even be argued that the subsequent vacuum in Australia's national energy policy can be traced at least in part back to my advisers' choice to emulate the government's favoured pathway by avoiding emphasis on alternative evidence.

Katy Wilkinson's ethnographic research into the United Kingdom's Department for Environment, Food and Rural Affairs (Defra) describes a policymaking process directed not necessarily by political choice, but by layers of filtering expertise among scientists and policy advisers:

> [W]e get experts together and we decide from an expert's point of view the answer to specific questions raised by policy colleagues … essentially there is a role for knowing who you need to bring together to be able to get a consensus view on what the scientific and veterinary issues are and then being able to explain that coherently to policy makers who actually can choose to ignore the advice that has been given to them. Their role is to seek advice from whatever sources they believe necessary and then to recommend what a particular policy should be. (Wilkinson 2011: 964)

A similar separation was observed in this case study between AEMO's advice that renewables were probably not to blame for the blackout and policy advisers' careful avoidance of having to make that claim themselves. In the frequent event of failing to construct persuasive evidence, Wilkinson's civil servants focus on rationalising their roles within the organisation:

> Defra policy makers and scientists alike express their powerlessness at the hands of bureaucratic procedure, suggesting that when they fail to act in a rational manner it is not their fault but the result of being swept up into the bureaucratic machine … What attraction does bureaucracy hold for officials (and advisers)? The key is in the sense of powerlessness … Bureaucracy affords the opportunity for officials to abdicate responsibility for the division's failings. It also helps these frustrated decision makers to retain a sense of place and worth in the organisation: the bureaucratic mode of ordering gives all participants a place in the bureaucratic system that does not depend on the subsequent utility of their contributions. For example, even the scientific advisers whose expertise is rarely used have a place in the bureaucratic organisation; whether their advice is used or not, they have fulfilled their 'function' simply by existing and providing advice. Bureaucracy does not weight the different contributions of its participants; the emphasis is on procedural regularity and order. (Wilkinson 2011: 968)

Thus, being ignored or rebuffed adds to a feeling of powerlessness, which is subsumed into bureaucratic identity. The way advice is produced, then, can be connected to an acceptance and even standardisation of failure.

Surveying another area of the same department, Claire A. Dunlop describes biofuels policymaking. Following the UK Government's 2008 demand that biofuels make up 2.5 per cent of road transport fuel sales, ramping up to 5 per cent by 2010–11, policy advisers set about assembling evidence to 'develop detailed policy strategy' (Dunlop 2010: 351–52), despite being 'aware that increased biofuels production raised potentially significant and environmentally deleterious countervailing risks' (p. 352). Further, advisers 'struggled to know both how to process the often inconsistent and conjectural evidence and the weight to attach to the risks being signalled' (Dunlop 2010: 352). This suggests that, in fulfilling the requirement to be responsive to Westminster governments' policy directions, expert advisers find it difficult to express conflicting evidence even when motivated to be objective.

Energy policy in Sweden, according to Katrin Uba, 'has arguably succeeded, to a greater extent than in other countries, in promoting renewable energy production and use' (2010: 6675). She notes that policies 'of this kind usually involve a broad participation by stakeholders and/or an extensive reliance on expert knowledge' and investigates whether this holds when considering committees of inquiry, which represent 'an important phase in the formulation of Swedish public policy' (Uba 2010: 6675). The members of committees of inquiry are

> named by the ministry responsible for the issue in question, but said members are free to seek out advice from any expert they deem appropriate … [Committee] members are usually politicians, civil servants, representatives of various state agencies, or representatives of private and public interest groups. (Uba 2010: 6675)

While committee independence and political interference have been raised as possible drawbacks, 'the extent of government control is limited due to the tradition of publishing the committee's report and of inviting interested actors … to comment on it'. Further, the 'responsible ministry then uses the report and the comments to formulate a government bill, which parliament discusses and usually accepts without major modification' (Uba 2010: 6675). Uba's research finds that, in terms of making renewable energy policy, committee structure can, for instance, be dominated by large industry, but 'it must compete with other stakeholders to have an impact', giving committee recommendations and reports a greater chance of nearing objectivity. Further, the prominent voices of uranium and fossil fuel producers, and those of the less-organised renewable energy producers, have 'not hindered the formulation of renewable-energy policies that many have characterised as "forerunner" and "pioneering"' (Uba 2010: 6682). This suggests that, despite a handful of downsides, Swedish committees of inquiry are an attempt at producing evidence for government that draws together a range of expertise, opinions and stakeholders, enabling policy to be made relatively contestably, thus raising the chances for robustness and limiting opportunities for interference and politicisation. Although Sweden is not immune to disagreement on energy policy, the 'involvement and co-operation of different actors has encouraged broader societal consensus … for a long period'. Indeed, the 'increasing engagement of experts, the predominance of state actors, and the relatively even balance among various stakeholders keeps the level of political conflict lower than in countries without such an institutional setting' (Uba 2010: 6682).

Although Australia's institutional setting accommodates inquiries using committee structures to inform changes in legislation or to review administrative matters, membership is drawn from the upper or lower houses of parliament, while stakeholder, expert, industry and community submissions are usually invited in writing and/or as part of public inquiries. With the chair and deputy chair positions usually drawn from each of the two major parties, outcomes and recommendations tend to represent political compromises rather than consensus on the best available evidence, particularly on issues marked by political haste, such as national security.[21] For example, the *Criminal Code Amendment (High Risk Terrorist Offenders) Act 2016*, which established a scheme for continuing to detain terrorist offenders even after the completion of their sentence, passed through an inquiry process via the Parliamentary Joint Committee on Intelligence and Security. Although credentialled external experts had serious misgivings, the Bill nonetheless passed with bipartisan support.[22]

Returning to the international context, a 2004 study of Dutch renewable energy policy finds that 'growth of the renewable energy market in the Netherlands has been limited', partly due to the Dutch Government failing to build 'confidence through stable policies' and reduce 'market uncertainties' (van Rooijen and van Wees 2006: 69). Presaging countless

---

21 Viewed alongside the paralysis in energy policy, it is astounding to see the amount of national security, citizenship and migration legislation that was passed under both the Abbott and the Turnbull governments. The Grattan Institute's *A Crisis of Trust* puts the number at 15 items in less than five years (Wood and Daley 2018).
22 For further information and submissions, see PJCIS (2016).

pleas for certainty on energy policy in Australia (for example, BCA 2018; NERA 2017; Watson 2018), Sascha N.M. van Rooijen and Mark T. van Wees suggest

> the effectiveness of policies to stimulate renewable energy is best guaranteed if governments create confidence among stakeholders. Uncertainties need to be minimised and actors should feel secure about the future developments in a policy. This means that governments should adopt clear and stable policy objectives and instruments. Any uncertainty on goals, vision and future direction will reduce the effectiveness of policies. Frequent shifts in policy have negative impacts, as they lead to uncertainties about the directions of policy. In the Netherlands, a stable climate for growing a renewable energy market has yet to be established. (2006: 69)

However, unlike Australia, where uncertainty in energy policy was effectively preserved by policy advisers who avoided making more of their knowledge known to the government, the Netherlands seems to be working on how to communicate uncertainty in a way that increases awareness of its policy implications. J. Arjan Wardekker et al. worked at the science–policy interface out of Utrecht University and the Netherlands Environmental Assessment Agency. According to the authors, the Environmental Assessment Agency had been 'actively reflecting on its assessment and communication of uncertainties over the past few years' (Wardekker et al. 2008: 629). To be fair, Australia's DEE has also reflected on uncertainty in its contribution to policymaking, as illustrated by its then secretary Gordon de Brouwer's 2015 speech on science in Australia's environmental policy.[23] Yet, following an international expert meeting exploring the issue of communicating uncertainty, Utrecht University and the Environmental Assessment Agency in 2008 went further by embarking on several experiments on the presentation and importance of uncertainty information among various policy actors, including policymakers and policy advisers. Their findings returned a mixture of responses. On the

---

23 De Brouwer argued for 'adaptive management' to manage uncertainty and risk in environmental policy—specifically, by taking 'a precautionary approach to environmental management. The precautionary principle argues that policymakers should be confident about the future environmental effects of an activity before allowing it, and should not wait for conclusive proof of environmental harm before adopting appropriate remedial measures'. He continued by illustrating adaptive management with three examples: threatened species, the Great Barrier Reef and coal-seam gas, which, beyond their explicatory value, underscored that risk and harm are matters of perspective (Department of the Environment 2015).

one hand, participants 'noted that providing uncertainty information prevents false certainty, waste of money, and decisions based on insufficient information'. On the other hand, according to the participants,

> it can lead to difficulties in negotiations and weaken policy proposals. An 'overdose' could, in their opinion, paralyse and lead to unnecessary discussion and delay of action. Selective and strategic use of uncertainty information was said to be a problem in many cases. Some participants also considered interpretation and use of uncertainty information to be difficult in their own daily practice. Preliminary results from another study indicate that policymakers often were not aware of uncertainty information, or did not know how to deal with it. Consequently, the actual use is limited. (Wardekker et al. 2008: 631)

However, despite some downsides, particularly in terms of achievement, it was found that, in situations where

> facts are uncertain, values in dispute, and the decision stakes high … explicit attention for uncertainty and knowledge quality is important. Policy processes demand information at short notice, but users of this information often do not have a clear view of the research behind it and its complexities, caveats and robustness. (Wardekker et al. 2008: 637)

Between the two distinct groups of policymakers and policy advisers:

> Policymakers were surprised by the many aspects of uncertainty, and policy advisors noted that policymakers tend to see numbers as 'solid facts'. Nuances in information may be obvious to scientists, but not to policymakers and, therefore, need to be made explicit. (Wardekker et al. 2008: 637)

The authors conclude that, even though uncertainty information can add complexity to already thorny problems, 'simply not providing such information or relegating it to background reports would not add to the quality of these decisions' (Wardekker et al. 2008: 637–38). Indeed, 'uncertainties can be highly policy-relevant' and can 'take the forefront in societal debate'. To prepare policymakers for such debate, not to mention equip them with the relevant evidence to be seen to make fully informed decisions, Dutch policy advisers are encouraged to 'provide information on the consequences for the solidity of the conclusions and the policy risk (probability and consequences) of wrong decisions' (Wardekker et al.

2008: 638). Although a willingness by one policy adviser to do this early was noted in my Australian case study, this was short-lived in the face of the more pressing need to be responsive to a particular political choice.

I have observed similarities with UK policymaking, perhaps showing the limitations of expectations of objectivity, independence, responsiveness and contestability at the same time, and contrasts with Sweden and the Netherlands. A final, intriguing example in my search for relevant international comparisons comes from Lebanon. A developing economy whose 'energy legislative, institutional and infrastructure frameworks [date] back to the post World War II era' (Khodr and Hasbani 2013: 629), and whose political context poses an obstacle to 'the development of evidence-based policy' and 'to energy policy making' (Khodr and Hasbani 2013: 639), may not educe the most instructive comparison with Australia. Indeed, of the factors that make up these obstacles—'sectarianism, corruption, lack of accountability and transparency, the politicization of policy and the absence of policy continuity' (Khodr and Hasbani 2013: 639)—Australia can really only be said to feature the last two. Yet, in their research—which asked 40 interviewees drawn from ministries and parliamentary committees why policymakers and researchers were 'not making better use of research to contribute to more evidence-based energy policies in Lebanon'—Hiba Khodr and Katarina Uherova Hasbani (2013: 630) found all their respondents named the political context as 'the most crucial domain in influencing the impact of research on energy policy'. Politicisation of energy policy is not uncommon internationally, nor does it automatically imply policy kinship with Australia. But the details are revealing:

> Due to the relatively short time in power, there is not a sufficient space for a healthy policy debate and discourse among policymakers: a two-years average term of government in power means one-year preparation, one-year action. The political life in Lebanon was described as a 'permanent election campaign'. Even when technical arguments are presented, they are not taken fully into consideration and decisions about projects are generally a reflection of political needs: Most policy discussions seem to be political with populist argumentation. A 'blame game' often takes place between ministries as one is blamed to be obstructing the work of the other … In fact, there is very limited policy debate behind closed doors; all issues become public and receive full media coverage. This again prevents the use of evidence-based arguments in policy decisions. (Khodr and Hasbani 2013: 635)

Although Australia's House of Representatives has a maximum term of three years, it is usually less than this and has been critiqued as too short (Bennett 2000). When one considers that the past decade has seen six prime ministers, terms can be even more truncated. Leadership instability, driven by internal party unrest, has given rise to the appearance of permanent election campaigns as leaders attempt to maintain their position (Bowman 2015; Coorey 2018; Strutt 2018). We have already seen that AEMO's technical reviews of the blackout could not have been considered seriously by ministers given the speed and populist timbre of their public statements. Indeed, the man who, as treasurer in early 2017, brought a piece of coal into the House of Representatives to tell delighted party members 'this is coal—don't be afraid' (Butler 2017) became Australia's prime minister until May 2022. Against this backdrop, it is not difficult to empathise with policy advisers choosing pragmatism over explaining complex technical subtleties. We also witnessed a 'blame game', not between ministries, but between federal and state governments regarding renewable energy targets. We do not know how much policy debate goes on behind closed doors, but the lingering resentment of deposed leaders has ensured most policy and political issues are played out under the media spotlight, often by way of leaks (Oakes 2010; Murphy 2018) or direct appeals to the public to head off internal dissent (Remeikis and Murphy 2018). In conditions like this, the cautious tone of AEMO's advice, for example, probably lacks the necessary force to help politicians cut through (and be seen to win) debates. 'Decisions on energy issues are therefore political to a great extent, which overrides evidence-based choices', note Khodr and Hasbani (2013: 635) in a statement that could easily apply to the Australian context.

Khodr and Hasbani also raise the related issue of continuity—confirmed by most of their respondents. While 'the prevailing nature of policy in Lebanon is that there is no policy continuity between consecutive governments, even within the same political party', the political system is also 'resistant to change and maintaining the status quo is the norm' (2013: 635). This seems a contradictory dynamic, in the sense that lack of continuity cannot simultaneously imply maintenance of the status quo. Yet this dynamic is present in my Australian example in the sense that frequent leadership change has required that things be seen to be done both differently and the same. For instance, in deposing the electorally popular but allegedly dysfunctional Kevin Rudd, Julia Gillard had to both acknowledge Rudd's achievements and propose to do better: 'I believed that a good Government was losing its way' (Gillard 2010). In our case, Turnbull had to both demonstrate that he was different to Tony Abbott (more progressive, less ideological) and repeatedly reassure those concerned about his past progressivism that he would maintain Australia's economic reliance on coal by being 'technology agnostic'[24] on energy. I have discussed this tension previously in connection with Turnbull's *kairotic* requirements. As such, Turnbull had to demonstrate a break with the policies of the Abbott government and maintain them. Turnbull's energy technology agnosticism was an attempt at straddling this divide.

Finally, Khodr and Hasbani note that Lebanese public institutions' lack of 'the appropriate mechanisms to integrate expert views and lack of political consensus on at least key policy elements is a serious issue' (Khodr and Hasbani 2013: 635). We have seen the lack of political consensus on energy and climate policy, which has persisted throughout Australia's leadership changes. The lack of consensus is apparent not just along party lines, of course, but also across the current rank and file of the governing party. Yet, after 10 years of shifting complexity across the political landscape, one might assume this is a new normal in Australia. It is worth asking why the APS continues to struggle to integrate expert views into its advice or whether, indeed, it is still realistic to expect it to do so. In other words, expecting the APS to provide both evidence-based *and* responsive advice could be unworkable in the sense that fear of losing relevance in an environment in which others can offer more acceptable advice will likely always entail the production of expertise that maintains favour.

Based on our knowledge of policy advice about South Australia's blackout and by appraising it against international examples, it appears that conditions for Australia's policy advice-giving are similar to the United Kingdom's, where pressure to confirm specific political choices by way of organising the evidence base and a willing acceptance of failure to do so were particularly noticeable. The Dutch and Swedish examples revealed jurisdictions mostly conscious about contestability, such as by acknowledging uncertainty and articulating its policy implications,

---

24 '[A]s the world's largest coal exporter, we have a vested interest in showing that we can provide both lower emissions and reliable base load power with state-of-the-art clean coal–fired technology. The next incarnation of our national energy policy should be technology agnostic. It's security and cost that matters [sic] most, not how you deliver it. Policy should be all of the above technologies, working together to deliver the trifecta of secure and affordable power while meeting our emission reduction commitments' (Turnbull 2017). The website from which the transcript of this speech was sourced features at least 21 instances of Turnbull's 'technology agnostic' phrase.

as well as by assembling a variety of viewpoints to arrive at agreed policy proposals. This was broadly in contradistinction to Australia. Finally, we also saw that over 10 years of political instability, as well as the APS's own acknowledged lack of strategic advisory capability, warrant comparison with aspects of Lebanon's public policy administration. One must ask whether Australia's approach to producing expert policy advice—so far removed from being frank and comprehensive—can remain tenable over time and whether it adequately serves the public interest. I will return to this in my conclusion.

4

Excess of Objectivity: Australian Intelligence Assessments of Iraq's Weapons of Mass Destruction

Introduction

This case study takes place in the period leading up to Australia's decision to join the United States and the United Kingdom in their 20 March 2003 invasion of Iraq to find weapons of mass destruction (WMD). While his allies George W. Bush and Tony Blair frequently signalled that an invasion was justified due to the clarity of their evidence, Australian prime minister John Howard also incorporated uncertainty and contestability into his case for convincing Australia to join them. Much more than his counterparts, Howard's rhetoric embraced the imperfection of evidence and, with it, capitalised on the doubt that surrounded it. This uncertainty was at least partially created by his two primary producers of evidence, the Defence Intelligence Organisation (DIO) and the then Office of National Assessments (ONA). Without them, it is unlikely Howard could have made his case in quite the way he did. The language of the rebuffed—at times inconsistent and often expressed with an 'excess of objectivity' (Sarewitz 2004: 388)—thus contributed to bolstering a useful political strategy. As we shall see, despite the differences in time, context and policy topic, this language helped Howard to politically utilise its inconclusiveness in much the same way it supported Malcolm Turnbull's position in the previous chapter.

My focus here will be specifically on material produced by the ONA, which assesses and analyses 'international political, strategic and economic developments for the Prime Minister and senior ministers in the National Security Committee of Cabinet' (ONA n.d.[c]), and DIO, whose efforts are directed at tactical, military matters for the benefit of the Minister for Defence and other government officials involved in international security matters, such as the minister for foreign affairs. ONA and DIO are Australia's only two intelligence assessment agencies, evaluating intelligence collected by at least three of the four intelligence collection agencies—the Australian Signals Directorate, the Australian Secret Intelligence Service (ASIS) and the Australian Geospatial-Intelligence Organisation[1]—as well as a variety of other sources. ONA 'bases its assessments on all sources of information … intelligence as well as diplomatic reporting, other government agencies' information and reporting, and material available from open sources' (ONA n.d.[c]), while DIO's intelligence evaluates 'information from a variety of sources, such as satellite surveillance, foreign newspapers and broadcasts, social media and human contacts'. DIO is an authority in its own right on 'chemical, biological, radiological and nuclear issues that may pose threats to Australia' (Department of Defence n.d.); ONA is a kind of umbrella organisation that sifts through all available information to produce wideranging assessments of relevance to the government. Overall, Australia's intelligence services are part of the 'Five Eyes' community—an intelligence-sharing alliance between Australia, Canada, New Zealand, the United Kingdom and the United States. Because the Middle East is not part of Australia's intelligence remit, in the leadup to the Iraq war, 'Australia relied on its partner agencies for approximately 97 per cent of the intelligence on Iraq; only about three per cent of this intelligence originated in Australia' (PJCAAD 2003: 46). This means that ONA and DIO assessments of Iraq's WMD had recourse to, and included, material and references from US and UK intelligence agencies.

---

1   The fourth, the Australian Security Intelligence Organisation (ASIO), is a collector of domestic intelligence, which is generally not shared with international intelligence agencies due to conflicting legislative requirements, such as protecting the privacy of Australian citizens.

Given the volume of inquiries into intelligence on Iraq (several of which will be discussed later in this chapter), some may wonder why more analysis is necessary. Why not choose another, less examined example of rebuffed advice such as those mentioned in my introduction? These are fair points. There are three reasons for choosing Australian intelligence assessments on Iraq. The first is that, although Australia only underwent one parliamentary inquiry into the nature of the intelligence assessments on Iraq, the material made available was rich enough for me to connect it to political statements and reactions in the front regions. This, in turn, made it possible to interrogate and establish rebuffal as directed by my framework. The second reason is I wanted to apply my framework to an example with which most readers would already be well acquainted, and for which numerous post-mortems could become part of the overall analysis. Even one of the most known events of the early twenty-first century, in other words, could still be illuminated in productive new ways. Finally, apart from a handful of exceptions (Gleeson 2014; McDonald and Merefield 2010), the role of Australia's own intelligence in constructing a case to invade with a specific focus on language has rarely been subject to sustained analysis.

Choosing an example drawn from the world of intelligence rather than policy per se provides several other insights germane to this book. The first is related to FOI. The assessments of the two agencies became public in 2003 following an inquiry into intelligence on Iraq's WMD by the Australian Parliamentary Joint Committee on ASIO, ASIS and DSD[2] (PJCAAD), a now superseded committee whose membership represented both houses of parliament, and whose chair and deputy chair were drawn from the government and the opposition, respectively. While this departs from my corpus operating under the 'shadow' of FOI legislation, here one has an opportunity to observe a language that presumes relative independence and a high degree of confidentiality, if not complete secrecy. This will ultimately offer an insight into how government advisers communicate without the pretext of being inhibited by FOI requirements. The second is that ONA and DIO are not, strictly speaking, APS agencies. ONA is bound by its own Act, the *Office of National Assessments Act 1977*, the *Intelligence Services Act 2001* and the *Public Governance, Performance and Accountability Act 2013*. DIO is covered under the *Intelligence Services Act* (ALRC 2010). None of these Acts talk explicitly about the nature

---

2   Defence Signals Directorate, which in 2013 became the Australian Signals Directorate.

of advice in terms similar to the *Public Service Act*'s requirements for frankness and objectivity. Again, far from clouding my framework and its objectivity schema, this represents a valuable variable in that it shows advice relatively free from such legislative provisos. Finally, intelligence and intelligence assessments are not policy advice because they usually form a kind of evidence base that feeds into policy advice. As Australia's 2017 *Independent Intelligence Review* puts it, the role of intelligence is to 'explain the forces at work in particular situations and thus to help government influence developments' (PM&C 2017: 33). Yet, as Prime Minister Howard implied after the release of Britain's Chilcot Inquiry report, intelligence and advice are somewhat interchangeable.[3] For the purposes at hand, the use of intelligence as an example in my examination of rebuffed policy language is instructive because it demonstrates that this type of knowledge is produced in ways that are very similar to those of policy advice.

In its decision to join the United States and the United Kingdom in their invasion of Iraq on 20 March 2003, the Australian Government effectively rebuffed several streams of advice. Primarily, it rebuffed assessments made by its own intelligence agencies, especially the DIO, which was reluctant to be definitive about the presence and immediacy of the WMD threat, particularly in relation to Iraq's potential nuclear capability. But there are additional layers of rebuffal, which include the Australian Government emulating the US Government's rejection of recalcitrant advice from the Department of State's Bureau of Intelligence and Research, the Department of Energy, the Air Force and even the more hawkish Central Intelligence Agency (CIA) (Hersh 2003). The Australian Government also rebuffed reports by the United Nations Monitoring, Verification and Inspection Commission (UNMOVIC) for Iraq and the International Atomic Energy Agency (IAEA), which offered a unique opportunity to gain firsthand insight into a country largely closed to other means of human intelligence collection. From this perspective, I will focus on the language of advice as it was articulated by Australia's intelligence agencies, with occasional recourse to that of other rebuffed actors. I will therefore look at excerpts of Australian assessments contained in the report of the PJCAAD inquiry, as well as statements by weapons inspectors Hans Blix and Mohamed ElBaradei and the CIA's 'National Intelligence Estimate'

---

3   Howard told journalists: 'If you wait for advice that is beyond doubt you can end up with very disastrous consequences' (Blackwell 2016).

of October 2002. To determine how they were rebuffed here in Australia, I will primarily analyse 'front region' speeches and statements by John Howard, who largely led the debate here, and his minister for foreign affairs, who helped enhance or amplify his message, as well as statements by US president Bush, US secretary of state Colin Powell and UK prime minister Blair's *Iraq's Weapons of Mass Destruction: The Assessment of the British Government*, known as the 'September Dossier'.

Discussion of Australian intelligence assessments

On 18 June 2003, just a few months after the invasion of Iraq and a fruitless search for WMD, the Australian Senate[4] referred the matter of intelligence on Iraq's WMD to the PJCAAD. The committee was to report on:

a) [T]he nature and accuracy of intelligence information received by Australia's intelligence services in relation to:

(i) the existence of,

(ii) the capacity and willingness to use, and

(iii) the immediacy of the threat posed by, weapons of mass destruction (WMD).

b) the nature, accuracy and independence of the assessments made by Australia's intelligence agencies of subparagraphs (a)(i), (a)(ii), and (a)(iii) above;

c) whether the Commonwealth Government as a whole presented accurate and complete information to Parliament and the Australian public on subparagraphs (a)(i), (a)(ii) and (a)(iii) above during, or since, the military action in Iraq; and

---

4   In Australia, 'the Senate' does not equate to 'the government' because the government does not usually have the majority of votes in the Senate: 'The proportional representation system of voting used to elect senators makes it easier for independents and the candidates of the smaller parties to be elected. In recent decades this has meant that the government party usually does not have a majority of votes in the Senate and the non-government senators are able to use their combined voting power to reject or amend government legislation. The Senate's large and active committee system also enables senators to inquire into policy issues in depth and to scrutinise the way laws and policies are administered by ministers and public servants' (for more, see Department of the Senate n.d.).

d) whether Australia's pre-conflict assessments of Iraq's WMD capability were as accurate and comprehensive as should be expected of information relied on in decisions regarding the participation of the Australian Defence Forces in military conflict. (PJCAAD 2003: x)

While each yields interesting insights in the PJCAAD report, words like 'accuracy', 'independence', 'complete' and 'comprehensive' stand out because they rephrase terms such as 'objectivity' and 'evidence', which I considered in the previous chapter. Of note is one of the PJCAAD's recommendations for the Australian intelligence community to 'examine their processes to ensure the maintenance of their independence and objectivity' (PJCAAD 2003: xiii). The report was completed in December 2003 and tabled in the Australian Parliament on 1 March 2004.

The material provided to the PJCAAD and used in its report spans the period 16 February 2000 to 11 March 2003 for ONA, and 16 February 2000 to 2 April 2003 for DIO. In each instance, the committee was given unclassified extracts: 26 from ONA and 14 from DIO, the latter telling the committee it had produced a total of 189 prewar assessments (PJCAAD 2003: 28). Being provided with such a small proportion of assessments, the committee noted, was different to similar inquiry processes in the United States and the United Kingdom: '[B]oth counterpart committees—in the United Kingdom, the Intelligence Services Committee and in the United States, the House Permanent Select Committee on Intelligence—were provided with *all* the pre-war intelligence assessments for scrutiny as part of the post-war inquiries' (PJCAAD 2003: 27; emphasis added).

PJCAAD chairman David Jull therefore recommended exercising caution when examining the material, noting the committee's conclusions 'must be qualified' (PJCAAD 2003: vii). This entails some caution for this book, too. Having access to only a slice of expert advice should temper speculation beyond what is offered. Nonetheless, as then director of ONA Kim Jones clarified, 'the selection provided was "a reasonable reflection of what we said"' (PJCAAD 2003: 27)—which means, one assumes, that what is visible in the report is representative of the material provided to the government at the time and therefore provides a good indication of how other, unseen material may have been expressed.

In its report, the PJCAAD differentiates between two phases of assessments. The first is from February 2000 to September 2002, during which ONA's and DIO's conclusions converged in how they qualified and nuanced the evidence of WMD in Iraq. This phase deemed intelligence on Iraq's purported nuclear program 'scarce, patchy and inconclusive' (PJCAAD 2003: ONA/DIO joint assessment, 19 July 2002, p. 29). ONA later noted that, although 'the case for the revival of the WMD programs is substantial', it was 'not conclusive' (PJCAAD 2003: ONA assessment, 12 September 2002, p. 29). In relation to chemical and biological weapons, ONA and DIO explained that Iraq 'most likely kept a sizeable amount of anthrax and other BW [biological warfare] agents concealed from UN inspectors' during United Nations Special Commission (UNSCOM) inspections between 1991 and 1998, which, on conclusion, revealed a variety of materials and weapons unaccounted for (Butler 1999).

Judging from what is observable, therefore, ONA and DIO more or less accepted that Iraq had probably maintained a chemical and biological weapons capability. Nonetheless, during the first reporting phase, the two agreed that Iraq's nuclear capacity was likely to be very limited. On 8 February, ONA referred to 'reports'—likely from US intelligence— pointing to Iraq's 'attempts to acquire aluminium pipes believed to be for gas centrifuges to make weapons grade uranium' (PJCAAD 2003: 30). Although this belief had been questioned, if not entirely debunked, in 2001 by a noted US centrifuge expert (PJCAAD 2003: 127), the two agencies simply noted that 'US agencies differ on whether aluminium pipes, a dual use item sought by Iraq, were meant for gas centrifuges' (PJCAAD 2003: ONA/DIO joint assessment, 19 July 2002, p. 30). This effectively softened the degree of dissent among US analysts around the only physical evidence for claims that Iraq was reconstituting its nuclear weapons program. However, both concluded that Iraq's nuclear program was 'unlikely to be far advanced' (PJCAAD 2003: 30).

On 6 September, ONA reported:

> Iraq is highly unlikely to have nuclear weapons, though intelligence on its nuclear programme is scarce. It has the expertise to make nuclear weapons, but almost certainly lacks the necessary plutonium or highly-enriched uranium … Iraq may be able to build a basic nuclear weapon in 4–6 years. (PJCAAD 2003: 30–31)

Yet, in the same report, ONA also firmed on Iraq's attempted acquisition of the aluminium tubes by stating that 'procurement patterns are consistent with an effort to develop an enrichment capability' (PJCAAD 2003: ONA assessment, 6 September 2002, p. 30). By 12 September, it argued that 'the case for the revival of the WMD program is substantial, but not conclusive' (PJCAAD 2003: ONA assessment, 12 September 2002, p. 29), which, although making its audience aware of the lack of conclusiveness, still gives greater weight to the substantiveness of the case.

The second phase, from September 2002 to March 2003, sees a departure in ONA's assessments towards language that was much more 'definitive' (PJCAAD 2003: 32), while DIO's remained largely the same as in phase one: 'sceptical and circumspect' (p. 36). On 12 September 2002, US President Bush addressed the UN General Assembly to lay out the US case against Iraq. In his address, Bush claimed 'Iraq has made several attempts to buy high-strength aluminium tubes used to enrich uranium for a nuclear weapon' (Bush 2002a). A day later, ONA stated 'there is no reason to believe that [Iraqi president] Saddam Hussein has abandoned his ambition to acquire nuclear weapons'. Although having an ambition is not the same as possession, this language of having 'no reason' to believe in a positive development left little room for doubt and leant rather heavily towards a fatalistic interpretation. In the same assessment, ONA stated that 'Australian intelligence agencies believe there is evidence of a pattern of acquisition of equipment which could be used in a uranium enrichment programme. Iraq's attempted acquisition of aluminium tubes may be part of that pattern' (PJCAAD 2003: ONA assessment, 13 September 2002, p. 32).

ONA effectively buried any trace of dispute—still present in its 19 July 2002 assessment—among intelligence experts on the purpose of the aluminium tubes.

In a radio interview on 13 September, the same day as the ONA assessment cited above, John Howard did not overtly refer to either uranium or aluminium tubes, but allowed their potential authenticity to sink in:

> **[Interviewer Jon] Faine:** George W. Bush and Tony Blair both said we have evidence that Iraq is assembling nuclear weapons. We already knew they had extended aluminium shafts and tubes. We already knew they employed nuclear scientists. We already knew all the things that George W. Bush mentioned at the United Nations. There is no new evidence.
>
> **Prime Minister:** But hang on, if your case is that Iraq has weapons of mass destruction, the fact that most of the evidence that Iraq has weapons of mass destruction is already in the public domain and accepted, doesn't destroy the argument that Iraq has weapons of mass destruction. What we're seeing here with the critics in

America and the critics of the Australian Government is this sort of leap of logic—because some of the evidence is old evidence, therefore it is no evidence.

Faine: No, the old evidence was inadequate evidence and we were told but wait, there's more.

Prime Minister: Well who said it was inadequate? (Howard 2002c)

Four days later, on 17 September 2002, the minister for foreign affairs, Alexander Downer, made the government's first major statement on Iraq in the House of Representatives. Ranging from the events of 9/11 and Iraq's history of using chemical weapons to tallying what remained unaccounted for following UNSCOM's departure in 1998 and Iraq flouting countless UN resolutions, and back to Iraq's chemical and biological stockpiles, Downer's speech finally settled on the alleged nuclear threat, borrowing heavily from ONA's 13 September assessment:

> As with chemical and biological weapons, the Australian government has no reason to believe that Saddam Hussein has abandoned his ambition to acquire nuclear weapons. All the circumstances suggest the opposite. Australian intelligence agencies believe there is evidence of a pattern of acquisition of equipment that could be used in a uranium enrichment program. Iraq's attempted acquisition of very specific types of aluminium tubes may be part of that pattern. Iraq still has the expertise and the information to reconstitute a nuclear weapons program and may have continued work on uranium enrichment and weapons design. And Iraq could shorten the lead time for producing nuclear weapons if it were able to acquire fissile material from elsewhere … The government's view is that there is good reason to be extremely worried about the status of Iraq's programs. (Downer 2002)

Let us briefly pause to think about the importance of nuclear weapons, which is suggested by Downer's verbatim use of ONA's assessment regarding the aluminium tubes. As Albright (2003) notes, '[p]eople in general fear nuclear weapons far more than other weapons of mass destruction', meaning the presence of chemical and biological weapons might be disturbing but less likely to shift public sentiment in the way an arsenal of nuclear WMD would. To substantiate the case for invading Iraq—which was difficult based on chemical and biological materials alone—the US, UK and Australian governments needed physical evidence of a nuclear program that could demonstrate the distinct possibility of Iraq becoming both a nuclear vendor to terrorists and a nuclear threat in its own right. As Albright continues elsewhere, 'the tubes were at the core' of making that case (Jackson 2003). US Vice President Dick Cheney hammered this home in a speech on 20 September 2002, in which he declared the tubes were 'irrefutable evidence' (quoted in Barstow 2004). Causing enough public anxiety to justify invasion therefore hinged on proving Iraq's intention to acquire the relevant nuclear materials. In this second phase of Australian intelligence assessments, ONA lent its expert authority to consolidating the credibility of that evidence.

By 20 September, ONA temporarily regained some of its scepticism when it cast doubt over the United Kingdom's September Dossier, stating it remained 'cautious about the aluminium tubes and the claim that Iraq has sought uranium from Africa' (PJCAAD 2003: 33). In October 2002, DIO stated: 'What is known about Iraq's programmes is as worrying as what is not known' (PJCAAD 2003: DIO assessment, 10 October 2002, p. 33). In relation to Iraq's chemical and biological weapons, it assessed: 'Iraq has the necessary civil, and possibly hidden military, assets to have resumed limited [biological weapons] production, although there is no specific evidence of this' (PJCAAD 2003: 37). By December, DIO concluded: 'There is no known CW [chemical warfare] production' (PJCAAD 2003: DIO assessment, 31 December 2002, p. 37). Regarding nuclear weapons, it argued:

> As a worst case—if Iraq had begun fissile material production after UNSCOM inspections ceased in 1998—it may be able to manufacture a crude nuclear weapon by 2006–2008. In the unlikely event that Iraq was to obtain fissile material from a foreign source, it would take 12 months to develop a nuclear weapon—assuming it already possessed a useable weapon design. (PJCAAD 2003: DIO assessment, 10 October 2002, p. 38)

In deeming the possibility of Iraq sourcing fissile material unlikely, DIO appeared to discount, without direct reference, Iraq's purported uranium purchases from Niger. In the same report, referring to purchases of dual-use items to produce weapons-grade uranium, DIO noted the intelligence was 'patchy and inconclusive' (PJCAAD 2003: 38). The sourcing of aluminium tubes is therefore potentially also discounted by DIO in its pronouncement that evidence of dual-use purchases was inconclusive. Yet this delicate phrasing probably did not resonate. Uranium from Niger and aluminium tubes became major examples of hard evidence for the United States and the United Kingdom, despite a series of credible entities disproving the existence of both. Indeed, evidence related to uranium was debunked at least six times between February 2002 and 2 March 2003, while the suitability of the aluminium tubes was very seriously questioned by US centrifuge experts and the US Energy Department and Bureau of Intelligence and Research on at least five occasions between late 2001 and February 2003 (in PJCAAD 2003: 123–30).

As noted above, ONA sifts through and assesses intelligence from multiple sources, including DIO. As the PJCAAD report points out, ONA's 13 September report was a compilation of intelligence community views on Iraq. In its submission to the PJCAAD, however, DIO noted 'the final product was not cleared formally by the contributing agencies', meaning DIO was left in the dark about how its views had been presented. It is possible, therefore, that ONA's phrase 'Australian intelligence agencies believe' overstated the unity among them. It is equally possible the phrase was preceded by words to the effect that, if one was to base one's case purely on a selection of material provided by allied intelligence, evidence could be said to exist. This 'evidence' could, in turn, be said to reveal a pattern. Whichever possibility is closest to the truth—and perhaps neither is—it is certain ONA's wording regarding Iraq's alleged pattern of acquisition, including of aluminium tubes, was reproduced verbatim in the minister's speech, turning what other experts deemed an unlikely scenario of fissile material acquisition into a real possibility.

DIO is one of the 'Australian intelligence agencies' referred to in the minister's speech. DIO's views during the time of Downer's speech— that is, between 19 July, when it assessed that Iraq's nuclear program was 'unlikely to be far advanced' (PJCAAD 2003: 30), and 10 October, when it concluded that intelligence on Iraq was 'patchy and inconclusive' (p. 38)—are not known. It is possible that, like ONA, it crafted advice during this time that was more suited to Downer's preference to heighten the nuclear threat. But all else being equal, it is more likely it continued to be sceptical, given the consistency of its advice throughout the remainder of the period assessed by the PJCAAD. If this is the case, on this crucial issue of the existence of physical evidence that could make the case for war, DIO's nuanced and qualified advice was rebuffed in favour of expertise that could publicly support the government's preference.

A second instance of rebuffal occurred later in this reporting phase. On 4 February 2003, the prime minister made a statement on Iraq to the Australian Parliament. Referring to intelligence, Howard said:

The Australian government knows that Iraq still has chemical and biological weapons and that Iraq wants to develop nuclear weapons.

We share the view of many that, unless checked, Iraq could, even without outside help, develop nuclear weapons in about five years.

Even before the report of the Head of the United Nations weapons inspection body there was compelling evidence to support these beliefs within the published detailed dossiers of British and American intelligence.

On the basis of the intelligence available, the British Joint Intelligence Committee judged that:

Iraq has a useable chemical and biological weapons capability, which has included recent production of chemical and biological agents.

Iraq continues to work on developing nuclear weapons—uranium has been sought from Africa that has no civil nuclear application in Iraq.

Iraq possesses extended-range versions of the SCUD ballistic missile in breach of Security Council resolutions, which are capable of reaching Cyprus, Turkey, Tehran and Israel.

Iraq's current military planning specifically envisages the use of chemical and biological weapons. In its view, Saddam Hussein is determined to retain these capabilities.

The analysis provided by the Director of US Central Intelligence reached similar conclusions—viz:

Iraq is reconstituting its nuclear weapons programme.

It has begun renewed production of chemical warfare agents, probably including mustard, sarin, cyclosarin and VX.

All key aspects—R&D [research and development], production, and weaponisation—of Iraq's offensive biological weapons programme are active and most elements are larger and more advanced than they were before the Gulf war.

The intelligence material collected over recent times, to which Australia has contributed, points overwhelmingly to Saddam Hussein having acted in systematic defiance of the resolutions of the Security Council, maintained his stockpile of chemical and biological weapons and sought to reconstitute a nuclear weapons programme. (Howard 2003a)

Certainly, Howard acknowledged that Australian intelligence had contributed to the collected material. Yet, except for a potential five-year horizon on nuclear weapons development, he referred exclusively to foreign intelligence. The PJCAAD also made this point:

> The statements by the Prime Minister … are more strongly worded than most of the AIC [Australian intelligence community] judgements. This is in part because they quote directly from the findings of the British and American intelligence agencies. In particular, in the 4 February speech to the House of Representatives, the Prime Minister quoted the findings of the Joint Intelligence Committee of the UK and the key judgements of the National Intelligence Estimate of the CIA. In both of these documents the uncertainties had been removed and they relied heavily on the surge of new and largely untested intelligence, coming, in the US at least, from Iraqi defectors. These dossiers comprised stronger, more emphatic statements than Australian agencies had been prepared to make. (PJCAAD 2003: 94)

This can be viewed as a rejection of Australian advice. In the leadup to this speech, ONA provided advice that 'an Iraqi artillery unit was ordered to ensure that UN inspectors would not find chemical residues on their equipment' (PJCAAD 2003: ONA assessment, 31 January 2003, p. 35) and 'Saddam is procuring equipment and antidotes to protect his own troops in a CBW [chemical and biological war]' (ONA assessment, 30 January 2003, p. 36). From an Australian perspective, this advice may have lent further credence, as well as immediacy, to Howard's references to chemical and biological weapons. Yet, it was publicly ignored in favour of much less ambiguous British and American intelligence.

Nonetheless, ONA may have notched up a small victory in Howard's insistence on referring to uranium being sourced from Africa. Even though on 20 September 2002 it remained 'cautious about the aluminium tubes and the claim that Iraq has sought uranium from Africa' (PJCAAD 2003: 33), by 19 December 2002, ONA pointed out that Iraq's 7 December declaration failed to explain its 'attempted procurement of aluminium tubes and its apparent effort to procure uranium outside Iraq' (p. 34). At this time, ONA was almost certainly aware of the intense dispute around both the tubes and the uranium, yet it clearly continued to think they should be mentioned. It is curious that Howard never referred to the tubes—notwithstanding his foreign minister doing so on 17 September—yet he seemed less concerned by references to African uranium. The British Joint Intelligence Committee report to which Howard referred mentions both.[5] Powell included only one reference to the tubes and none to uranium in his address to the United Nations Security Council (UNSC) the following day, 5 February 2003.

ONA's position was clearly complicated. Across the reporting period, one can see shifting positions, ranging from caution to support for policy positions. As a direct report to the prime minister, as well as in its role as premier assessor with access to the dominant US and British intelligence discourse, ONA would have found it difficult to remain completely removed from the pressure of the government's plainly visible policy preference. Oscillating between caution and support may have been a symptom of its increasingly complex role—on the one hand, describing what it could and could not observe, while on the other, responding to the expectations of its primary customer, the prime minister. Based on what one can discern from its language, this complexity does not bear as heavily on the more technically expert DIO.

Perhaps surprised by Downer's September claim that Iraq may revive its nuclear weapons program, DIO intoned in not one but two assessments that '[w]e assess Iraq does not have nuclear weapons'—the first on 10 October and the second on 31 December 2002 (PJCAAD 2003: 38). This contradicts Howard's statement that Iraq was 'reconstituting its nuclear weapons programme'. Also on 31 December, DIO claimed '[t]here is no known CW [chemical warfare] production', 'Iraq is assessed as unlikely to carry out an offensive first strike on coalition forces' and '[t]here has been no known offensive [biological weapons] research and development since 1991, no known BW [biological warfare] production since 1991 and no known BW testing since 1991' (PJCAAD 2003: 38). This refutes Howard's statement that Iraq had produced chemical and biological agents, that it planned to use them and that they were all active. On Scud missiles, DIO and ONA noted in July 2002, Iraq had in the past built missiles with a range that could, indeed, reach Israel, but '[m]ost, if not all, of the few that are still hidden away are likely to be in poor

---

5   '[T]here is intelligence that Iraq has sought the supply of significant quantities of uranium from Africa … Iraq has also made repeated attempts covertly to acquire a very large quantity (60,000 or more) of specialised aluminium tubes' (FCO 2002: 25–26).

condition' (PJCAAD 2003: ONA/DIO joint assessment, 19 July 2002, p. 39). All these, it could be argued, are at odds with Howard's depiction of certainty and immediacy. This represents the second rebuffal.

Howard made three further statements on Iraq. The first was an address on Iraq to Australia's National Press Club on 13 March 2003. He then made a statement to the House of Representatives on 18 March in which he moved that previous UNSC resolutions 'provide clear authority for the use of force against Iraq' (Commonwealth of Australia 2003), based on legal advice he tabled as part of this statement. Finally, he made a televised address to the nation on 20 March to announce the Australian Government was committing troops to disarm Iraq. In the leadup to these three statements, ONA's and DIO's reporting continued along similar, bifurcated lines. ONA endorsed Powell's statement to the UNSC as 'confirmation that Iraq has WMD, since Iraq's concealment and deception are otherwise inexplicable' (PJCAAD 2003: ONA assessment, 6 February 2003, p. 35). Just less than a fortnight later, ONA confirmed that intelligence 'points to continuing Iraqi concealment and deception, confirming Saddam has something to hide' (PJCAAD 2003: ONA assessment, 18 February 2003, p. 35) and, by mid-March, it claimed 'Baghdad remains defiant and claimed it has no WMD to declare: US and UNMOVIC assessments say the opposite' (ONA assessment, 11 March 2003, p. 35).

On 24 February 2003, DIO simply noted: 'There is no reliable intelligence that demonstrates Saddam has delegated authority to use chemical or biological weapons (CBW) in the event of war' (PJCAAD 2003: DIO assessment, 24 February 2003, p. 40). Nonetheless, although it continued to raise the lack of hard evidence, DIO also echoed the logic of other actors in the Iraq war narrative who deemed history a reliable indicator of future outcomes: 'Despite the lack of firm evidence, precedent suggests that this is a likely scenario. During the 1991 Gulf War, Saddam authorised Iraqi commanders to use CBW if Saddam was killed or coalition forces entered Baghdad' (PJCAAD 2003: DIO assessment, 24 February 2003, p. 40).

Turning to Howard's statements, one notices a focus on the intentions of terrorists, particularly Al-Qaeda, and various rogue nations to acquire WMD. His speech to the National Press Club, and its subsequent Q&A with the assembled press, insinuated a link between terrorist groups and Saddam's WMD, referring to 'the intelligence community's professional assessment', which 'is based on the full range of intelligence material available' and sourced from 'secret intelligence' as well as 'the public domain' (Howard 2003b). His subsequent exchange with two journalists is worth quoting in full here.

The first, Catherine McGrath, asked the prime minister about the link between terrorists and Iraq, which he largely ignored:

> **JOURNALIST:** Prime Minister, Catherine McGrath from the AM, PM and World Today programmes. Can I ask you, you opened your speech today by talking about terrorism, terrorist groups and you identified Osama bin Laden, you talked about his appalling track record. You then spoke about Iraq and said that if Iraq is not stopped that's the green light for weapons to pass from terrorists to Iraq. Can I ask you, you've made a link between the terrorists' requests, the terrorists' desire but you haven't made a strong link between Iraq or provided any proof that Iraq is seeking to deliver its weapons to terrorists. Can I ask you a two-part question—do you have any evidence that you can provide now? Secondly, what about other countries that hold nuclear weapons that may provide opportunities for terrorists, for example, Pakistan which some could argue would have more chance of passing them on?

> **PRIME MINISTER:** Well, can I start with the other countries that have them. I mean, we regret very much that Pakistan and India have nuclear weapons, we made that very clear. I mean, I do have some warm regard for the courage and the stance of [Pakistan's president] General Musharraf in the war against terror. I have great admiration for the risks that he's taken and the strength he's displayed. India and Pakistan, to my knowledge, didn't sign the nuclear non-proliferation treaty and they don't, to my knowledge, have the same track record as Iraq. I mean, to compare a country like India which is the probably the—I mean, it's the largest functioning democracy in the world—with Iraq is very, very unfair. And equally, although Pakistan has not had the same familiarity with parliamentary democracy as India, it is nonetheless in many other ways a very, very good international citizen. So, I don't think you can ... and I think it's very unfair on both India and Pakistan to draw that analogy. Catherine, with respect I think you leapt over one of the things I said. I mean, my argument is this in relation to Iraq. Iraq is demonstrably, to use my language, a rogue state. If we don't make sure that Iraq is disarmed, that of itself will encourage other rogue states to acquire and develop weapons of mass destruction and the more of those states that acquire, the greater inevitably is the likelihood that those weapons are going to get into the hands of terrorists. And when you have on top of that clear evidence, that I mentioned today, that Al Qaeda—

the most lethal of the international terrorist organisations—wants to get its hands on, and in fact is doing its own work in relation to those weapons, you know, that to me is pretty compelling. Now, you say proof, I mean as I say, I can't prove before an Old Bailey or a Central Criminal Court jury but can I say to you again, I mean if the world waits for that, it's too late. I mean, that is I said a Pearl Harbour [sic] situation. (Howard 2003b)

The second journalist, Laurie Oakes, suggested to Howard he had not answered McGrath's question:

> JOURNALIST: Laurie Oakes, Nine Network, Prime Minister. I don't think you answered Catherine's question, so before I ask mine I'll ask hers in a slightly different way. We read in the morning papers that you were going to present today evidence from our intelligence agencies of a link between Iraq and terrorists. What happened to that evidence? Why isn't it in your speech? And since you've made no attempt at all to demonstrate a link, are we to assume there is none? And then my question after you've answered that—the speculation that the US and its allies will stop seeking a fresh UN resolution against Iraq before launching military action, Spain one of the co-sponsors has indicated there's not much point if it's not going to get through. Is that your information and how do you feel about that?

> PRIME MINISTER: Well, Laurie, in answer to the second question—I've had a number of discussions about what's happening in the UN, the latest information I have is that there is still a very concerted effort being made to get a resolution through. Now, it's a fluid situation, things can often change but they're still trying very hard. As for the first question, well I read what was in the paper this morning and I'm not entirely responsible for what's in the newspapers, although I'm sometimes responsible for some of it. I'm perfectly happy to plead guilty to that. What I endeavoured to do today was to do two things—to establish clear evidence that terrorist groups wanted weapons of mass destruction and I think I did that and I think I did that quite convincingly. I've never represented to anybody that we could produce what I called Darlinghurst or Old Bailey proof.

> JOURNALIST: … you didn't need six intelligence agencies to tell you Osama bin Laden wanted nasty weapons.

> PRIME MINISTER: Well, no, I didn't but I think by the reaction of some people, they did. (Howard 2003b)

Even when two attempts were made to try to evince an admission about the evidence base for war—which hinged on the existence of deployable, preferably nuclear, WMD in Iraq—Howard claimed his evidence was both clear and incomplete, which turned the element of doubt into a strength. That is, by referring to the devastating fact of Pearl Harbor, which represents one of the worst intelligence failures in US history, and linking it to the potentially ruinous requirement for an absence of doubt in the case of Iraq, Howard effectively demerited the argument that absolute proof was needed to invade. As he was to later suggest, waiting for such proof can—and has—led to disaster. Committed to war, Howard must nonetheless have understood there were very credible doubts about Iraq having any WMD. Even while he publicly rebuffed those doubts in the sense that they were never publicly foregrounded, he assumed a kind of precautionary rhetoric to convince Australians that the world could not afford to wait for certainty.

In his 18 March address to the Parliament, Howard returned to 'available' intelligence—that is, what he could see, as his evidence base: 'The available intelligence indicates that, since the departure of inspectors in 1998, Saddam has continued to work on his chemical and biological capabilities and has maintained his nuclear aspirations.'

And: 'Intelligence analysis tells us that Saddam Hussein considers these weapons programs to be essential both for internal repression and to fulfil his regional ambitions' (Commonwealth of Australia 2003: 12507–8).

These statements are not reflected in the Australian material and may be sourced from overseas or older intelligence. Howard's address to the nation two days later revisited the threat of WMD falling into the hands of terrorist networks: '[T]he possession of chemical, biological, or even worse still, nuclear weapons by a terrorist network would be a direct and lethal threat to Australia and its people' (Howard 2003c).

Howard worked hard after 9/11 to insinuate a connection between terrorism and WMD. As Gleeson puts it:

> Almost certainly an attempt to ride the wave of popular support for the war on terror, Howard tried to make the link in a number of ways leading up to the war … Whether or not he sincerely believed this to be the case, Prime Minister Howard clearly wanted Australians to view involvement in Iraq as a natural extension of the nation's commitment to the War on Terrorism. (2014: 135–36)

In laying the groundwork for the case to invade Iraq as the next step in the 'war on terror', Howard, like his US counterpart, frequently linked Saddam to terrorism. For instance, in January 2002, Howard asserted that 'the campaign against terrorism doesn't end with a successful operation in Afghanistan' (Howard 2002a). In September that year, he claimed that

> when you have a country [Iraq] that is threatening and has the capacity to deliver destruction on other countries, September 11 has told us that we should not assume it won't happen to you … That is the September 11 link, if I can put it that way. (Howard 2002b)

Linking the two, therefore, was not a new motif for Howard. Yet, it remained unaccompanied by any references to intelligence or evidence and was left to linger in the subjunctive. Later during the same 20 March address, he referred to intelligence, if only to rebuff Australian input:

> A key element of our close friendship with the United States and indeed with the British is our full and intimate sharing of intelligence material. In the difficult fight against the new menace of international terrorism there is nothing more crucial than timely and accurate intelligence. This is a priceless component of our relationship with our two very close allies. There is nothing comparable to be found in any other relationship—nothing more relevant indeed to the challenges of the contemporary world. (Howard 2003c)

Why talk about the nature of the intelligence-sharing relationship on the day of the invasion? Referring to intelligence then, as elsewhere, served as a legitimising force in committing a country to war. It is here also portrayed as a symbol of survival in a world fraught with new risks. Yet, with only 3 per cent of intelligence coming from Australia, and its intelligence agencies remaining somewhat unconvinced of immediate intervention, one cannot help but conclude that Howard's very conspicuous lauding of the 'timely and accurate' intelligence of his friends—without whom we might never have known the true extent of Iraq's evil—represents a rejection of his own intelligence experts. Howard's 13 March and 18 March statements find their apotheosis on 20 March and together represent the third rebuffal.

Table 4.2, at the end of this chapter, reproduces excerpts of the Australian intelligence assessments quoted here and lines them up with domestic statements—that is, statements made by Foreign Affairs Minister Downer and Prime Minister Howard, as well as international statements by the

US leadership, the United Kingdom's September Dossier and weapons inspections bodies UNMOVIC and the IAEA. This highlights some of the differences between them as I move ahead in my analysis.

The text

Overall, DIO was rebuffed on specific evidence, while both DIO and ONA were ignored as war drew closer in favour of US and British intelligence. The first time DIO was rebuffed in favour of ONA, Downer cited the acquisition of aluminium tubes as evidence of a 'pattern of acquisition of equipment that could be used in a uranium enrichment program'. Other than referring to the dispute among US agencies regarding the tubes, DIO did not directly assess them (as far as can be determined from the material available). Nor is DIO's reporting immediately before Downer's speech visible. It is, however, entirely plausible that not much changed in DIO's outlook between declaring, on 19 July 2002, that intelligence on Iraq's nuclear program was 'scarce, patchy and inconclusive' and 31 December 2002, when it assessed that 'Iraq does not have nuclear weapons'. In Prime Minister Howard's hands, one observes a different approach to Downer's. Perhaps aware of the imprecision of the evidence, Howard seemed to publicly ignore Australian intelligence entirely, yet still used its uncertainty to his advantage. He made the case for war exclusively based on US and British intelligence in his 4 February speech and, in three major public statements on 13 March, 18 March and 20 March, emphasised indirect links to terrorism. His final public statement to the nation concluded with a tribute to his close friends, the United States and the United Kingdom.

Let us now return to the questions my framework asks of the text:

1. *Kairos*: What effect does time have on the advice?
2. Context: How does context potentially affect language—and does language affect context?
3. Awareness of self and audience: How is the advice conceived, how is it framed and what does its audience do with it?
4. Response: What is the political reaction to the advice and how is it formed?

In the case of Iraq, it is useful to begin with context drawn from the front regions. For the purpose at hand, this includes statements about terrorism, Australia's alliance with the United States and Iraq's history. On 11 September 2001, Howard was in Washington, DC, on a visit to the United States to mark the fiftieth anniversary of the signing of the Australia, New Zealand and United States Security Treaty (ANZUS Treaty). After the third plane crashed into the Pentagon, the US Secret Service whisked Howard to a safe house, where he dictated a letter to President George W. Bush: 'In the face of an attack of this magnitude, words are always inadequate in conveying sympathy and support. You can however be assured of Australia's resolute solidarity with the American people at this most tragic time' (Howard 2013b: 447).

In Howard's telling, being 'in Washington meant that I absorbed, immediately, the shocked disbelief, anger and all of the other emotions experienced by the American people' (Howard 2013b: 448). This was a time 'for a 100 per cent ally, not a 70 or 80 per cent one' (Howard 2013b: 452), and he resolved there and then to stand with the United States, barely pausing to conclude: 'Having experienced 9/11, who could blame Americans for thinking that the next time a hijacked plane headed for a tall building, it might contain a chemical, biological or even nuclear weapon' (p. 495).

On this day, Howard normalised the link between terrorism and WMD as a natural conclusion. On 14 September 2001, Article IV of the ANZUS Treaty was invoked, meaning Australia was effectively on standby should the United States request military assistance.[6] Just over a year later, on 12 October 2002, 88 Australians lost their lives after a bomb exploded in a nightclub in Bali, Indonesia, which personalised Australia's experience of international terrorism. Although Australia's alliance with the United States was formalised 50 years earlier, in 2001, the alliance deepened as the two nations resolved to defeat any further attempts to harm 'our way of life' and zeroed in on Iraq as a threat to that:

> Supporting the United States in Afghanistan, and later in Iraq, was more than giving expression to our most important alliance relationship; it signalled a determination on our part to participate in an aggregate response to the terrorist threat ... Saddam had

6   'Each Party recognizes that an armed attack in the Pacific Area on any of the Parties would be dangerous to its own peace and safety and declares that it would act to meet the common danger in accordance with its constitutional processes' (see JFADT 1997).

not been involved in September 11, but his regime was listed by the US State Department as a state sponsor of terrorism because of support for other terrorist groups. He had the potential to facilitate a future terrorist outrage. (Howard 2013b: 497)

Following President Bush's 12 September 2002 address to the United Nations, the UNSC passed Resolution 1441 on 8 November 2002, enabling weapons inspectors to return to Iraq on 27 November 2002. Before and after the passing of Resolution 1441, the rhetorical efforts of Australia's political leadership to convince voters of the case to invade relied on absence and not knowing: the location of what the previous UNSCOM mission had been unable to find before its departure in 1998, what Iraq did between 1998 and the resumption of inspections by UNMOVIC in late 2002 and construing UNMOVIC's efforts as insufficient in terms of knowing the extent of Iraq's current capabilities. In addition, Iraq's history of human rights abuses, as well as known use of chemical weapons in its war with Iran, were used as reliable indicators of future behaviour.

These three contexts—fear of the unknown (both in terms of terrorism and what, if anything, Iraq was hiding), emotional connections to powerful friends and the impulse to view history as capable of helping determine the future—combine into a powerful backdrop against which to view the construction of intelligence assessments. Indeed, each context emerged into plain sight from September 2001. Each is also connected to timing. Fearing the unknown—whether Iraq had WMD, whether terrorists might get their hands on them, whether terrorists were plotting further attacks—as well as the pressure from governments to produce evidence that could prevent attacks would have made a formidable combination in adding to the urgency under which intelligence agencies were likely already operating, particularly after 9/11 and the Bali bombings. As the PJCAAD-recommended Inquiry into Australian Intelligence Agencies noted in 2004: '[A]ssessments staff were working extended hours over long periods and operating under significant time pressures' (Flood 2004: 29).

Australia's connection to the United States is here also linked to *kairos*. In his autobiography, Howard alludes to a cool relationship with the administration of President Bill Clinton, particularly when Clinton refused to commit US troops to the Australian-led peacemaking taskforce in East Timor in 1999, which Howard reports left him 'stunned' (Howard 2013b: 405). Already disposed towards Bush by 'a natural sympathy',

Howard admits that, although 'publicly neutral, privately I had wanted Bush to win' the 2000 US election (Howard 2013b: 543). Indeed, he later enthused: 'We were closer friends than any other two occupants of the leadership positions we once respectively held' (Howard 2013b: 540). Howard's presence in the United States in September 2001—originally to reaffirm the ANZUS alliance, only to then witness an unprecedented attack on his friends—meant he was ideally placed to pledge support, solidarity and a promise to stand ready when asked, no matter the request. He had, as an Australian documentary series put it, 'a ringside seat during one of the most dramatic moments in history' (ABC TV News and Current Affairs 2008). By quickly invoking Article IV of the ANZUS Treaty on 14 September, Howard not only aligned Australia with the United States in case of armed attack, but also hitched it to America's conception of itself as the world's only superpower—a beacon of the right way to view reality.

This view is particularly evident in the National Security Strategy of the United States, which Bush released in September 2002:

> The United States possesses unprecedented—and unequaled—strength and influence in the world. Sustained by faith in the principles of liberty, and the value of a free society, this position comes with unparalleled responsibilities, obligations, and opportunity. The great strength of this nation must be used to promote a balance of power that favors freedom. (The White House 2002)

Claiming the right to strike pre-emptively any adversary threatening the United States, its friends or allies,[7] the Bush doctrine gave voice to a philosophy that had percolated for some time among neoconservatives in the White House leadership team. As Robert Manne has argued, 9/11 presented those individuals with a 'historic chance' to advocate, once and for all, for 'the end of the Iraqi regime' (Manne 2003: 12–14). It was, in other words, a '*kairotic* moment'—an opportunity afforded by time and events. As David Zarefsky puts it:

---

7   'We must adapt the concept of imminent threat to the capabilities and objectives of today's adversaries. Rogue states and terrorists do not seek to attack us using conventional means. They know such attacks would fail. Instead, they rely on acts of terror and, potentially, the use of weapons of mass destruction—weapons that can be easily concealed, delivered covertly, and used without warning … The United States has long maintained the option of preemptive actions to counter a sufficient threat to our national security. The greater the threat, the greater is the risk of inaction—and the more compelling the case for taking anticipatory action to defend ourselves, even if uncertainty remains as to the time and place of the enemy's attack. To forestall or prevent such hostile acts by our adversaries, the United States will, if necessary, act preemptively' (The White House 2002).

> [M]any [advocates of US military action in Iraq] believed that the first President Bush had erred in bringing the Persian Gulf War of 1991 to a close with Saddam Hussein still in power. This was the opportunity to finish the job. What made this a kairotic moment, creating the opportunity to mobilize public opinion in support of the goal, was … the psychological effect of September 11, 2001. (2007: 275)

This sense of something that was overdue, justified, somehow preordained and inevitable extends to Australia as well. By tying Australia to the United States in this complex mix just days after 9/11, Howard signalled he would accept any future eventuality and any logic and evidence that might accompany it. Eva Horn goes so far as to suggest that 9/11 became 'an epistemologically operative moment' in the sense that it marked 'a rupture between a *before* and a *from now on*' (2013: 330). She cites the 2002 National Security Strategy's rhetorical contrasts between enemies of the past and those of the present and future to illuminate how these new threats can be justified:

> The question is not *What happened?* but *What will happen from now on?* … It is as if 9/11 could only be presented as part of a scenario (both present and future) that suggests, introduces, and ultimately justifies possible new threats and types of warfare. (Horn 2013: 330)

Howard's rhetoric similarly highlights the potentially greater risk of a 'next time'—something as bad or worse than 9/11, and Saddam's, or any rogue actor's, 'potential to facilitate a future terrorist outrage'. In this, the events that followed 9/11, like Iraq, are part of an inexorable and defensible sequence, in which uncertainty represents the spur to action.

A final point regarding time concerns troops being deployed to the Middle East. As Howard recalled:

> The optimum time for an invasion of Iraq could be February/March 2003. The American troop build-up began in October. They and their British allies faced the twin challenges of time and weather. Iraq is impossibly hot for most of the year. It is prohibitively so from April onwards for a period of three or four months. I knew that if an invasion were to take place then it could not be later than March 2003 … I also knew that if our forces were to be given every opportunity to prepare in theatre, thus minimising the likelihood of casualties, then they should be pre-positioned by early February at the latest. (2013b: 507)

As it transpired, Australian troops deployed on 23 January 2003 (The Age 2003). The shrinking time horizon extending no further than late March was surely another worrisome ingredient in the pressure on intelligence assessors and advisers to point to something that troops could find.

Finally, deeming Iraq's past behaviour a good indicator of its future intentions made the case of contextualising Iraq's suspect present behaviour significantly easier to prosecute. Even though it fails to account for the fact that Iraq's past behaviour was born of different foundations to projected future behaviour (Mearsheimer and Walt 2009), this strangely reassuring supposition was not only persuasive, it also lent considerable support to the notion that future behaviour could be curtailed by pre-emptive action. As WMD were not found, and as coalition troops were not attacked by Saddam, it became clear the idea of history and future being somehow the same was wrong. Conflating them at the time, however, suited a scenario of inexorability and added to the time-based anxiety surrounding the uncertainty that an immediate threat could materialise.

Regarding time and context, then, one finds pressure to help prevent future attacks; solidarity with whatever way the United States chose to justify its destined influence and strength; sweltering, impatient troops who would have had to leave, somewhat ignominiously, by March 2003 if war did not eventuate; and the vitalising power of the notion that past behaviour reliably indicates future behaviour. Each of these, separately and combined, surely represented a potent force in influencing how advice was manufactured. Can one see traces of their influence, both temporal and contextual, in the language of our intelligence assessments as the months wore on? And did the language of the assessment agencies colour the rhetoric of Australian decision-makers?

In the case of ONA, these influences are clear. On 12 September 2002, the day ONA assessed that 'the revival of the WMD program is substantial, but not conclusive', President Bush (2002a) addressed the UN General Assembly to proclaim 'the history, the logic, the facts lead to one conclusion: Saddam Hussein's regime is a grave and gathering danger'. The following day, ONA conceded 'there is no reason to believe that Saddam Hussein has abandoned his ambition to acquire nuclear weapons', before composing the basis for Downer's speech concerning Iraq's 'attempted acquisition of aluminium tubes'. Given the most forceful intelligence was coming from US agencies, it is possible Downer required the added imprimatur of Australian assessments to imbue his words with the kind of 'independent' expertise that would help the Australian Government to not only line up with the United States but also corroborate its conclusions. As the PJCAAD pointed out, ONA returned to a more prevaricating tone on 20 September when it claimed it remained 'cautious about the aluminium tubes and the claim that Iraq has sought uranium from Africa'. Yet, by 6 February 2003, it seemed all but convinced by context when it noted that secretary of state Powell's statement to the UNSC on 5 February provided confirmation that Iraq had WMD. No similar assessment by DIO was included in the material provided to the PJCAAD, so it is impossible to know how it viewed Powell's statement.

Another example of ONA being influenced by the dominating context comes on 11 March 2003, when it claimed: 'Baghdad remains defiant and claims it has no WMD to declare: US and UNMOVIC say the opposite.' This is likely a reference to the 7 March UNSC meeting at which Blix and ElBaradei provided updates of their work. Far from 'saying the opposite', Blix said:

> Inspection work is moving on and may yield results … One can hardly avoid the impression that, after a period of somewhat reluctant cooperation, there has been an acceleration of initiatives from the Iraqi side since the end of January. This is welcome, but the value of these measures must be soberly judged by how many question marks they actually succeed in straightening out. This is not yet clear. (Blix 2004: 209–10)

Blix was clearly unable to provide a glowing picture of a compliant and disarming Iraq; he did not have sufficient evidence to make such a definitive call. His language therefore conveyed cause for encouragement because of recent activity but remained circumspect. Ever the diplomat, Blix's language tried to communicate both cautious optimism and risk, which made it palatable for a range of audiences but also easy to misconstrue. The subtlety of his information, which tried to express a range of probabilities, was easily—perhaps not even unreasonably—reinterpreted by those, like ONA, who were willing to move UNMOVIC's account towards a more conspicuous, negative impression. This is symptomatic of a broader rejection of language that allows nuance and detailed accuracy to dominate at the expense of clarity and forthrightness. The UK Government's failure to make a convincing case not to leave the European Union in 2016 is a case in point, and there are others.

For example, Mark Thompson illustrates this point with the UK Government's attempt to reform parts of its National Health Service, where a clause in the reform Bill led to both wilful and unintentional misinterpretation by those opposed to it. When those opponents looked to be succeeding, proponents complained about detail being ignored and the truth being sacrificed (Thompson 2016: 117–20). Yet, what this also shows is that such complexity seems to offer an invitation to oversimplification by, on the one hand, those who may not have the time or capacity to come to grips with the detail and, on the other, those who can steer the paradoxical ambiguity of that intricacy towards advancing whatever standpoint they want to emphasise.

While ONA was influenced by the dominant rhetorical context that recommended war and found it easy to reinterpret and simplify Blix's somewhat oblique statement to the United Nations, it did not seem to heed the rather more unequivocal statements of ElBaradei when he announced the IAEA had found neither evidence nor indications of a nuclear weapons program (Blix 2004: 178, 211). Perhaps US Defence Secretary Donald Rumsfeld's famous phrase that 'the absence of evidence is not evidence of absence',[8] used in a speech on 6 June 2002, was particularly persuasive among some of the intelligence assessors.

DIO's language, on the other hand, does not appear to have been subject to the same kind of influencing contexts as ONA's. Rather, DIO seems to have deliberated over the available information and found it inconclusive despite those contexts. That is, far from denying a threat existed, DIO acknowledged the risks: Iraq had hidden assets, it could potentially make a nuclear weapon by 2006–08 (both on 10 October 2002) and the precedent of having used chemical and biological weapons could recur (24 February 2003). This does not imply the same kind of pivots seen from ONA. Indeed, DIO's acknowledgements of potential danger gave

---

8   'There are things we know that we know. There are known unknowns. That is to say there are things that we now know we don't know. But there are also unknown unknowns. There are things we don't know we don't know. So when we do the best we can and we pull all this information together, and we then say well that's basically what we see as the situation, that is really only the known knowns and the known unknowns. And each year, we discover a few more of those unknown unknowns. It sounds like a riddle. It isn't a riddle. It is a very serious, important matter. There's another way to phrase that and that is that the absence of evidence is not evidence of absence. It is basically saying the same thing in a different way. Simply because you do not have evidence that something exists does not mean that you have evidence that it doesn't exist. And yet almost always, when we make our threat assessments, when we look at the world, we end up basing it on the first two pieces of that puzzle, rather than all three' (Rumsfeld 2002).

its expert advice a more realistic, credible edge when it also stated that evidence surrounding the aluminium tubes was 'patchy and inconclusive' (10 October 2002), that Iraq did not 'have nuclear weapons' (10 October and 31 December 2002) and that there was no reliable evidence of Saddam using chemical and biological weapons now (24 February 2003). These pronouncements were made against the backdrop of mounting claims from both sides of the Atlantic that Iraq was well advanced in building deployable, nuclear-capable weapons. Amid this portentous discourse, and with only weeks to go before the commencement of war, DIO continued to preface its own assessments with words like 'there is no reliable intelligence', 'despite the lack of firm evidence' and a Rumsfeldesque 'what is known about Iraq's programmes is as worrying as what is not known'.

As the PJCAAD (2003: 29) report points out, before September 2002, the assessments of the two agencies were qualified. Indeed, during this time, one sees joint assessments in which the two agencies together mention gaps in intelligence and dissent among US intelligence agencies, particularly regarding the purpose of the aluminium tubes. After September 2002, ONA becomes more definitive, while DIO remains, as noted, 'more sceptical and circumspect' (PJCAAD 2003: 36). Its qualifiers about the lack of firm and reliable evidence suggest an ongoing acknowledgement of gaps and dissent almost right up to the beginning of the war. It is useful to pause here to explore how acknowledging these uncertainties contributed to DIO being rebuffed.

As agencies charged with assessing material of strategic interest from both open and covert sources, ONA and DIO included their conclusions on those uncertainties until September 2002, with DIO continuing to include them until the war. What are the implications for language that reveals uncertainty, even disagreement? Did conveying uncertainty and disagreement—the absence of consensus about the evidence that Iraq could and would deploy nuclear weapons—weaken DIO's legitimacy? Moore argues that revealing how consensus is arrived at can help encourage acceptance of findings or decisions. He suggests that, typically, 'the language of consensus hides the fact that a process of collective decision is taking place'. By neglecting to lay bare how conclusions were arrived at, such language makes it easy for audiences to suspect 'that the reason for the consensus must be something other than that they have converged on the truth' (Moore 2017: 144). Therefore, 'to give confidence to those outside, it is necessary to show that strong alternatives were considered'

(Moore 2017: 130). This implies there is a benefit in being upfront about dissent because it can strengthen the credibility of an argument, such as by demonstrating 'agreement among experts in which it is evident that a minority went along with the group judgement because of the "exhaustion of acceptable objections", and not necessarily because they truly believe or were convinced'. Such a process 'could make the collective judgement of experts more robust than the presentation of a position of apparent unanimity' (Moore 2017: 145).

While it is not possible to judge exactly how DIO laid out its reasons for circumspection, it frequently alluded to a lack of unanimous evidence, thereby coming as close to Moore's revealed decision-making process as can be observed in the available material. In other words, DIO came as close to presenting a collective judgement as anyone in this debate, avoiding the overconfident position of 'apparent unanimity'. Perhaps ironically, it achieved the opposite of making expert judgement more robust. This does not bode well for advisers who try to construct transparent and openly imperfect evidence for decision-making. However, this does not necessarily mean that advice presented without provisos about its limitations is more likely to be used. In fact, the uncertainty expressed by the language of a rebuffed DIO was extremely useful in how Australia's political leadership framed the decision to invade Iraq.

This leads to one of my framework's last questions about the text itself: how advice was framed. In the six months before the invasion on 20 March 2003, ONA's advice frame came to be more aligned with the discourse of Australia's allies, whose predominant narrative was one of a gathering danger the world could no longer ignore. With this, the discourse created an exigency that advisers to governments committed to this narrative would have found very hard to resist. DIO's frame was not like this. It did what advice committed to impartially evaluating evidence should do if it wants to be objective: it acknowledged the existence of doubt.

One encounters this frame repeatedly in other expert advice, particularly in science and economics. Reports by the Intergovernmental Panel on Climate Change, for example, speak of average temperatures during the latter part of the twentieth century as '*very likely* higher than during any other 50-year period in the last 500 years and *likely* the highest in at least the past 1,300 years' (IPCC 2007; emphasis in original), while the International Monetary Fund (IMF 2018) suggests that 'upside and downside risks are broadly balanced over the next several quarters, but risks farther down the road are skewed to the downside'. These are, in other words, the best calls that can be made as truthfully as possible at this time by most involved experts. They are offered in good faith and submit themselves as material—perhaps an evidence base—for others to operationalise. Indeed, Blix's words on Iraq's progress are of a similar nature, but this kind of language is easy to disrupt.

In the short review 'When Doubt Becomes a Weapon', Wynne (2010) considers that 'because uncertainty arises in any scientific study, powerful elites find it easy to derail policies by representing the justificatory knowledge as inadequate'. In this field, as in economics and other complex policy areas, 'the ingrained assumption that scientific evidence is the only authority that can justify policy action—scientism—is what renders both policy and its supporting science vulnerable to the dogmatic amplification of doubt' (Wynne 2010: 441).

When I constructed my framework for rebuffed advice, I discussed this assumption in relation to policy advice as an institution or edifice whose adherence to objectivity and evidence presumes its world view is obvious and shared. This is partly why it is easy to reject or reinterpret. Wynne continues:

> The doubters' success lies in the way that policy questions are framed, with science placed at the centre. If a policy commitment is reduced only to a question of whether the science is right or wrong, then evidence can easily be made to unravel. (2010: 441)

John Howard seems to have understood this. That is, while intelligence was frequently referred to as evidence, its actual content was not central in the Australian context. It was outweighed by references to other inputs, such as the nature of Australia's relationship with its allies, the national interest, the Anzac tradition (Gleeson 2014; McDonald and Merefield 2010) and, perhaps most crucially, the notion that, if one is serious about averting disaster, evidence will very likely have to be incomplete. As such, Howard avoided the unravelling of evidence because he was clear about intelligence *not* being a question of right or wrong. His policy commitment—to invade Iraq with his allies—therefore remained intact.

As this section draws to a close, let us consider whether ONA's and DIO's language coloured the rhetoric of Australian decision-makers, which is closely related to the question of how their audience reacted to that advice. Certainly, we saw ONA's words reproduced verbatim in Downer's speech to parliament, but this does not mean its language influenced his. As the PJCAAD noted, ONA's assessment was 'made at the request of the Department of Foreign Affairs and was intended to be the basis of the Ministers' speeches' (2003: 54). This means ONA simply provided what had been asked of it and may even have written this material in a particular style or following specific directives.

DIO's language, however, did colour the government's rhetoric—by its absence. That is, DIO's absence from government discourse—particularly Howard's last major statements on Iraq on 13 March, 18 March and 20 March—is reflective of the government's rejection of the objectivity frame and the language that underpinned it. The way Howard spoke in each major statement suggests he was aware of DIO's—and others'— dissenting views, and carefully avoided explicitly referencing their content. Indeed, his references to evidence became scarcer as war approached; when it is mentioned, only US and British intelligence is included. As discussed above, there is an emphasis on emotion and friendship and the invaluable contribution the allies make to facing a dangerous new enemy. Clearly, none of this was present in DIO's provided advice. Of course, political rhetoric does not have to be slavishly tied to advice provided by bureaucrats, nor should it if it aspires to have any poetry. But one is left with the impression that in the case of Iraq, which so strongly relied on showing off evidence, Australia studiously avoided it, as if its prime minister had not seen any Australian intelligence agency's advice at all. Yet, as I have already suggested, it provided Howard with a basis for incorporating doubt into his strategy that action on Iraq was imperative. Thus, its public absence strongly affected his rhetoric, and it continued to be strategically valuable well beyond 2003.

For example, in 2013, to mark the 10-year anniversary of the Iraq war, Howard delivered a retrospective speech at the Lowy Institute in Sydney. Speaking of the 'eternal dilemma of intelligence', he said:

> Intelligence assessments never produce evidence beyond a reasonable doubt. Almost always, the art of intelligence assessment involves assembling a mosaic from varying, incomplete and sometimes contradictory sources. To insist on such a standard of proof would certainly avoid an Iraq-style intelligence failure, but could have other consequences. (Howard 2013a)

In this 10-year interim, Howard explicitly acknowledged that intelligence cannot be perfect and the burden of assembling the mosaic is a matter of judgement. To insist on a complete picture could end in disaster, but if that is the required level of proof then perhaps Iraq could be deemed an intelligence failure. This logic shows almost no shift from his position that insisting on 'Old Bailey proof' could end in another Pearl Harbor, and again insinuates that those who insist on such proof risk unprecedented bloodshed. Nonetheless, for a politician not known for changing his mind, the words 'Iraq-style intelligence failure' do suggest a small change in rhetoric, if only to shift blame away from the government and towards intelligence assessments. By 2016, at the conclusion of Sir John Chilcot's *Report of the Iraq Inquiry* in the United Kingdom, Howard became more defensive when he stated: 'There was no lie. There were errors in intelligence, but there was no lie' (ABC News 2016).

As we have seen, casting intelligence as mistaken was made considerably easier by intelligence language that tried its best to be qualified, nuanced, objective and judicious. This is a devastating blow for expert advice provided to governments—at least when it attempts to be balanced and impartial. It is clear the frame of objectivity creates a tension for civil servants, including intelligence assessors. If alerting policymakers to uncertainty is a part of being objective, the possibility that acknowledgement of uncertainty leads to bolstering unfounded consequences could grow in frequency.

The micro-context

I will now move on to the institutional aspects of this case study. Here, my framework asked:

1. Expectations: What are the expectations—legislated and/or institutional—of the adviser?
2. Culture: Does culture influence the language of the policy adviser?
3. Effect on knowledge: How might this bear on how policy expertise is constructed and communicated?

In relation to expectations, I will briefly return to three revealing details: the absence of disclosure by way of FOI legislation, the fact that ONA and DIO are not bound by the *Public Service Act*, and the similarity between intelligence and policy advice. Regarding the absence of FOI obligations,

I observed a mode of expression that can be reasonably confident it will not be aired publicly or with the negative scrutiny usually afforded policy advice when it is released under FOI legislation. It would therefore not be unreasonable to assume that such advice has fewer of the qualities that make other policy advice rebuffable, such as 'having no confidence in its own truth' and expressing 'a kind of powerlessness' (Button 2013: 168). If objections to the stifling effects of FOI obligations are well founded, I should, by rights, have found a language in these excerpts that was frank and fearless.

Superficially, one might say ONA's language could be described in this way. Despite raising the inconclusive nature of the available intelligence until about September 2002, its subsequent assessments became firmer. Yet, this does not imply a trajectory towards frankness. Rather, one might conclude (with the benefit of hindsight) that it suggests capitulation to the political context. While this could be representative of being responsive to government direction, ONA's language appeared to reinterpret UNMOVIC's account of Iraq's cooperation to align it more closely with political interpretations. To be fair, it would have been difficult and even unwise to sustain a nuanced position when pressure was so high: time was running out, Saddam Hussein was a known aggressor and there were still many gaps left to fill. Yet, as was the case with DIO, it was possible to be clear about the lack of clarity. It was also possible to continue to provide a view that ran counter to the majority. There is an element of fearlessness in this given the strength of the context and political expectations at the time. As such, it could be claimed that DIO did try to speak truth to power. That is, despite the weight of the government's predisposition, DIO chose to continue to alert policymakers to the uncertainty surrounding Iraq and, in so doing, was providing impartial advice.

To borrow a phrase coined by Greg Thielmann, the former director of Strategic, Proliferation and Military Affairs at the US Bureau of Intelligence and Research, DIO chose to be 'feckless and ignored' over being 'wrong and unobjective'.[9] One might say that, based on the example of Iraq, objections to FOI as a constraint on candidness do, indeed, hold

9   In an interview with Harry Shearer about his involvement in US intelligence assessments of Iraq's capabilities, Greg Thielmann said: '[W]e would rather be feckless and ignored than wrong and unobjective' ('Open/Interview with Greg Thielmann (from The Arms Control Association), Part I', 27 January 2013, available from: harryshearer.com/le-shows/january-27-2013/).

up. That is, agencies that are not subject to FOI laws can speak more openly than their APS counterparts. Yet, the more politically deferential language of ONA does not bear this out. As Richard Mulgan puts it:

> [C]onfidentiality is not a guarantee of objectivity, as for instance in the alleged bias of the Office of National Assessments reports, which were not destined for any public dossier but were still written with an eye to not upsetting ministers. (2007: 582)

In addition to being exempt from FOI legislation, ONA and DIO are, as mentioned earlier, not bound by the *Public Service Act*. Instead, the *Office of National Assessments Act* as it applied during the period under consideration stipulated that the agency 'assemble and correlate information relating to international matters that are of political, strategic or economic significance to Australia', 'prepare reports in relation to such of those matters as are of current significance' and 'furnish reports prepared, and assessments made' in relation to such matters (Federal Register of Legislation 1977). Similarly, while the *Public Service Act* clarifies the role of secretaries as principal policy advisers to their ministers, the role of ONA's director-general is not articulated to the same degree. Although they may be asked to prepare a report by a minister or prescribed Commonwealth officer to assist 'in the formation of policies', they are broadly independent: '[T]he Director-General is not subject to direction in respect of the content of, or any conclusions to be reached in, any report or assessment under this Act' (Federal Register of Legislation 1977). The *Intelligence Services Act*, under which DIO operates, provides the legislative basis for all intelligence agencies' operational conduct and does not stipulate how to articulate information. One might therefore conclude that, although legislation exists to ensure their products find an appropriate balance 'between the right of a community to public safety … and the right of individuals in that community to their freedom and privacy' (PM&C 2017a), the way ONA and DIO compose them is not prescribed in their respective legislative instruments.

Importantly, however, ONA has something most other public-sector agencies do not: the gift of independence, bestowed on it by the first Royal Commission on Intelligence and Security, led by Justice Robert Hope. Indeed, ONA's website proudly proclaims that, as a result, it is 'the only intelligence assessment agency in the world with statutory independence protecting the integrity of its analysis' (ONA n.d.[b]). In its examination of the independence of DIO's and ONA's intelligence assessments, the PJCAAD report accepted the agencies' 'declarations that there was no overt pressure from Government to change assessments', but stated that changes 'did occur in the nature and tone of some assessments', specifically in the tone of ONA's assessments of 12 and 13 September 2002 (that is, between asserting that the case for Iraq's WMD revival was inconclusive and having no reason to believe Saddam had abandoned his nuclear ambitions). The committee considered the change so sudden that 'ONA, at least unconsciously, might have been responding to "policy running strong"' (PJCAAD 2003: 54).

The theme of independence is taken up by former head of ONA and senior diplomat Philip Flood in his 2004 inquiry into Australia's intelligence agencies, which was announced in response to the PJCAAD's report. Flood suggested 'it is not reasonable to expect an intelligence agency to comment on the manner in which the government chooses to use … intelligence' (2004: 31), such as during the clearance process for public speeches. Yet, if expert advice is to be independent in a way that protects the 'integrity of its analysis', commenting on its potential misinterpretation while it is not too late, such as during the drafting stages of a speech and before public delivery, should be part of its role. While Mulgan does not blame ONA officials for allowing ministerial speeches to misrepresent material, he notes that this puts them in a difficult ethical position:

> Once any false attribution of certainty to official reports becomes part of the public record, public servants can themselves become complicit in maintaining a public falsehood. If they keep their counsel as loyal public servants, they are acquiescing in a deceit and lending it credence, thus in effect becoming party to the deceit. (2007: 581)

Expectations and culture seem to come into play here. Although independent, 'ONA is not', its director-general declares on its website:

> a policy agency, though we aim to contribute to policy development; we are a government body and part of the Australian Intelligence Community. We are staunchly objective in our analysis; in fact the independence of our judgments is enshrined in law. The insights into world affairs we provide to the Government help it to develop and implement effective policy responses that advance Australia's interests. (ONA n.d.[a])

We do not know whether this is how ONA described itself during the leadup to the war in Iraq. It is possible that descriptions of itself, such as they might have been in 2002 and 2003, were less effusive, given most intelligence agencies had either a limited or no online presence. Yet, in Flood's diagnosis of the effectiveness of the two agencies, ONA enjoyed 'a very strong reputation', which can bring some downsides in terms of excessive self-confidence and reluctance to discuss its findings with others. A similar predicament came into view in my consideration of Australia's Treasury in Chapter 2. It is possible ONA's self-perception had an impact on the way it approached assessments on Iraq. Among Flood's proposals for change are 'clearer identification of the basis for judgments in reports', 'a more systematic approach to challenging assumptions', 'more rigorous and consistent testing of sources' and 'greater use of external expertise' (2004: 101)—all of which indicate a deficiency in the pre-review environment. This implies that ONA's reliance on reputation may have come at the possible expense of rigorous analysis and questioning of the status quo. This suggests that, despite being free of the constraints of FOI that allegedly prevent other APS agencies from being candid, ONA's perceptions of its reputation and independence may have prompted a culture marked by homogeneity and conformism. Mulgan considers the Flood report's indication of a 'lack of "a rigorous culture of challenge" in the ONA' may even imply 'a characteristic that could encourage voluntary politicization' (2007: 578).

For DIO's part, Flood's comments suggest organisational issues and confusion about its responsibilities and the breadth of its functions. Claiming that its focus had become too diffuse, he also notes its level of contestability was healthy and it had fostered a culture of critical inquiry (Flood 2004: 119, 126, 127). Both are probably symptoms of belonging to a very large organisation and servicing a variety of customers, both military and civilian, each with specific needs and strongly separate identities. It is difficult to surmise from this how DIO perceived itself at the time; today, its website states that its 'mission is to provide the best intelligence possible to the intelligence consumer' (Department of Defence n.d.). Nonetheless, its frequent questioning of the evidence on Iraq in the face of noisy counterviews suggests an organisation that felt relatively independent, secure in its technical abilities and open to other views, albeit stretched across too many areas. The flipside to this is an agency too close to its technical expertise and not sufficiently attuned to political requirements. However, while the overall tone of Flood's analysis evokes an atmosphere of organisational difficulties, the written content of DIO's 2002–03 Iraq assessments in large measure represents much of what is expected of its APS counterparts: objective, apolitical and based on the best available evidence.

This takes us to the correlations between policy advice and intelligence. Much like those covered under the *Public Service Act*, which calls secretaries of departments the 'principal policy advisers' to their respective ministers, the directors-general of ONA and DIO are similarly expected to provide high-quality expert advice to their respective ministers. The *2017 Independent Intelligence Review* proposes that the role of intelligence is to 'explain the forces at work in particular situations and thus to help government influence developments' (PM&C 2017a: 33). While it describes policy and intelligence as related, it also points to a tension between intelligence assessments and policymaking. On the one hand, 'if the content of intelligence assessments is influenced by preordained policy priority and preferences, those assessments lose their credibility'. On the other, 'if intelligence assessments are seen as disconnected from the difficult but necessary choices involved in policy-making, or from the timing of major policy decisions and direction-setting, those assessments become increasingly irrelevant' (PM&C 2017a: 38).

To make things even knottier, '[p]olicy decision-making and intelligence assessments need to be connected even when policy preferences and intelligence assessments do not coincide' (PM&C 2017: 39). As former ONA director-general Allan Gyngell (2017) puts it, this wording 'glides a little too easily over some quite basic tensions between the principle of independence … and pressures for greater policy relevance'. The complexities inherent in balancing such dissonant criteria suggest that both intelligence and policy advice struggle to provide policymakers with responsive but objective information.

So, what is intelligence—and the institutions charged with formulating it—expected to do? In his inquiry, Flood suggests 'intelligence is only one of a range of factors that influences the policy decisions of governments, and it is rarely the decisive factor'. In conjunction with other sources, it can provide warning of conflict or terrorist plans, help interpret the environment, support military operations or foreign policy and provide knowledge about adversaries. However:

> In so far as it seeks to forecast the future, assessment based on intelligence will seldom be precise or definitive. This is particularly so when it seeks to understand complex developments and trends in future years. Greater precision is sometimes possible in relation to intelligence's warning function—highlighting the possibility of a specific event in the near term future (eg a terrorist attack).

> But even in this field, precision will be hard to achieve. Intelligence will rarely provide comprehensive coverage of a topic. More often it is fragmentary and incomplete. (Flood 2004: 7)

Paradoxically, intelligence is often thought of as a higher power—evidenced by criticism of intelligence failing to detect all terror plots. Flood argues that assuming that intelligence is omniscient and should present a complete picture is fraught:

> The history of major intelligence failure—the failure to detect plans for the World Trade Centre attack in 2001, Iraq's intention to invade Kuwait in 1990, the imminent collapse of the Berlin Wall in 1989 or, much earlier, the failure to anticipate the strength of Turkish forces in the Dardanelles in 1915 or Japanese plans for Pearl Harbour [sic]—provide a cautionary lesson for any policymaker who believes intelligence is always accurate or that it can provide guarantees. (2004: 8)

John Howard had it both ways when he acknowledged that intelligence can be incomplete even while invoking it in ways that implied an objective evidence base. This use of intelligence helped him maintain a credible position both before and after the war. That is, Howard's claim that there were errors in intelligence followed a similar rhetorical path to his prewar acknowledgement that it was incomplete. Intelligence assessments therefore played a dual role as both a source of insight and a purveyor of doubt, even misinterpretation. In this, the expectations and uses of intelligence are double-edged.

This, of course, is the case with all expertise enmeshed in policymaking. As Boswell notes:

> [E]xpert knowledge can lend authority to particular policy positions ... drawing on expert knowledge can be said to have a symbolic rather than a substantive value: it enhances the credibility of agencies or policy positions ... It is not so much content of knowledge that is being valued, as the signal it conveys about the credibility of an organization or its policies. (2009: 7–8)

The symbolic value of being seen to draw on expert advice was evident in Howard's use of it (as, indeed, it was in Blair's, Bush's, Powell's and Downer's). Beyond Boswell's conception of the symbolic usefulness of expert knowledge, such knowledge can continue to be useful even as it threatens to no longer impart credibility. In other words, it was possible for Howard to maintain the same viewpoint by acknowledging the imperfection of his advice and making it known he was following it in good faith. The only shift needed was to stretch that imperfection towards error.

While both intelligence and policy advice can be used in symbolic ways to signal their users' credibility, intelligence does differ from policy advice in the way it suggests a deeper knowledge—that is, by way of its ostensible capacity to listen in and watch reality unobserved, particularly via signals and image collection. In my case study, intelligence was invoked politically as a kind of symbol of objectivity, which hinted, by extension, at an ability to reveal a pure, unalloyed kind of evidence that is as close to the truth as we can ever know. Horn puts it this way:

> With its bureaucratization as state knowledge, intelligence became more than a form of knowledge, more than even a branch of science: it became an encyclopedic archive of many different disciplines and types of knowledge—a metascience, ranging from political science and conflict psychology to nuclear physics. It increasingly relies on public sources (television, newspapers, the Internet, statistical yearbooks, maps, professional publications, etc.) … Intelligence is like a classified encyclopedia of the world, knowledge about everything, but not for everyone. (2003: 66)

In its assumed ability to know everything, therefore, it can be construed as omniscient. Table 4.1 presents this across a variety of statements from each of the three allies.

Table 4.1 Allies' statements implying omniscience of intelligence

Tony Blair's foreword to the United Kingdom's September Dossier	'[T]he assessed intelligence has established beyond doubt' that Saddam will continue to develop nuclear weapons; some WMD will 'be ready within 45 minutes of an order to use them'.
George W. Bush	'[K]nowing these realities'; 'facing clear evidence of peril'; 'the facts lead to one conclusion'.
Dick Cheney	'[T]here is no doubt that Saddam Hussein now has weapons of mass destruction'; aluminium tubes are 'irrefutable evidence'.
CIA National Intelligence Estimate	'Iraq has continued its Weapons of Mass Destruction (WMD) program.'
Alexander Downer	There is 'no reason to believe that Saddam Hussein has abandoned his ambition to acquire nuclear weapons'; 'Australian intelligence agencies believe there is evidence'; the 'Australian government believes there is good reason to be extremely worried'.

| John Howard | The 'Australian government knows ... that Iraq wants to develop nuclear weapons'; 'compelling evidence ... within the detailed dossiers of British and American intelligence'; 'there is nothing more crucial than accurate and timely intelligence'. |
| Colin Powell | 'What we are giving you are facts and conclusions based on solid evidence'; 'these are not assertions. These are facts.' |

Note: For references, see Table 4.2 at the end of this chapter.

It is interesting to note that the last of these statements, from US Secretary of State Colin Powell's 5 February 2003 address to the UNSC, has been cited as the most convincing case for war (Barker 2003), even by ONA whistleblower Andrew Wilkie, who suggested:

> Powell made probably the most comprehensive and persuasive case for the invasion of Iraq ... The 5 February presentation in New York was a powerful performance by Bush's most credible player, so much so that on one estimate the pro-war sentiment among editorial writers for large US newspapers doubled overnight (rising to three-quarters in favour) ... Powell ... unveiled an impressive collection of communications intercepts and grainy satellite photographs. (2004: 78–79)

While Powell also relied on intelligence from human sources—supplied by defectors in whom other leaders placed too much faith and most of which was later exposed as false or exaggerated (Jervis 2006; Hartnett and Stengrim 2004; Hersh 2003)—it is probable his special persuasiveness came mostly from him illustrating his case with signals and imagery intelligence. As Horn suggests when comparing human intelligence with imagery:

> [T]he uncertainty of fallible human reasoning that burdens HUMINT [human intelligence], is contrasted with the image–technological intelligence of IMINT (imagery intelligence) as a supposedly more objective process. Under the eye of the camera, the space of intelligence becomes smooth, homogenous, and dreamily transparent. From above—and the higher up the better—nothing can be hidden; it is the wish for absolute clarity fulfilled. (2003: 78)

Policymakers framed intelligence in much the same way—as all-seeing and all-knowing—and used language that anchored this evidence in the present, not the hypothetical. Despite formulations around what intelligence should realistically be expected to do, there is symbolic value in conceiving of intelligence as capable of foreseeing disaster and catastrophe. This becomes particularly evident when intelligence is seen to fail, such as the then-recent failure to foresee the events of 9/11. Yet even despite the overwhelming tragedy associated with this failure, intelligence continued to inspire confidence, even faith:

> After 9/11 the intelligence services have become more popular as never before. True, after the terror attacks they were charged with unresponsiveness and failure to predict or prevent, but today they appear to be the only force available to fight the diffuse and impenetrable network of fundamentalist terror. Thus the social and the political status of the intelligence services—especially in America but not just there—has fundamentally changed. (Horn 2003: 59)

As we saw, Howard used the trust inspired by this conception of intelligence several times, even if mostly from non-Australian sources, to make the case that invading Iraq was necessary to triumph over this encroaching terror. Ironically, he inflated the social and political status of his intelligence community with his credibility-bestowing references to the crucial nature of 'timely and accurate intelligence', only to devalue it as errors in intelligence when later called on to account for his policy decisions. With this, he both capitalised on its reputation and undermined it.

Despite being used politically in ways that insinuated omniscience, as well as bearing the totality of culpability in Australia, such expectations are unrealistic, as we saw from comments by Flood and the *2017 Independent Intelligence Review*. The former pointed to the incidence of assessments being comprehensive as an exception to the rule that sees them more commonly 'fragmentary and incomplete', while cautioning policymakers against the presumption of accuracy and guarantees (Flood 2004: 7–8). Indeed, Howard himself echoed this sentiment when he adroitly suggested that his reason for joining the invasion of Iraq was made in full knowledge, perhaps even because, of intelligence assessments 'never produc[ing] evidence beyond a reasonable doubt. Almost always, the art of intelligence assessment involves assembling a mosaic'. This described intelligence as an illuminating influence for policymaking, but also warned against the twin hazards of excessive independence and kowtowing to political influence. Instead, policy and intelligence needed 'to be connected' even when they did not match up (PM&C 2017a: 39). This enigmatic connectedness seems to be the epitome to which intelligence might aspire.

'Policymakers,' Joshua Rovner notes, 'need intelligence to help them manage ambiguity and reduce uncertainty' (2011: 1). To be helpful, intelligence should understand the policy world and, with that awareness, be able to clarify ambiguity so that effective and relevant policy can be made. As Rovner continues:

> What would intelligence–policy relations look like in the ideal? To start with, intelligence analysts would feel free to produce objective estimates on important issues without concern for policy preferences. They would also feel free to offer bad news without fear of recrimination. At the same time, policymakers would have the freedom to criticize intelligence products that they felt were sloppy, inaccurate, or otherwise unhelpful, and to demand better analyses without being accused of pernicious meddling. In sum, we can imagine a relationship characterized by healthy tension: intelligence and policy would routinely challenge one another in the best sense of the world. (2011: 2)

This healthy tension of connectedness without sycophancy may well be the sweet spot for intelligence agencies, particularly those close to policymakers. Yet, 'it is difficult to sustain this sort of healthy tension', because

> intelligence work is somewhat akin to scholarship, but policy work is action-oriented. Intelligence analysts are comfortable with uncertainty, but policymakers cannot let uncertainty get in the way of making decisions. Intelligence officials believe they provide a unique product, but policymakers do not always agree. (Rovner 2011: 2)

For these reasons, instead of connectedness, 'friction is the norm' (Rovner 2011: 2). It is interesting to see a reflection of DIO in Rovner's characterisations of intelligence. One might even recognise ONA in his descriptions of policymakers in the sense that the agency seemed to anticipate policymakers' needs and expectations for action, certainty and specific viewpoints. Moreover, ONA seemed to pre-empt friction to preserve connectedness by aligning with government views from September for the crucial last six months before the war. By remaining scholarly and unruffled by uncertainty, DIO fractured its connectedness to policy relevance.

Expectations and culture—one might call them the organisational social context—had an influence on the language of my intelligence experts/advisers. We saw various accounts of independence, as well as the expectation to be objective without being so far removed from policy preferences as to be unable to contribute to policymaking. Through Gyngell and Rovner, we also noticed this tension could, in practice, be irreconcilable and that trying to connect intelligence with policy was probably a symptom of maintaining relevance but also entailed becoming more politically implicated. In this, intelligence and policy advice share the same concern.

As Australia's premier intelligence agency with a reputation for high-quality advice, ONA, it might be concluded, was more concerned with the need to be 'connected even when policy preferences and intelligence assessments do not coincide' than DIO, whose quiet technical expertise may have been 'seen as disconnected from the difficult but necessary choices involved in policy-making'. Yet, even while it is tempting to propose that ONA's reputationally connected culture may have influenced its increasingly certain and confident language, and that DIO's culture of contestability was reflected in its more open-ended language, neither overtly strayed from what was expected of it: DIO tried to remain neutral and independent of policy preferences; ONA was pragmatic in its approach to the haziness between independence and political responsiveness. What was different was their interpretation of that framework and their role within it. Each approach, however, met a similar fate.

While the PJCAAD report alluded to potential politicisation in its finding that ONA's tone changed from the time material was submitted to the time it appeared in ministers' speeches, the Flood Inquiry found no evidence of political pressure. However, given the expectation that awareness of policy is necessary if one is to be relevant, each agency must have been reasonably attuned to the government's policy preferences. I established this in my discussion of time and context and confirmed that ONA's language was more strongly resonant of political preferences than DIO's. I am not proposing that ONA was therefore subject to overt political interference, but rather that politicisation, such as it was, would have occurred as a more internalised construct, similar to my case study on renewable energy. As Mulgan suggests, the distortion of material such as ONA's does not have to be a result of direct political pressure:

> It is more likely to be indirect and unstated, the result of officials anticipating unfavourable reactions to unpopular advice. If public servants believe they will be penalized by their political masters if they tell the unvarnished truth, they will tend to tailor their evidence to what they believe the government wants. (2007: 577)

Rovner calls this 'soft politicisation' and it is useful to examine it more closely to see whether it or its objective but more removed counterpart has more impact. Rovner explains that soft politicisation occurs when intelligence officials seek to prevent 'isolating themselves from the policy process and sacrificing any possible influence over policymakers' judgment'. It 'does not mean outright pandering, but it does constrain intelligence leaders from being blunt about estimates that are frankly at odds with policy beliefs and preferences' (Rovner 2013: 56). He illustrates this with several examples: US Director of Central Intelligence (DCI) John McCone's revision in 1963 of pessimistic appraisals of progress in the Vietnam War; DCI Richard Helms's backing down from estimates that Viet Cong numbers in 1966 were much higher than publicly claimed; and DCI George Tenet's promise to provide material that would help make White House statements more compelling in the leadup to the war in Iraq in 2003 (Rovner 2013: 58–61).

Rovner finds that, despite their soft politicisation, none of these examples preserved 'healthy intelligence–policy relations' (2013: 61). Indeed, McCone's relationship with the administration deteriorated, becoming dysfunctional by 1964; Helms was pushed out of decision-making processes, culminating in his dismissal in 1972; and Tenet's relationship with the White House 'sunk to a new low' when the intelligence community was blamed for bad estimates (Rovner 2013: 61–63). Any purported benefits of soft politicisation, Rovner argues, are not supported by the evidence and point to several adverse implications, among them that '[p]oliticized intelligence tends to present conclusions with an unrealistic sense of certainty even when the underlying information is incomplete or unreliable' (2013: 66). This was certainly borne out in ONA's later assessments. Another implication, he notes,

> is that policymakers will overreact to estimates that confront their own views. Long stretches of soft politicization may accustom them to intelligence that supports their beliefs and preferences. A sudden change in intelligence might cause them to suspect that intelligence is no longer interested in supporting policy but is actively opposing it. Alternately, they might fall victim to familiar psychological problems associated with incorporating dissonant information. Individuals typically struggle with news that contradicts their pre-existing beliefs. Rather than viewing such news objectively and reassessing their own beliefs, they are likely to ignore it or manipulate the new information so that it fits into their worldview. (Rovner 2013: 66–67)

This may have been the case with DIO's assessments. It is not difficult to imagine Australia's policymakers—accustomed to the certainty of British and US intelligence, as well as ONA's diminishing doubts—giving DIO's views short shrift because they did not accord with their beliefs, preferences or world views. From the material made public during the PJCAAD process, there is a good indication that DIO's offerings were much less certain, frequently failed to confirm the dominant view and were, of course, ignored. By judging them alongside Rovner's exploration of soft politicisation, it is clear neither the language of politicised nor the language of unpoliticised assessments secured lasting political support. Perhaps most importantly, even while ONA's certainty and DIO's doubts helped fuel Howard's rhetorical strategy, neither ONA's softly politicised language nor DIO's language of objectivity prevented them from becoming the official fall guys of Australia's Iraq policy outcomes.

The macro-context

When I constructed my framework for assessing rebuffable advice, I asked how the institutional environment of administrations connects to notions of objectivity and evidence, among others. Here, my framework asked:

1. Engagement with objectivity and evidence: Is the spectre of 'objectivity' present in policy advice? How does the advice engage with or construe the notion of evidence?

2. International comparisons and contexts: What do international comparisons tell us about Australia's rebuffed advice? Are contexts and circumstances similar or is Australia unique?

I have alluded to the conception that intelligence is somehow panoptic and even omniscient, ostensibly rendering it a more objective input to policymaking than other types of expert advice. Although careful to clarify realistic expectations of intelligence as an explainer, rather than as a predictor (PM&C 2017a: 31), Australia's 2017 intelligence review imbues intelligence with a similar knowingness when it suggests that it 'can provide hard evidence about the often harsh realities of how the world works, how states and other actors pursue their goals, and what those goals are' (pp. 31, 32). This indicates an uncritical acceptance of intelligence as a window on a clearcut reality. In other words, even though this review, representing the latest Australian Government thinking on intelligence at the time of writing, understands that intelligence should not always be an input into policy decisions,[10] the production of intelligence as absolute knowledge is not probed critically. This seems to imply an implicit acknowledgement of intelligence as a vessel for facts.

But the production of intelligence as agreed knowledge is not as straightforward as that. Writing in the US context, Brendan McQuade, for instance, calls intelligence 'a weakly autonomous form of knowledge production shaped by struggles within the bureaucratic field to control the definition and distribution of public goods' (2016: 262). In this description, intelligence offers information that settles into single meaning in the aftermath of interpretative tussles. Florin Poenaru, examining Romania's secret police archives, sees intelligence as a form of anthropological knowledge in the way 'knowledge is defined, accumulated and used'. He posits that both intelligence and anthropology are 'involved in processes of "translating" the surrounding world in specifically codified languages and both share the ambition of rendering visible the hidden' (Poenaru 2017: 113). Here, both ethnography and intelligence assessment become written accounts 'about an observed reality' and, in this, not merely describe reality but also create it (p. 114). Although the intelligence practices of a former authoritarian state can be expected to offer different observations of reality to their contemporary democratic peers, their aim to uncover and deduce reality for the benefit of the state is surely a shared one. In both accounts, intelligence is ultimately produced as an expression of reality: in the United States, as a contribution to political objectives; in Romania, as a co-creator with the state.

How, then, is intelligence produced in the Australian context? There is only one unclassified, contemporaneous account—that of ONA whistleblower Andrew Wilkie, who resigned from ONA on 7 March 2003 due to what he saw as insufficient evidence to invade Iraq. Wilkie describes how ONA intelligence assessments are initiated, drafted and approved:

> At weekly meetings, the senior management of ONA plan in detail which reports will be prepared, when and by whom … Once tasked, analysts develop their assessments to a polished draft stage. Each analyst has two computer terminals … The classified machine is a treasure trove, providing ready access to HUMINT,

10 In statements such as: '[I]t is vital that intelligence assessments not only "speak truth to power" when the intelligence evidence exists but also that they indicate when definitive judgments are not possible because the intelligence evidence (derived from either open or covert sources or both) is incomplete, contradictory, unreliable or inconsistent' (PM&C 2017a: 38).

intercepted communications and imagery, and diplomatic cables, as well as to much of the output of most American, Australian, British and Canadian intelligence agencies …

All of ONA's draft assessments are subjected to a rigorous editing and clearance process. The relevant Branch Head, the Deputy Director-General and the Director-General all review the draft in detail, and other intelligence agencies as well as relevant policy departments such as Foreign Affairs are often invited to comment. The Director-General's role is particularly significant, going well beyond simply authorising the release of assessments. He personally adjudicates who will write what and when, and he edits in detail the final draft, even to the point of literally standing behind an analyst and supervising the detail and shape of the final version. (2004: 5–36)

The shape and form of assessments are similarly codified:

All are rigidly capped in length and written in simple terms for the benefit of the non-experts who will read them; often only the most basic explanation of the issue at hand is provided. Adding to the pressure to condense was John Howard's personal direction that ONA's reports be produced in a larger 13-point script so they would be easier for him to read. (Wilkie 2004: 35)

Despite the tightly managed process and restrictions on length, 'there is never enough information available to be sure of everything, yet the document produced will likely make an important contribution to the government's decision-making' (Wilkie 2004: 36).

These excerpts suggest intelligence assessments are produced both meticulously and narrowly: with access to a plethora of material but drafted under strict conditions and closely directed by a small group of overseers. Further, although Wilkie elsewhere mentions access to open-source information, much of the assessment process appears to find its primary material from secret intelligence. That, of course, is an obvious source for intelligence assessments, but it points to a sameness of terminology, style, observation and even world view, with important contextualisers and alternative evidence potentially left out. Wilkie's excerpts lead to several other observations. Ultimate authority over drafts by one person, the leader, adds to homogeneity and encourages writers to draft in the style of the final arbiter. Inviting external others to comment on drafts, although an important component of contestability, also, at least in this instance, suggests assessments may be subject to (re)direction by policy agencies. I do not suggest this is a bad thing; simply that it adds to funnelling a single viewpoint. Brevity—emphasised by Philip Flood as both a strength and a weakness—complicates how much shade can be given to an issue. Finally, despite the 'treasure trove' of classified material, there is insufficient information for certainty even though the overall tone and length of assessments can encourage governments to make very substantial decisions based on their contents.

Particularly in ONA's case, the material made available to the PJCAAD indicated authority and assumed a tone of fact. For example, 'procurement patterns are consistent with an effort to develop an enrichment capability', 'the case for the revival of the WMD programs is substantial' and 'there is no reason to believe Saddam Hussein has abandoned his ambitions' insinuate careful consideration. That is, determining consistency in procurement activities implies lengthy examination and finding patterns, making a substantial case suggests the accumulation of material into a solid whole, while having 'no reason' to believe hints at exhaustive analysis of alternatives, none of them persuasive. The implied exhaustive nature of ONA's language leaves no room for the possibility that its claims could be wrong. Further, there are no qualifiers that suggest these may be interpretations. As such, the reader is left with the strong impression they are facts. Even DIO's mainly inconclusive assessments exuded a factual quality: 'Iraq *has* the necessary civil, and possibly hidden military, assets *to have resumed* limited [biological weapons] production' (emphasis added), before adding 'although there is no specific evidence of this' (PJCAAD 2003: 37).

Considering this and the way ONA produces its special kind of knowledge remind one of Stone's statement that 'facts do not exist independent of interpretive lenses, and they come clothed in words and numbers' (1997: 307). Further, far from being independently objective, determining facts is a social process:

> What we think of as facts—statements about the true state of the world—are produced in social processes. Most of our knowledge and ideas about the world come not from direct observation but from social knowledge, from the accumulation and presentation of observations and beliefs. (Stone 1997: 308)

Yet, in my chosen texts, I have not been able to observe an acknowledgement or clarification of how the conclusions to assessments have been drawn. Instead, terminology and style are repetitive, which certainly implies consistency, but also suggests the increasing consolidation of facts and, with them, implicit agreement that they depict reality.

In this, the intelligence I have examined certainly attempts to fulfil its function as a provider of 'hard evidence'. However, unlike many other types of expertise, intelligence does not invite peer review or other measures of contestability. Functioning as 'hard evidence' is therefore epistemologically problematic. Horn considers intelligence to be 'a very specific kind of expert knowledge' and quite unlike any other type of expertise:

> [S]ecret intelligence is exclusive in a much more radical way than scientific, economic or technological expertise. That is why, despite the lurid associations one might have in mind when it comes to the world of espionage and secret agents, secret intelligence can be used as a paradigmatic example for the difficulties and fallacies arising in the creation, processing and assessment of highly exclusive knowledge. (2010: 2)

Further, given its exclusivity, intelligence expertise and its purported objectivity cannot be assessed in the same way as other types of expertise:

> How can we assess the expertise of an expert? Only another expert can. But again, in the case of highly secret and illegally obtained knowledge, there is often only one single expert on the very information in question: the person who produced it. It is therefore extremely hard to estimate the veracity of information. (Horn 2010: 28)

This inability to verify was the case with much of the intelligence on Iraq, particularly assessments based on human intelligence produced by the United States and the United Kingdom. Like Wilkie, Horn[11] describes a similarly closed production environment:

> To deal with these questions that have a tendency of bordering on unsolvable dilemmas, intelligence services have been organized in a complicated and highly compartmentalized form. Information will never (or only in a tightly controlled way) circulate inside the administration, it will mostly be dealt with by one specialized unit. It will also never circulate outside the house … While in academic research, research results or arguments will always

---

11   Horn, a German academic, became a committee member of the Gesprächskreis Nachrichtendienste in Deutschland (Discussion Group on German Intelligence) following an approach by Germany's secret service over a prescient essay she wrote on intelligence success and failure just before 9/11. The Gesprächskreis is a group in the public domain founded by Germany's intelligence community to 'contribute to constructive and open dialogue about secret intelligence services' (my translation; Hage 2004).

have to be widely circulated, evaluated and discussed within the scientific community, in the intelligence community there is no such thing as a peer review. (2010: 28)

This lack of circulation and openness to exchange leads to operating in a vacuum, even blindness:

The more limited the access to a certain kind of knowledge, the more the circulation and critical assessment of knowledge and expertise is stymied, the more this paradoxically creates all sorts of epistemological pathologies: not just utter errors, but … a blindness that consists in asking the wrong questions or searching for answers in the wrong places … Perhaps the real danger lies … in experts blinded by their own expertise and its dazzling exclusivity. (Horn 2010: 31)

Horn's conclusions are supported by a former intelligence analyst. In her examination of Swedish intelligence, Gunilla Eriksson views intelligence as a knowledge producer, and considers that 'intelligence analysis contains assumptions and valuations that eventually lead to an established knowledge-steering political worldview' (2016: 11). In critically reading intelligence products, she highlights some peculiarities:

For instance, the text of the assessments seemed to contain a high degree of repetitiveness in wording and substance. Furthermore, the conclusions seemed to be articulated as objective truths. They were formulated with objective truth claims and the arguments and evidence in support of the conclusions were mostly diffuse or hidden in the background of the text. Moreover, many of the assessments often came to the wrong conclusions (history being the judge). (Eriksson 2016: 2)

Although her primary focus is the Swedish Military and Security Directorate's estimates on the North Atlantic Treaty Organization (NATO), Russia and terrorism, the similarity with many of the intelligence assessments I have considered here is uncanny. In her interviews with the directorate's staff, Eriksson finds analysts who, like Australia's, 'are guided by principles of objectivity and impartiality' (2016: 112). The complexity these principles exert over the production of intelligence does not go unnoticed:

The analysts perceive that they are expected to reveal the only way that an event may be understood, and to depict and describe the way things really are. At the same time, the analysts themselves are sceptical of the possibility of the 'one truth', yet it is this single possibility that is the ideal end result of their analysis. (Eriksson 2016: 112)

The way Australia's Swedish counterparts circumvent this convolution is to 'adapt to the expectation of finding the one truth by suppressing their analytical contribution and presenting analysed and interpreted materials as accumulated information and facts, rather than interpretations' (Eriksson 2016: 112).

Eventually, even unconfirmed information can become fact, as this statement by one of Eriksson's interviewees suggests:

Within the organisation, and it's probably the same for all organisations that are doing this kind of thing [intelligence], it [information] becomes facts over time. Although it [the information] has not been substantiated or confirmed, it sort of gains a life of its own and then finally becomes facts. As long as nobody questions it. And then we'll add some new information that has not had time to become facts yet ... We make some sort of distinction even if we are not that clear about how. There are many assumptions that have become facts. (Eriksson 2016: 113; insertions in original)

It is not hard to imagine that a lack of peer review or systematic contestation leads to assumptions becoming facts over time, and Eriksson considers the conventions surrounding the production of intelligence have contributed to some of its failures. That is, the requirement for, and practices applied on behalf of, objectivity have rendered much intelligence indistinct and untransparent, which, in turn, has hampered the production of objective advice:

Although the intelligence service's prime purpose is to provide policymakers with objective, impartial intelligence to help them make informed decisions, this study suggests this is sub-optimised. This study suggests that the biggest threat to objectivity and impartiality is the indistinctiveness in the analytical and interpretative processes for the assessments. (Eriksson 2016: 204)

Eriksson makes several suggestions for reform, such as a more '*reflective* approach to knowledge production' and '*explicitness* in various aspects of knowledge production' (Eriksson 2016: 211–12; emphasis in original). Given time and executive will, these would undoubtedly have an impact on the presentation of intelligence knowledge. Yet, as an input into government decision-making, intelligence, like policy advice, serves an important symbolic function as the proof or evidence that provides justification for political decisions. Despite Australia's intelligence not being used, simply invoking it and letting it hint at reality were powerful and eminently useful at the time. Despite being merely symbolic, this usefulness continued even when intelligence could no longer authenticate government actions and assumed its role as scapegoat. Objectivity and the language burdened with representing it are therefore indispensable political tools, because they can be construed as interchangeably neutral, ambiguous or wrong. How or even whether they can be improved or achieved is probably irrelevant to political actors given the importance of their symbolic political function (as opposed to their actual substance). When submitted or presented as the basis for government decision-making, expertise as a representation of evidence or objectivity is performative and enables governments to engage in what Edelman has called 'a dramaturgy of objective description' (1988: 115). The edifice of objectivity—with its virtues *and* shortcomings—thus facilitates the enhancement and maintenance of political credibility, often at the expense of its supporting actor: the bureaucracy.

Mulgan highlights the implications for bureaucrats charged with providing objective advice. Asking '[w]hat counts as truth or objectivity in advice', Mulgan (2007: 570) contends that '[c]areer public servants ... are held to higher standards of objectivity' than politicians, and 'can be relied on for honest judgments', which is 'evident from the way in which politicians themselves publicly rely on the supposed objectivity of their official advisers' (p. 576). One reason is to be able to 'disown responsibility in case the information later turns out to be incorrect', another is to 'vouch for the reliability of the information' (Mulgan 2007: 576). We saw this, too, in intelligence agencies' dual role. Objectivity may impart credibility, but, Mulgan argues, if advice is 'distorted to suit the government's political interests, the public is being deliberately deceived through a form of misrepresentation in which politically partisan opinion is being passed off as objective and politically neutral' (2007: 576). Over time, the expertise and credibility of the civil service itself will corrode. When 'politicians, instead of taking responsibility for such material themselves, explicitly attribute it to their officials, they are trading on, and abusing, the integrity of the public service' (Mulgan 2007: 577). Without safeguarding a degree of independence:

government departments may be under pressure to resort to 'spin' if they suspect their advice is destined for the public arena. Over time, these trends will undermine the very reputation for objectivity upon which politicians rely when they attribute statements to their officials. A cynical public, when offered a statement such as 'my department assures me' or 'our intelligence sources tell us', will simply treat it as yet more government spin. (Mulgan 2007: 583)

The language of the rebuffed is not the same as spin, in the sense that the former evades stable meaning while the latter is skewed towards specifics. Yet Mulgan highlights a phenomenon similar to what I have problematised as the language of rebuffed policy advisers: a language that seems to invite governments to ignore or reinterpret advice should political circumstances necessitate it. This language is not capable of safeguarding the integrity and independence of those who reason in the public interest.

My framework's questions asked whether the spectre of objectivity was present in the advice I examined and how that advice engaged with or construed the notion of evidence. We saw advice that was presented as an objective view of reality in its assumptions around Saddam Hussein's intentions, ambitions and storage of unaccounted-for weapons. Both ONA and DIO presented these assumptions as largely undisputed information, yet DIO was alone in alerting its readers to the tenuousness of its conclusions given the scarcity of evidence. One could conclude that representations of reality in the advice of both agencies took a shared objectivity as a given, but only DIO explicitly confronted the possibility that its evidence could be deficient. While neither was ultimately used by the prime minister, they served three important symbolic functions: one, they provided an ostensible evidence base from which to invoke objective knowledge of 'things as they really are' so the government's actions could be normalised as the next logical steps; two, raising doubts about doubtful evidence facilitated a political strategy that made it hard to discount the government's preferred position; and three, having wrongly portrayed 'things as they really are', the evidence could be discounted and kept at arm's length from decision-makers.

Can international comparisons shed further light on Australia's rebuffed advice, and can they help identify whether there are specific Australian characteristics in how it deals with rebuffed advice? I have already considered the language of the intelligence assessments of Australia, as well as some of those of the United States and the United Kingdom.

We know Australia's international coalition partners used their respective assessments to enable a stronger rhetoric about specific 'evidence', lending their decision-making—or decision-justification—processes an aura of greater certainty. When it became clear the Iraq Survey Group would not find WMD in Iraq, George W. Bush and Tony Blair, like Howard, encouraged interpretations of intelligence, rather than policy, failure. In December 2015, Blair said in an interview 'the intelligence we received was wrong' (Maynard and Agencies 2016) and, in July 2016, at the conclusion of the Iraq Inquiry, he reiterated that 'intelligence assessments turned out to be wrong' (Reuters 2016). For his part, Bush reminisced that 'the biggest regret of all the presidency has to have been the intelligence failure in Iraq' (Spillius 2008). Howard, as we know, referred to 'errors in intelligence' while maintaining his cognisance of uncertainty by adding 'when you're dealing with intelligence it's hard to find a situation where advice is beyond doubt' (Sunshine Coast Daily 2016).

Beyond encouragement by the three leaders to view the evidence base as faulty, all three coalition partners underwent public inquiry processes to investigate the accuracy and adequacy of intelligence. In the United States, the report on the 'U.S. Intelligence Community's Prewar Intelligence Assessments on Iraq' prepared by the Senate Select Committee on Intelligence (SSCI) reported on 9 July 2004, while the 'Report to the President of the United States, The Commission on the Intelligence Capabilities of the United States Regarding Weapons of Mass Destruction' concluded on 31 March 2005. The SSCI report focused largely on intelligence collection and analysis, specifically in relation to the CIA's National Intelligence Estimate of October 2002. It was tasked with considering the 'objectivity, reasonableness, independence, and accuracy of the judgments reached', whether 'these were properly disseminated to the executive and legislative branches' and whether 'any political pressure affected these assessments' (SSCI 2004: 1). A second reporting component was to 'cover the more politically contentious issues', such as 'whether public statements, reports and testimony regarding Iraq by U.S. Government officials made between the Gulf War period and the commencement of Operation Iraqi Freedom were substantiated by intelligence information'. This second reporting component was 'quietly shelved' (Phythian 2006: 404) after the 2004 elections, but, at the beginning of November 2005, 'with popular sentiment turning rapidly and keenly against the worsening quagmire in Iraq … the SSCI announce[d] it was recommencing Phase II' (Glees and Davies 2006: 870). The reports of this second phase were released in four sections from 2006 to 2008; the final section, published on 5 June 2008, determined that, in making the case for war, 'the Administration repeatedly presented intelligence as fact when in reality it was unsubstantiated, contradicted, or even non-existent' (SSCI 2008). Further, the report concluded that the US Administration's public statements were 'contradicted by available intelligence' and not reflective of 'the concerns and uncertainties expressed in the intelligence products' (SSCI 2008). Nonetheless, there was 'no question we all relied on flawed intelligence' (SSCI 2008).

For its part, the WMD commission's report was 'not authorized to investigate policy-maker use of intelligence' (Phythian 2006: 404). This means that, until 2006, both US investigations avoided examining the role of policymakers in presenting intelligence as fact, thereby circumventing making judgements about them and directing most if not all of the focus towards administrative accountability. Mark Phythian, following Richard Betts' claim that intelligence failure is most often due to 'the decision makers who consume the products of intelligence services', suggests 'any post-mortem that fails to address [policymakers'] role and instead seeks solutions through organizational reforms is self-defeating' (Phythian 2006: 402). As such, he considers the US inquiries until 2006 to be one-sided and inadequate. It is possible he would make similar claims about Australia's inquiries. After 2006 and by 2008, legislative oversight in the United States did address that role, and it did so substantially. Yet, it is curious that the notion of flawed intelligence continued to circulate in 2008 despite the SSCI ultimately finding that responsibility for turning a language of uncertainty into facts rested with the administration.

Three major inquiries took place in the United Kingdom—Australia's only Westminster coalition partner: the *Report of the Inquiry into the Circumstances Surrounding the Death of Dr David Kelly, C.M.G.* (aka the Hutton Inquiry), which reported on 28 January 2004; the *Review of Intelligence on Weapons of Mass Destruction: Report of a Committee of Privy Councillors to the House of Commons* (the Butler Report), 14 July 2004; and *The Report of the Iraq Inquiry* (the Chilcot Report), 6 July 2016. The first of these was an inquiry into the suicide of former British weapons inspector David Kelly. Its terms of reference were to investigate 'the circumstances surrounding the death of Dr Kelly'—essentially to investigate whether Kelly's alleged tip-off to the BBC that the government had 'sexed up' the September Dossier (particularly its claim that weapons were deployable within 45 minutes) set off a chain of events that led to his death. The Hutton Inquiry judged that the question of whether intelligence was 'of sufficient strength and reliability to justify … military action' (Hutton 2004: 320) fell outside its terms of reference and sidestepped the issue of who was accountable for constructing an actionable evidence base. In its final conclusions, the inquiry provided a reading of the term 'sexed up', which it saw as

> capable of two different meanings. It could mean that the dossier was embellished with items of intelligence known or believed to be false or unreliable to make the case against Saddam Hussein stronger, or it could mean that whilst the intelligence contained in the dossier was believed to be reliable, the dossier was drafted in such a way as to make the case against Saddam Hussein as strong as the intelligence contained in it permitted. If the term is used in this latter sense, then because of the drafting suggestions made by 10 Downing Street for the purpose of making a strong case against Saddam Hussein, it could be said that the Government 'sexed-up' the dossier. However in the context of the broadcasts in which the 'sexing-up' allegation was reported … I consider that the allegation was unfounded as it would have been understood by those who heard the broadcasts to mean that the dossier had been embellished with intelligence known or believed to be false or unreliable, which was not the case. (Hutton 2004: 321)

Mulgan proposes that, had Lord Hutton been wholly committed to uncovering the manifestation of 'sexing up', he would have widened his comments regarding the drafting of the dossier by asking for 'a case "as strong *or as weak* as the evidence properly permitted"' (2007: 575; emphasis in original). This author agrees. However, Lord Hutton's 'strong' interpretation does point to a view that governments' inflation of advice is accepted as ordinary. In other words, the report expects that governments regularly stretch the evidence base for policy as far as possible before it technically becomes a lie. Further, Lord Hutton suggests the government 'believed' the intelligence to be 'reliable', which seems to implicitly place the burden of meaning on the agencies.

The Butler Report's terms of reference are similar to those of the PJCAAD:

> [T]o investigate the intelligence coverage available in respect of WMD programmes in countries of concern and on the global trade in WMD, taking into account what is now known about these programmes; as part of this work, to investigate the accuracy of intelligence on Iraqi WMD up to March 2003, and to examine any discrepancies between the intelligence gathered, evaluated and

used by the Government before the conflict, and between that intelligence and what has been discovered by the Iraq survey group since the end of the conflict; and to make recommendations to the Prime Minister for the future on the gathering, evaluation and use of intelligence on WMD, in the light of the difficulties of operating in countries of concern. (Butler 2004: 1)

Lord Butler's conclusions are not unlike those of the PJCAAD; his report, for example, found 'no evidence of deliberate distortion or of culpable negligence'; 'no evidence of JIC [Joint Intelligence Committee] assessments and the judgements inside them being pulled in any particular direction to meet the policy concerns of senior officials on the JIC'; and concluded 'that the intelligence community made good use of the technical expertise available to the Government' (2004: 152).

On the use of intelligence, and with the September Dossier as its example, the Butler Report paints a picture of division between 'dispassionate assessment' and government 'advocacy' (Butler 2004: 78). For instance, while Lord Butler appreciates the Joint Intelligence Committee did its 'utmost' to provide its government with assessments that 'properly' reflected 'the judgements of the intelligence community', this was likely to 'have put a strain on them in seeking to maintain their normal standards of neutral and objective assessment' (Butler 2004: 78). This seems to suggest being 'neutral and objective' is somehow difficult, perhaps even impossible, when in proximity to 'advocacy'. Yet, surely the 'objective assessments' of any knowledge producer serving the government are always in close proximity to advocacy; indeed, one might say this proximity is their bread and butter.

The report considers the government displayed 'mistaken judgement' in its public release of the dossier under the authorship of the JIC, and that the JIC itself exhibited 'serious weakness' by failing to make 'warnings on the limitations of the intelligence underlying its judgements ... sufficiently clear' (Butler 2004: 78). This is odd given the report also considers that, when 'material from JIC assessments' was translated 'into the dossier', 'warnings were lost about the limited intelligence base on which some aspects of these assessments were being made' (Butler 2004: 78). Rather than being contradictory, however, this suggests that whatever warnings were present, they were made neither vehemently nor often enough, which echoes the Hutton Report's implication that administrators should ensure evidentiary language is not only clearly transmitted to, but also unequivocally understood by, governments.

Lord Butler also recognises that the JIC and its September Dossier were used by the government to give it additional authority and the hue of objectivity: '[T]he advantage to the Government of associating the JIC's name with the dossier was the badge of objectivity that it brought with it and the credibility which this would give to the document' (2004: 78).

This resulted in more weight being placed 'on the intelligence than it could bear' (Butler 2004: 154). To avoid this in future, Lord Butler concludes:

> [I]f intelligence is to be used more widely by governments in public debate in future, those doing so must be careful to explain its uses and limitations. It will be essential, too, that clearer and more effective dividing lines between assessment and advocacy are established when doing so. (2004: 155)

The Butler Report thereby identifies a responsibility for governments to treat evidence inputs and advice in a particular way when using them in public and expects them to clarify that those inputs are separate from advocacy. In other words, input sourced from suppliers of objective information must stay separate from political language. It would certainly be more comprehensive for governments to treat the evidence that leads them to, or justifies, actions or decisions in a mode more akin to academic referencing. But is this practical? Who is to judge whether the manner of referencing is sufficient? And is this not how governments did proceed—that is, by making a show of their inputs coming from intelligence agencies? The intelligence assessments, characterised by Lord Butler as uncertain evidence, were easily utilised in political advocacy to invade Iraq, not because governments failed to reference inputs or highlight limitations, but because they did. This is not especially unorthodox, as assessments or policy advice tend usually to be in the mix of advocacy for political decisions. Indeed, intelligence and policy advice are produced by personnel within public administrations solely for use by a single customer—the government—for policy formation and decision-making. While it is reasonable to expect governments to resist interfering in the knowledge-construction process while it is in their administrators' hands, once that knowledge has been delivered to the customer, a key measure of its success is influencing the policy process. So, the aim is really to connect with policy, rather than to stay separate.

Steering away from comprehensive scrutiny of policymakers, Lords Hutton and Butler infer administrators were neither clear nor sufficiently persistent in communicating that their uncertainty needed to inform decision-making in a more fundamental way. For its part, the later Chilcot Report sets out in detail decision-making in the UK Government covering the period from when the possibility of military action first arose in 2001 to the departure of UK troops in 2009. It covers many different aspects of policy and its delivery. (Committee of Privy Counsellors 2016: 4)

As such, it records government processes and decisions from a more expansive viewpoint than its predecessors. Called by Robert Jervis 'the mother of all post-mortems', the Chilcot Report is vast and comprehensive, yet reveals 'no bombshells; we do not have to relearn the history'. This, Jervis proposes,

> should not be a cause for disappointment because the point of inquiries like these is to lay out the historical record and reach sensible judgments, not to be original. The fact that there are so few revelations is reassuring in showing that in an open society, it did not require an investigation as long and thorough as this one to bring out a good account of what had happened. (2017: 287)

Its key findings on the matters that concern this section on international contexts and circumstances—specifically, how each jurisdiction managed subsequent perceptions of failure and where it placed the burden of accountability for language use that stimulated political decisions— underline Jervis's claim. That is, despite the plethora of material, Chilcot's findings echo those of previous inquiries that there was no improper political influence.[12] However, '[t]he assessed intelligence had *not* established beyond doubt either that Saddam Hussein had continued to produce chemical and biological weapons or that efforts to develop nuclear weapons continued. The JIC should have made that clear to Mr Blair' (Committee of Privy Counsellors 2016: 116; emphasis in original).

As it happened, the JIC did not make that doubt clear. Indeed, as Chilcot implies, the JIC stood by while its advice became evidence: 'The Government's strategy reflected its confidence in the Joint Intelligence Committee's Assessments. Those Assessments provided the benchmark against which Iraq's conduct and denials, and the reports of the inspectors, were judged' (Chilcot 2016).

---

12 'There is no evidence that intelligence was improperly included in the dossier or that No.10 improperly influenced the text' (Committee of Privy Counsellors 2016: Vol. 4, p. 115).

One is left with the impression that Rovner's 'soft politicisation' played a role here, too. In other words, it is possible the JIC feared rejection— such as was happening at the time in relation to advice about internal strife and regional instability, for example[13]—and moved to prevent this by allowing the inconclusive nature of its advice to flourish. Even though British policymakers' inexact use of unripe advice is portrayed damningly in the Chilcot Report, it, like its predecessors, places much of the onus of accountability for the establishment and maintenance of facts on administrators. Chilcot differs, however, in including observations on the role of ministerial advisers, particularly that of Blair's director of communications and strategy, Alastair Campbell. While he does not draw conclusions about the propriety of Campbell's involvement in making decisions, Chilcot's description of events involving Campbell are instructive in relation to the role of ministerial advisers in the formation of expert advice.

Describing a meeting to discuss the September Dossier, the Chilcot Report provides a statement by John Williams, press secretary of the UK Foreign and Commonwealth Office. Williams notes of the meeting:

> It was clear that no decision had been taken about who would produce the dossier. [JIC head] John Scarlett said that intelligence had no experience of writing documents for publication and would need the help of a 'golden pen'. He turned to me. Alastair Campbell did not take this up. At the end of the meeting I asked Alastair what his intention was. He said he was inclined to give the task to the No.10 Strategic Communications Unit … When I reported this … to the Foreign Secretary and Michael Jay, they were clear that the dossier must be produced by the Foreign Office, not No.10, and I should be the 'golden pen'. (Committee of Privy Counsellors 2016: 153 (s. 4.2))

What follows are detailed accounts of the development of the dossier, shepherded by Campbell, in close agreement with his prime minister, particularly in relation to tone, objectivity and credibility. While this does not reveal a single moment in which a ministerial adviser influenced the reaction of his or her minister, it is informative that the cultivation of close associations between ministerial advisers and civil servants in the construction of their advice is a valuable tool in giving birth to evidence.

---

13   'The risks of internal strife in Iraq, active Iranian pursuit of its interests, regional instability, and Al Qaida activity in Iraq, were each explicitly identified before the invasion' but were ignored (Chilcot 2016).

Despite being more of a co-produced document, the dossier's ascribed author was the JIC and, as we saw, this was optically desirable to give the political decision to go to war the semblance of fact and objectivity. While the UK Government may have used the dossier with less precision than it ought, public inquiries of this nature tend to place great emphasis on the production of knowledge. In instances where a policy has been perceived as a failure and invites formal scrutiny, one might therefore say the burden of accountability rests heavily on those responsible for output rather than outcome. This is probably partly due to the comparative ease of making suggestions for improving the executive branch of government. Chilcot, for instance, proposes that lessons 'for any similar exercise in future would be':

> The need for clear separation of the responsibility for analysis and assessment of intelligence from the responsibility for making the argument for a policy.
>
> The importance of precision in describing the position …
>
> The need to identify and accurately describe the confidence and robustness of the evidence base …
>
> The need to be explicit about the likelihood of events …
>
> The need to be scrupulous in discriminating between facts and knowledge on the one hand and opinion, judgement or belief on the other.
>
> The need for vigilance to avoid unwittingly crossing the line from supposition to certainty, including by constant repetition of received wisdom. (Committee of Privy Counsellors 2016: 131–32)

Given the preceding discussion—particularly around the reticence to be candid, the eagerness to be responsive, the acceptance of 'objectivity' as an undisputed marker of reality, the development of assumptions into facts as well as the potential for soft politicisation and being scapegoated for failure—it is difficult to imagine an environment in which civil servants become clearer, more precise, more robust, more explicit, more scrupulous and more vigilant in the presentation of their advice. This situation is not only politically useful; it also keeps public accountability problematic.

The tendency of public inquiries to make suggestions for improving how knowledge is produced is probably also partly due to how terms of reference are established, at least in Westminster-style jurisdictions.[14] As McConnell et al. suggest, such inquiries or investigations can perform three functions:

> First, investigations may have a *symbolic* role, through an appearance of expert and learned individuals being given the freedom to construct an impartial and reasoned account of what went wrong, who or what is to blame, and what should be done ... Second, there is a *learning* role. A purpose of inquiries is to establish the causes of failure in order to produce recommendations which are part of a learning process to ensure that a similar failure does not happen again—or if it does, society is much better placed to cope ... Third, there is the *realpolitick* [sic] perspective. Here, investigations perform a crucial role in the protection and maintenance of key office holders. Therefore, establishing a particular format of inquiry can assist in protecting office holders from scrutiny, apportioning blame elsewhere, or even putting an issue into the 'freezer' to avoid taking difficult decisions until a later date when the issue may (somehow) become more manageable. (2008: 605; emphasis in original)

One can see a combination of all three functions in the inquiries under consideration, although charges of the last are more pronounced. As *The Guardian* put it at the release of the Chilcot Report:

> A government whose members were complicit in the matter under investigation (Gordon Brown financed and supported the Iraq war) defined his terms of reference. This is a fundamental flaw in the way inquiries are established in this country: it's as if a defendant in a criminal case were able to appoint his own judge, choose the charge on which he is to be tried and have the hearing conducted in his own home. (Monbiot 2016)

A similar complaint has been made in the Australian context regarding the 'Report of the Inquiry into Certain Australian Companies in Relation to the UN Oil-for-Food Programme', also known as the Cole Inquiry, in 2006:

---

14 Although in the US context, the composition of committees tends to have a similar effect (see, for instance, Phythian 2006; Glees and Davies 2006).

There is a time-honoured pattern with politically charged 'independent' investigations. The government of the day first of all clears the decks, it defines very tight terms of reference, appoints the correct man for the task (when can you remember it being left to a woman?), sets an impossible deadline for the reporting date and provides a measly budget for the whole exercise. (Ackland 2006)

These comparisons are instructive. With limited remits, these inquiries may not have gone far enough to more tangibly examine the role of policymakers and their use of expert advice. Although this did not seriously hamper Chilcot's strong conclusions about policymakers, such as finding the UK Government 'chose to join the invasion of Iraq before the peaceful options for disarmament had been exhausted', each of the aforementioned inquiries made much of intelligence agencies' weakness in challenging their governments', as well as their own,[15] predispositions. This leads to the observation that those producing knowledge for government use are expected to set the record straight, which is a legitimate expectation. Administrators should be accountable if they are aware their knowledge is being misinterpreted. This is an important point in considering language, both for the rebuffed and for the unrebuffed, in that passive acceptance of remodelled advice can be viewed as coming very close to providing the wrong advice in the first place—which the interpretation of 'flawed intelligence' makes clear.

In the Australian context, the report of the PJCAAD—requested on 18 June 2003 and delivered in December 2003—was the first of the coalition partners' inquiry processes. Despite the report's timeliness, Australian intelligence was not publicly released, nor was all of it provided to the PJCAAD committee, as noted earlier. Further, Australia's reviews were not as wideranging as its counterparts', excluding scrutiny of the role of policy advisers, government ministers and ministerial advisers. Nonetheless, the 2003 PJCAAD made recommendations about the capacity and independence of the intelligence agencies, while alluding to the possibility of ONA being influenced by 'policy running strong'— perhaps a form of anticipatory compliance. In judging whether the Australian Government itself presented accurate information in making its case for war, the committee made several observations, including that

---

15   Chilcot is particularly strong on this: 'There was an ingrained belief in the UK policy and intelligence communities that: Iraq had retained some chemical and biological capabilities; was determined to preserve and if possible enhance them—and, in the future, to acquire a nuclear capability; and was able to conceal its activities from the UN inspectors' (2016).

the Australian prime minister and other ministers did not use the highly charged language of their coalition counterparts and the government's claims about Iraqi WMD reflected ONA's views after its 13 September 2002 assessment. Without explicitly saying so, this seems to insinuate that both moderate language and adhering to ONA assessments equate to accurate presentation of information. Yet, it is another of the committee's observations that is of more interest here, and it relates to the agencies' checking of accuracy in ministerial speeches, which I briefly discussed earlier. Nonetheless, it bears teasing out some of the detail.

The committee wrote that ONA checked each of the prime minister's speeches

> for the accuracy of the references to intelligence information; they sought to indicate any errors in the factual information. Their definition of accuracy specifically excluded any views on the broader policy issues. This is consistent with their role of not providing policy advice. However, accuracy must also encompass whether the picture being presented is complete. Ignoring significant elements of fact or opinion when citing intelligence assessments can have a distorting effect. A true and accurate interpretation must consider the total balance of the points of view being adduced in support of a policy. (PJCAAD 2003: 93–94)

On the prime minister citing British and American intelligence, the committee was told the judgements quoted in the speeches

> were not necessarily ones that [ONA] might have made, but that, as they were made on the basis of material ONA had not seen, the quotations in the speeches were not questioned. They were considered accurate quotations, in the sense of transcriptions, from the British and US documents. In response to a question about the threat of Iraq's WMD being 'real and unacceptable', [Director-General of DIO] Mr Lewincamp thought it was not a judgement that DIO would have made. (PJCAAD 2003: 94–95)

This implies a passive approach to checking accuracy and communicating instances of inaccuracy. Further, when British and American intelligence was contained in Australian speeches, fact-checking extended purely to proofreading quotations, rather than raising doubts about their content. These conclusions are similar to Chilcot's lessons for improvement and carry the added weight of Australian agencies not questioning the evidence base of international counterparts.

As stipulated by its terms of reference, the subsequent 2004 Flood Inquiry restricted its recommendations largely to organisational issues relating to Australia's foreign intelligence community. While thoughtful and comprehensive, the report nonetheless pours cold water on the PJCAAD's implied suggestion that agencies that provide their expertise to government decision-making processes by checking the accuracy of government documents be more assertive in pointing to distortions of fact. As we saw, Flood considered 'it is not reasonable to expect an intelligence agency to comment on the manner in which the government chooses to use ... intelligence' (2004: 31). We saw far more substantial expectations in the British context.

Flood acknowledged that a review such as his had 'the full benefit of hindsight' and he recognised that assessment agencies produced 'much to commend their efforts' (2004: 27). Yet, he concluded that '[t]here has been a failure of intelligence on Iraq WMD'. Carefully measured, the Flood Inquiry moves along a vacillating trajectory. On the one hand, 'ONA's and DIO's key judgements on Iraq's WMD capabilities were relatively cautious', while on the other, 'ONA and DIO ... failed to judge accurately the extent and nature of Iraq's WMD programmes' (2004: 25). Further, 'ONA and DIO assessments represented reasonable and relatively cautious conclusions' (Flood 2004: 27), yet '[i]ntelligence was thin, ambiguous and incomplete' (p. 34). Seemingly contradictory, both are nonetheless possible. Yet, it is difficult to reconcile the relationship between cautious conclusions and inaccurate judgements. Flood also points to systemic weaknesses, such as 'failure rigorously to challenge preconceptions or assumptions about the Iraqi regime's intentions ... Iraq's WMD capabilities and the threat posed by Saddam' (2004: 25).[16] This lack of challenge and contestation is partly borne out by the material I have considered, yet we also know that, even when DIO doubted various assumptions—such as the presence of nuclear weapons—they were ignored in public.

---

16   For its part, the Chilcot report notes: 'At no stage was the proposition that Iraq might no longer have chemical, biological or nuclear weapons or programmes identified and examined by either JIC or the policy community' (Committee of Privy Counsellors 2016).

The reviews following the invasion of Iraq offer valuable insights into how three jurisdictions dealt with the language of specific types of knowledge. They all gravitated strongly towards holding intelligence advisers accountable and conveyed a sense that language starts with administrators—even those who are rebuffed and subsequently excluded from the public sphere where policy has already been decided. They all make suggestions as to how to improve intelligence as an evidence base, ranging from collection practices to organisational issues. Some of them even acknowledge the limitations of such improvements. As Jervis notes in a comparison of the reviews (preceding Chilcot):

> Despite the many errors, most of the [intelligence community's] general conclusions, although wrong, were reasonable. Indeed the Flood Report 'acknowledges that it is doubtful that better process would have changed the fundamental judgments about the existence of WMD'. In places, the WMD Commission comes close to seeing this, and the Butler Report can be read in this way as well. SSCI strongly implies the opposite. (2006: 46)

Taking the Flood Report as the beacon for acknowledging a counterfactual should be cause for celebration in the Australian context. After all, it suggests that Australian accountability mechanisms might be uniquely capable of making robust and impartial evaluations. However, this bequeaths a potentially unpopular absolution on those involved in the formation of faulty judgements and threatens to undermine the very reason for having an inquiry in the first place. Jervis puts it this way: 'To have admitted that, although errors were made and the process could be improved, no conceivable fix would have led to the correct judgment would have been met with incredulity and undercut the recommendations' (2006: 46).

Thus, recommendations, conclusions and findings are formulated with a principal focus on how government agencies are organised. This implies some quite fundamental shortcomings in how accountability mechanisms such as public inquiries proceed. I have already identified a few, such as bias and lack of contestability, and Jervis proposes several others:

> The investigations are marred by political bias and excessive hindsight. Neither the investigations nor contemporary intelligence on Iraqi WMD followed good social science practices. The comparative method was not utilized, confirmation bias was rampant, alternative hypotheses were not tested, and negative evidence was ignored. (2006: 3)

In comparing expert advice and subsequent accountability processes, one must remember the United Kingdom and the United States did not rebuff the advice of their intelligence agencies as Australia did; rather, they stretched it out of its original shape. This is important; the advice that was not rebuffed in the United States and the United Kingdom was more or less supportive of the government position, while Australia's was inconsistent in this respect. This is why, in pledging support to any US position as far back as 14 September 2001, John Howard had no choice but to cite his counterparts' intelligence rather than his own, which was not unequivocally corroborative. However, his own, Australian-produced intelligence caused him to construct a strategy of doubt that was more explicitly utilised in making his case for war than his counterparts. As such, the language of Australian intelligence assessments made it possible for him to remain untouched by accountability mechanisms— even allowing for their restricted terms of reference—in the sense that he could truthfully claim to have been aware of all the evidence, whether certain or uncertain, and that he reflected those views publicly. With the implication that he followed this intelligence in good faith, this gave his claim of errors in intelligence, rather than in his own political decision-making, a dexterous ring of truth.

Table 4.2 Intelligence, advice, events and public statements relating to Iraq, 2002–03

Date	ONA	DIO	Joint ONA/DIO	Public domestic/international event/material
11 September 2001				9/11 attacks
14 September 2001				ANZUS Treaty invoked
19 July 2002			Intelligence on Iraq's nuclear program is 'scarce, patchy and inconclusive'. Iraq 'most likely kept a sizeable amount of anthrax and other BW [biological warfare] agents concealed from UN inspectors' between 1991 and 1998. Iraq's nuclear program is 'unlikely to be far advanced'. 'US agencies differ on whether aluminium pipes, a dual use item sought by Iraq, were meant for gas centrifuges.' 'Most, if not all, of the few [Scud missiles] that are still hidden away are likely to be in poor condition.'	
26 August 2002				US Vice President Dick Cheney: '[T]here is no doubt that Saddam Hussein now has weapons of mass destruction' (Cheney 2002).
September 2002				National Security Strategy of the United States 2002 released.

Date	ONA	DIO	Joint ONA/DIO	Public domestic/international event/material
6 September 2002	'Iraq is highly unlikely to have nuclear weapons, though intelligence on its nuclear programme is scarce. It has the expertise to make nuclear weapons, but almost certainly lacks the necessary plutonium or highly-enriched uranium ... Iraq may be able to build a basic nuclear weapon in 4–6 years.' '[P]rocurement patterns are consistent with an effort to develop an enrichment capability.'			
12 September 2002	'[T]he case for the revival of the WMD programs is substantial, but not conclusive.'			US President George W. Bush addresses UN General Assembly: '[T]he history, the logic, the facts lead to one conclusion: Saddam Hussein's regime is a grave and gathering danger' (Bush 2002a).
13 September 2002	'[T]here is no reason to believe that Saddam Hussein has abandoned his ambition to acquire nuclear weapons.' 'Australian intelligence agencies believe there is evidence of a pattern of acquisition of equipment which could be used in a uranium enrichment programme. Iraq's attempted acquisition of aluminium tubes may be part of that pattern.'			

Date	ONA	DIO	Joint ONA/DIO	Public domestic/international event/material
17 September 2002				Australian Foreign Minister Alexander Downer: 'As with chemical and biological weapons, the Australian government has no reason to believe that Saddam Hussein has abandoned his ambition to acquire nuclear weapons. All the circumstances suggest the opposite. Australian intelligence agencies believe there is evidence of a pattern of acquisition of equipment that could be used in a uranium enrichment program. Iraq's attempted acquisition of very specific types of aluminium tubes may be part of that pattern. Iraq still has the expertise and the information to reconstitute a nuclear weapons program and may have continued work on uranium enrichment and weapons design. And Iraq could shorten the lead time for producing nuclear weapons if it were able to acquire fissile material from elsewhere.... The government's view is that there is good reason to be extremely worried about the status of Iraq's programs' (Downer 2002).
20 September 2002	ONA 'remains cautious about the aluminium tubes and the claim that Iraq has sought uranium from Africa'.			US Vice President Cheney: The aluminium tubes are 'irrefutable evidence' (quoted in Barstow 2004).
24 September 2002				The United Kingdom's September Dossier includes claims about uranium from Niger and aluminium tubes; also claims some of Iraq's WMD are ready to deploy within 45 minutes.
October 2002				US troops begin build-up.

Date	ONA	DIO	Joint ONA/DIO	Public domestic/international event/material
7 October 2002				US President George W. Bush: 'The evidence indicates that Iraq is reconstituting its nuclear weapons program ... Knowing these realities, America must not ignore the threat gathering against us. Facing clear evidence of peril, we cannot wait for the final proof – the smoking gun – that could come in the form of a mushroom cloud' (Bush 2002b).
10 October 2002		'[W]hat is known about Iraq's programmes is as worrying as what is not known.' 'Iraq has the necessary civil, and possibly hidden military, assets to have resumed limited [biological weapons] production, although there is no specific evidence of this.' 'As a worst case – if Iraq had begun missile material production after UNSCOM inspections ceased in 1998 – it may be able to manufacture a crude nuclear weapon by 2006–08. In the unlikely event that Iraq was to obtain fissile material from a foreign source, it would take 12 months to develop a nuclear weapon – assuming it already possessed a useable weapons design.' Intelligence on purchases of dual-use items for the production of weapons-grade uranium is 'patchy and inconclusive'. 'We assess Iraq does not have nuclear weapons.'		CIA's National Intelligence Estimate: 'Iraq has continued its weapons of mass destruction programs (WMD) in defiance of UN resolutions and restrictions ... Most agencies believe that Saddam's personal interest in and Iraq's aggressive attempts to obtain high-strength aluminium tubes for centrifuge rotors ... provide compelling evidence that Saddam is reconstituting a uranium enrichment effort for Baghdad's nuclear weapons program ... all key aspects – R&D, production, weaponisation – of Iraq's offensive BW [biological warfare] program are active and that most elements are larger and more advanced than they were before the Gulf war' (quoted in PJCAAD 2003: 139–41).

Date	ONA	DIO	Joint ONA/DIO	Public domestic/international event/material
11 October 2002				Bali bombings
8 November 2002				UNSC Resolution 1441.
27 November 2002				UNMOVIC and IAEA inspections commence.
19 December 2002	Iraq's 7 December declaration to UNMOVIC inspectors fails to explain its 'attempted procurement of aluminium tubes and its apparent effort to procure uranium outside Iraq'.			
31 December 2002		'[T]here is no known CW [chemical warfare] production.' 'We assess Iraq does not have nuclear weapons.' '[T]here has been no known offensive [biological weapons] research and development since 1991, no known BW [biological warfare] production since 1991 and no known BW testing since 1991'.		
23 January 2003				Australian troops deploy.
28 January 2003				US President George W. Bush's State of the Union address: 'Year after year, Saddam Hussein has gone to elaborate lengths, spent enormous sums, taken great risks to build and keep weapons of mass destruction. But why? The only possible explanation, the only possible use he could have for those weapons, is to dominate, intimidate, or attack' (Bush 2003).

Date	ONA	DIO	Joint ONA/DIO	Public domestic/international event/material
30 January 2003	'Saddam is procuring equipment and antidotes to protect his own troops in a CBW [chemical or biological war]'.			
31 January 2003	'[A]n Iraqi artillery unit was ordered to ensure that UN inspectors would not find chemical residues on their equipment.'			
4 February 2003				Australian prime minister John Howard: 'The Australian government knows that Iraq still has chemical and biological weapons and that Iraq wants to develop nuclear weapons. We share the view of many that, unless checked, Iraq could, even without outside help, develop nuclear weapons in about five years. Even before the report of the Head of the United Nations weapons inspection body there was compelling evidence to support these beliefs within the published detailed dossiers of British and American intelligence' (Howard 2003a).
5 February 2003				US Secretary of State Colin Powell addresses United Nations, claiming 'not assertions' but 'facts corroborated by many sources', including about the acquisition of aluminium tubes. 'What we are giving you are facts and conclusions based on solid evidence' (Powell 2003).
6 February 2003	Colin Powell's 5 February statement to the United Nations provides 'confirmation that Iraq has WMD, since Iraq's concealment and deception are otherwise inexplicable'.			

Date	ONA	DIO	Joint ONA/DIO	Public domestic/international event/material
14 February 2003				Head of UNMOVIC Hans Blix tells UNSC: 'One must not jump to the conclusion that [WMD] exist. However, that possibility is also not to be excluded … Without evidence … confidence cannot arise' (Blix 2004: 177). IAEA head Mohamed ElBaradei says there are no 'unresolved disarmament issues' (cited in Blix 2004: 178).
18 February 2003	Intelligence 'points to continuing Iraqi concealment and deception, confirming Saddam has something to hide'.			
24 February 2003		'[T]here is no reliable intelligence that demonstrates Saddam has delegated authority to use chemical or biological weapons in the event of war.' 'Despite the lack of firm evidence, precedent suggests that this is a likely scenario. During the 1991 Gulf War, Saddam authorised Iraqi commanders to use CBW [chemical or biological weapons] if Saddam was killed or coalition forces entered Baghdad.'		

Date	ONA	DIO	Joint ONA/DIO	Public domestic/international event/material
7 March 2003				Heads of UNMOVIC and IAEA present reports to UNSC. Blix: '[A]fter a period of somewhat reluctant cooperation, there has been an acceleration of initiatives from the Iraqi side since the end of January. This is welcome, but the value of these measures must be soberly judged by how many question marks they actually succeed in straightening out. This is not yet clear' (Blix 2004: 210). ElBaradei: '[A]fter three months of inspection, IAEA has found no evidence or plausible indication of a revived nuclear weapons program. Aluminium tubes are not likely to be related to manufacture of centrifuges and the alleged contract to source uranium from Niger is not authentic' (cited in Blix 2004: 210–11).
11 March 2003	'Baghdad remains defiant and claims it has no WMD to declare: US and UNMOVIC say the opposite.'			
13 March 2003				Prime Minister Howard's speech to National Press Club, followed by Q&A: '[Y]ou say proof, I mean as I say, I can't prove before an Old Bailey or a Central Criminal Court jury but can I say to you again, I mean if the world waits for that, it's too late' (Howard 2003a).
18 March 2003				Howard: 'The available intelligence indicates that, since the departure of inspectors in 1998, Saddam has continued to work on his chemical and biological capabilities and has maintained his nuclear aspirations.... Intelligence analysis tells us that Saddam Hussein considers these weapons programs to be essential both for internal repression and to fulfil his regional ambitions' (Commonwealth of Australia 2003: 12507–8).

Date	ONA	DIO	Joint ONA/DIO	Public domestic/international event/material
20 March 2003				Howard: '[T]he possession of chemical, biological, or even worse still, nuclear weapons by a terrorist network would be a direct and lethal threat to Australia and its people ... A key element of our close friendship with the United States and indeed with the British is our full and intimate sharing of intelligence material. In the difficult fight against the new menace of international terrorism there is nothing more crucial than timely and accurate intelligence. This is a priceless component of our relationship with our two very close allies' (Howard 2003c).

5

The Language of the Unrebuffed

Contemporaneous comparisons

The language of Australia's expert policy advice should not be judged by only a handful of examples that demonstrate ineffectiveness. We need to be able to investigate, as far as possible, whether a language of the unrebuffed is different—that is, whether it features characteristics that invite stable meaning and clear interpretation by its government audience. This chapter considers three contemporaneous Australian examples that appear to find some basis in unrebuffed policy advice: amendments to Australian citizenship, marriage equality and the legal basis for military action in Iraq. I investigate whether such advice is the language of persuasive advisers and whether it features additional, or entirely different, factors compared with that in this book's three primary case studies. I find that, even while they represent contemporaneous policy 'wins', my unrebuffed examples display a similarly constrained mode of advice-giving to those of the rebuffed.

This is baffling. Are the findings from each the same because they have used the same document-led approach using my tripartite framework? To test whether those findings are robust, I juxtapose them with two short comparisons borrowing from Rhodes' (2018: 8) 'bricolage' to find 'other ways of "being there"' by switching to a different methodology. That is, I will briefly consider interviews I conducted with Australian policy advisers reflecting on the introduction of a consumption tax in the late 1990s, as well as Dutch policy actors who worked on prison reforms throughout much of the 2000s. These show us another style of policy advising with which to test my hypothesis.

Readers may recall that the tenth and last question of my framework (see Chapter 2) asked whether viewing unrebuffed advice alongside contemporaneous rebuffed advice could shed further light on the advice that was not accepted. Will this line-up help us see why some advice is overlooked but other advice is not? Two policies that are now implemented bookend the advice on renewable energy that we considered earlier. One, the *Australian Citizenship Amendment (Allegiance to Australia) Act 2015*, which gives the relevant minister the power to strip dual nationals of their Australian citizenship if s/he determines they have engaged in terrorist conduct, passed into law on 11 December 2015. The other, which amended the *Marriage Act 1961* to redefine marriage as a union between two people, became legal on 9 December 2017. I will discuss each in turn before considering unrebuffed advice as it connects to intelligence assessments of Iraq. Here, I will look at contemporaneous advice that provided the legal basis for Australia's deployment of military forces to Iraq.

For now, I will return to the time frame of South Australia's electricity blackout. The citizenship Bill was introduced into parliament in June 2015 and was 'resoundingly criticised for its poor drafting and unclear operation' (Pillai 2015b). It was then referred to the Parliamentary Joint Committee on Intelligence and Security with a view to proposing amendments. Consisting of government and opposition members, the committee returned with 'a serious and responsive report' containing '27 recommendations for change' (Thwaites 2015), such as Australia's commitment to the United Nations' 1961 Convention on the Reduction of Statelessness as only applying to dual, not sole, nationals. The Bill subsequently passed into law with bipartisan input and support, partly based on 43 submissions from legal experts, human and civil rights organisations, community stakeholders and others. Inspired by the earlier Swedish example of co-produced energy policy decisions, one might expect the final legislation to reflect an amalgamation of stakeholder opinions and the evidence base, particularly in terms of the strength of its legal basis. However, in addition to wide criticism of its perceived flaws—such as the lack of mechanisms for determining whether terrorist conduct has occurred (Irving 2015), revoking only dual nationals' citizenship despite identical conduct by a sole national incurring a law-and-order response (Thwaites 2015) and its retrospectivity applying to cases where individuals had previously been convicted and sentenced to at least 10 years' imprisonment (Pillai 2015a)—the legislation has also drawn condemnation for its potential unconstitutionality. Specifically, it has been noted that the legislation likely breaches 'the separation of powers' in that 'the courts would not be involved in determining whether terrorist conduct had occurred' (Irving 2015), thereby effectively renouncing 'our own ability to bring a person to justice for breaking our laws' (Vines 2015) and giving 'the executive federal judicial power which would make it unconstitutional' (CEFA 2015). In June 2022, Australia's High Court ruled that the law was 'constitutionally invalid' (SBS News 2022). Four months later, in October 2022, the government announced it would again 'legislate to allow courts to strip terrorist suspects' citizenship' even after the High Court ruling in June 2022 (Karp 2022).

Despite its subsequent seesawing, the law's originally successful passage in 2015 nonetheless suggests that whatever policy advice was provided to government by its public servants was broadly influential. Before I unpack this, I will briefly discuss marriage equality. Following more than a decade of parliamentary attempts to overturn the *Marriage Act*, in August 2015, then prime minister Tony Abbott declared his government would 'go into the next election with a commitment to put this to the people', even though his party room had just confirmed that marriage was 'between a man and a woman' (Parliament of Australia 2015: 8092). Perhaps as planned, putting this to the people became a fraught and drawn-out issue as government ministers argued about whether it should take the form of a referendum or a plebiscite.[1] Choosing one or the other was said to be politically driven: government ministers closer to the centre preferred the relative ease of a plebiscite as the 'plainly appropriate method', while those further to the right favoured the relative complexities of a referendum as 'a much better chance of holding it off' because it needed 'to be carried by a majority of states as well as an overall majority' (Grattan 2015). After deposing Abbott just a month later, Malcolm Turnbull promised to hold a national plebiscite after the federal election in 2016. Following

---

1 A referendum 'is a vote to change the Constitution, subject to strict rules … Legally a referendum to decide the Commonwealth's power over same-sex marriage is not necessary. The High Court has determined that, in the same-sex marriage case, the federal Parliament has the power to legislate with respect to same-sex marriage'. A plebiscite 'is a vote by citizens on any subject of national significance but which does not affect the Constitution. Plebiscites are normally advisory and do not compel a government to act on the outcome' (Neilsen 2016).

Turnbull's narrow election victory in July 2016, the government began the process of arranging a plebiscite. On 14 September 2016, Turnbull introduced the Plebiscite (Same-Sex) Marriage Bill 2016 in the House of Representatives, where it passed in October 2016. It was defeated twice in the Senate, in November 2016 and again on 9 August 2017 (McKeown 2018). That day, the government directed the Australian Bureau of Statistics to conduct a voluntary postal survey, which opened in September and closed in November 2017. The results—61.6 per cent in favour—were announced on 15 November 2017 and legislation to amend the *Marriage Act* finally passed both houses of parliament on 7 December 2017 (SSCFPA 2018).

Marriage equality is now law in Australia. While this represents a national success, it is less clear whether this extends to success in policymaking. For example, considering the *Marriage Act* can be changed by a simple act of parliament—as, indeed, it was in 2004 by then prime minister John Howard to 'make it absolutely clear that Australia will not recognise same-sex marriages' (McKeown 2018)—the protracted way the policy stumbled towards eventual implementation could have been avoided. Further, the cost of conducting the survey ($80.5 million) (ABS 2018: 56) and, perhaps most importantly, the distress caused to the community (Brown 2017; Cook 2017; Heydt 2017) had needless impacts. Both policies discussed here, however, represent successful implementation of policy change.

I will now consider the policy advice that supported the government's decision-making. At the outset, it should be clarified that in neither case is it known exactly what policy advisers provided to government; no related material has been made publicly available. We do know, however, what was *not* contained in policy advice about changes to citizenship and marriage equality. To give an adequate description of this absence, one needs to go back to 14 October 2016, just 16 days after South Australia's blackout, when Solicitor-General Justin Gleeson SC appeared before a Senate committee on legal and constitutional affairs in response to an amendment drafted by Attorney-General George Brandis that stopped the solicitor-general from advising anyone in government without the attorney-general's approval (Tingle 2016). Until that point, the role of the solicitor-general had been to act as the Commonwealth's counsel and to appear on its behalf 'in most matters in the High Court of Australia' (Attorney-General's Department n.d.). Although the solicitor-general furnishes opinions on questions of law 'referred to him by the Attorney-General' and, as such, functions as the 'second law officer of the Commonwealth of Australia', they are also the 'most independent lawyer in Australian Government Service' (Barratt 2016). In Gleeson's own words, the job involves looking

> at a proposed policy and see whether it complies with the Constitution and whether it complies with the statute of law. If it does not, can it be modified to be brought within the law? There are times when any government lawyer, but particularly a Solicitor-General, has to give the hard news that it is his or her view that a particular policy if turned into legislation would be struck down by the High Court. (Senate Legal and Constitutional Affairs References Committee 2016a: 4)

Brandis's direction to amend Gleeson's legal services was viewed as highly contentious, not least by Gleeson himself, who said he regarded it 'as a threat to the independence of the office' (Senate Legal and Constitutional Affairs References Committee 2016a: 6).

During the 14 October Senate committee proceedings, Gleeson provided further information about his exclusion when he described advice he had given or had sought to give on matters related to citizenship amendments and marriage equality. On citizenship, he noted:

> My concern in relation to the citizenship bill was that I had provided a lengthy advice in respect to that proposal in 2014, and apparently within the department of immigration in the first half of 2015 a substantial change was made to that proposal. No-one had come back to me for advice, and it was only by accident that I learnt that the proposal had been radically changed. The issue I was raising was that if I had been asked to advise on legislation, proposed legislation, which is then amended there ought to be further Solicitor-General advice on the relevant version of legislation so that no-one can be misled as to exactly who was advising on the document. My concerns with citizenship were that I was brought into the process, taken out of the process and then brought back into it in unsatisfactory circumstances. (Senate Legal and Constitutional Affairs References Committee 2016a: 12)

A key point here is Gleeson's expert advice underwent significant changes within the department—presumably, at the hands of public officials working on citizenship policy. Although his expertise bracketed the beginning and end of the advisory process, it was not included when decisions were being made. This suggests its use was purely symbolic and, much like the use of the Australian Energy Market Operator's statements in my chapter on renewables, lent the department's advice the hue of evidence without incorporating that evidence into the substance of policy decisions. Gleeson's testimony also suggests departmental policy advisers knew exactly what the government required and accordingly excluded Gleeson's advice.

In a 12 November 2015 letter to the attorney-general, which was included in Gleeson's written submission to the Senate hearing, he detailed that

> the Bill which was introduced into Parliament some 24 hours later reflected new changes that were made without seeking my further advice. However, a written statement was later made by you to [Shadow Attorney-General] Mark Dreyfus QC, and ultimately published as an appendix to the Advisory Report of the Parliamentary Joint Committee (Joint Committee), that I had advised that 'there is a good prospect that a majority of the High Court would reject a constitutional challenge to the core aspects of the draft Bill' … In this morning's *Sydney Morning Herald*, the Prime Minister is reported to have made the following statements about the current version of the Bill before Parliament:
>
> The Government's advice is that the [citizenship] laws, if challenged in the High Court, would be upheld. But of course, advice isn't always born [sic] out …
>
> [The Bill has] gone through a proper process now, and we are confident that it would survive a High Court challenge, but only time will tell.
>
> Those statements, in context, are capable of being understood as statements about the Solicitor-General having advised on the current Bill. If so understood, they are inaccurate. (Senate Legal and Constitutional Affairs References Committee 2016b: 19–20)

In other words, despite Gleeson's only sporadic input, the government's public statements on the citizenship Bill strongly implied the solicitor-general's independent advice validated the current Bill's constitutionality and had even been submitted as evidence to the joint committee deliberating its fate. Appearing to draw on independent government advisers is thus useful in lending authority to government proposals even if advice is sought only rarely or perfunctorily. We saw a similar phenomenon in the previous chapter, where political statements gave the appearance of intelligence insights without really using the insights that had been provided by expert advisers.

On marriage equality, Gleeson told the hearing:

> My concern in relation to marriage equality was that during the second half of last year, when that matter was being considered within government, no-one came to me. My concern was very much that had that matter proceeded through to legislation, had it been under challenge in the High Court, it would be important that the primary government lawyer, who was expected to defend the legislation in due course in the High Court, had had inadequate opportunity to advise on it during the process. (Senate Legal and Constitutional Affairs References Committee 2016a: 12)

As a key adviser in each matter, the solicitor-general was either not consulted or was consulted only irregularly, with a final decision falsely presented as bearing his independent imprimatur despite his frequent absence from that process. Further, although his advice was originally sought in the citizenship matter, the proposal underwent significant changes 'within the department of immigration' (Senate Legal and Constitutional Affairs References Committee 2016b: 12), suggesting departmental policy advisers contributed to reshaping the Bill, perhaps to align it more closely with the government's disposition. This suggests departmental advice was not rebuffed because it excluded vital (but uncomfortable) evidence. Finally, the politically appointed attorney-general's legal services amendment seeking to remove the statutorily appointed solicitor-general's ability to consult with others in government without prior consent suggests the independence of advice is deemed subordinate to political will (even while that independence can be symbolically useful).

In my chapter on South Australia's blackout, I explored several weeks in the life of Australia's federal renewable energy policy setting and found it characterised by advisers' excision of unpalatable knowledge. In this chapter, I have so far considered two contemporaneous policy 'wins' and found a related mode of advice-giving prevailed. This similarity suggests policy advice and political objectives can align when the former is incomplete. While policy advice on the blackout was largely marked by departmental policy advisers' almost instinctive mode of 'knowing what not to know', the input of the solicitor-general on matters clearly linked to his advisory capabilities was simply not sought or sought only fleetingly. In other words, to respond to political objectives, these advisers either constrained themselves or constrained the input of evidence—the solicitor-general's—destined for political decision-makers.

This example also suggests governments can be reasonably sure their departmental policy advisers are unlikely to give them difficult written advice, while those, such as the solicitor-general and AEMO, who are further removed from government, ostensibly more independent and filtered by those advisers, are simply not included. In comparing these two, one also finds departmental policy advisers utilising once-removed expertise—from AEMO and the solicitor-general—as an input that symbolised evidence, facilitated the carrying out of their functions as purveyors of objective advice and created a buffer by which to minimise their direct accountability. In comparing examples of rebuffed and unrebuffed advice from within the same time frame, I have found a similar cultural impetus: an ingrained administrative milieu accustomed to limiting 'knowing in some directions' (Vaughan 1999: 931), which excludes either their own or relevant others' expertise if it is deemed politically discomfiting. My findings on rebuffed advice thus appear to extend to its unrebuffed counterpart.

This provides several insights into how policy advice escapes being rebuffed by its ministerial audiences. One is that potentially disagreeable expertise, which is more likely to be given the further away it resides from government, needs to be excluded to maintain the clarity of political policy preferences. A second is that being called independent is useful in helping governments signify objectivity if that type of advice does not put forward complicating or contrary views that might dilute or undermine the government's policy objectives. A third is that those objectives can appear to be within the law provided they are insulated from truly independent appraisal. A fourth is that ambiguity can operate as a safeguard not just against rebuffal, but also against other career consequences. To be more specific, being publicly unambiguous about the true content of one's advice can be career-limiting; Gleeson, like Clean Energy Finance Corporation CEO Oliver Yates, resigned shortly after his Senate appearance, on 24 October 2016.

In the chapter on intelligence about Iraq's WMD, we encountered a language marked by equivocation clothed in the appearance of independence. We saw that advice was accepted when it helped governments make their case to invade—perhaps most spectacularly illustrated by Colin Powell's 5 February 2003 speech to the United Nations in which he grouped experts who disagreed with the political argument that the centrifuges were capable of enriching uranium with the Iraqi government: 'Other experts, and the Iraqis themselves, argue that they are really to produce the rocket bodies for a conventional weapon, a multiple rocket launcher' (Powell 2003).

As Hersh reported in 2003, this demonstration of rebuffing unpopular expertise was the culmination of lengthy rhetorical battles within the Bush administration. To contest and challenge more circumspect assessments of Iraq's capabilities, the Pentagon's Office of Special Plans (OSP) sourced its own intelligence and, as an adviser who had worked with the OSP told Hersh, it

> cleaned up against [the] State [Department] and the C.I.A. There's no mystery why they won—because they were more effective in making their argument … They out-argued them. It was a fair fight. They persuaded the President of the need to make a new security policy … The [CIA] was out to *disprove* linkages between Iraq and terrorism. If you've ever worked with intelligence data, you can see the ingrained views at C.I.A that color the way it sees data … [The OSP] put the data under the microscope to reveal what the intelligence community can't see. (Hersh 2003; emphasis in original)

The OSP thus presented a dominant discourse that was compelling, urgent, all-seeing, powerfully argued and that undermined the intelligence community's doubts. The clarity of the OSP's intelligence was thus essential in representing an evidence base that could justify war.

A somewhat reminiscent dynamic played out in the Australian context, where advice provided to the government by officials from the attorney-general's and foreign affairs departments on the legality of invading Iraq went on to be used in a prime ministerial speech and tabled in parliament on 18 March 2003 (Commonwealth of Australia 2003). There have been dissenting views about the appropriateness of this advice, not least that the government did not pursue the correct channels in seeking advice, such as—unsurprisingly—the solicitor-general (see, for instance, Barratt 2016). These views are reasonable, particularly when one remembers that departmental policy advisers have seemed more likely to provide the type of advice that further-removed advisers, like the solicitor-general, will not. Yet it is also worth looking at the opening paragraph of the advice itself, which is starkly different to the cautionary tone of Australia's intelligence assessments:

> We have been asked whether, in the current circumstances, any deployment of Australian forces to Iraq and subsequent military action by those forces would be consistent with Australia's obligations under international law. The short answer is 'yes'. Existing United Nations Security Council resolutions provide

> authority for the use of force directed towards disarming Iraq of weapons of mass destruction and restoring international peace and security in the area. This existing authority for the use of force would only be negated in current circumstances if the Security Council were to pass a resolution that required Member States to refrain from the use of force against Iraq. (Quoted in SMH 2003)

Even allowing for the government seeking this advice for only one specific purpose, its vigour is in striking contrast to some of the excerpts encountered in my case studies. It is interesting to compare it with my earlier negative-gearing example, which was similarly requested for a single reason. Certainly, Treasury's advice modelled the opposition's policy while the advice at hand effectively sanctioned the government's oft-stated policy preference. The rhetorical difference between them, however, is vast. While the language of Treasury's piece revealed policy actors who seemed studiously unaware of the broader context, the language of Prime Minister Howard's legal advice was direct, persuasive and aware of the context in which it was being requested. This advice is also different to Gleeson's in that it was asked for and tailored precisely to government requirements. Knowing it would be accepted gave it the authority to be forceful and compelling and that strength, in turn, furnished the government with unequivocal information that helped frame the invasion as based on not only evidence but also the law, as both true and just. Policy and politics were mutually reinforcing.

There are other examples of rebuffed and unrebuffed advice within this approximate time frame, some of it straddling both domains. For example, the advice provided to the Australian Government regarding kickbacks paid by the then Australian Wheat Board to Iraq in the years leading up to the invasion is representative of the grey area created by tentative advice. Between 2000 and 2001, Australian diplomatic cables reporting potential irregularities in the Wheat Board's transport payments to Iraq seem to have been ignored by their administrative and ministerial audiences until disaster threatened (in the form of media exposure and the 2005–06 royal commission in Australia following the US Volcker Inquiry). When it struck, it was claimed some advice had been lost while the remainder was cast in a light that enabled the government to interpret it as proof it was unaware of the whole matter (see, for instance, Bradford 2006).

The administrative milieu of limiting 'knowing in some directions' is almost certainly a display of responsiveness to political expectations and all my examples are instances of this. Facing a choice between contrary candour and resigning one's position, on the one hand, and compliance and self-preservation on the other, this language and the culture from which it emerges exhibit an entirely reasonable preference for the latter. Relying on administrators to choose the latter, government ministers can be confident their policy advisers will continue to work hard to not embarrass them by giving them divergent or unpalatable advice. To fulfil expectations of objectivity and impartiality, policy advisers' language will increasingly bear signs of equivocation at best or excision at worst. They will operate in a twilight zone, where they go through the motions of reasoning in the public interest but their advice is constrained and tractable. Viewed in this way, it is really neither here nor there whether advice is objective, evidence-based, impartial or candid.

Triangulation

The above is not to say that objective and comprehensive policy advice does not exist, nor that government decisions are never based on such advice. Rather, it means my examples overwhelmingly did not demonstrate any such scenarios. Nonetheless, this is still an unsettling finding that requires further testing. Has my methodology—of utilising written material obtained through FOI or review processes—cast the net wide enough? Even though it has proved useful and productive because it has given us insights into advice constructed in its 'natural habitat' (inasmuch as this can be said to exist), I have essentially studied the construction of written knowledge at arm's length. Although I attempted to find ethnographic and other accounts to provide a thicker understanding of policy environments, I have not given policy advisers themselves an opportunity to reflect on their practices more directly.

Certainly, my at times forensic textual analysis enabled significant discoveries. Yet, while deep, perhaps my analysis was not broad or diverse enough, and thus returned the same or similar results across my case studies. If so, other methods should be used to triangulate my research. Writing about the interpretative approach as one that 'does not necessarily favour particular methods' or 'prescribe a particular toolkit for producing data', Rhodes (2018: 7–8) proposes a 'menu' of tools (in his case, 'ethnographic tools') with which to find 'other ways of "being there"' to recover meaning from policymaking. As a case in point, Boswell's work on anti-obesity advocacy in the United Kingdom and Australia draws on 'over 1000 documents, 25 hours of video footage and 36 semi-structured interviews' to determine how 'actors engaged in this policymaking network experienced and perceived the process and their role in it' (Boswell 2018: 124). Following in their footsteps, I propose briefly switching to interviews as part of my toolkit in piecing together the rest of my story about the rebuffed.

Unlike close textual analysis, interviews can offer valuable firsthand explorations of the 'activities and role perceptions of civil servants in their daily routines' (Geuijen et al. 2008: 25), in which interviewees can produce 'situated accounts' about 'their social reality' (Alvesson 2003: 17). Perhaps such accounts—as fallible as my principal methodology but ostensibly adding a more lived context—can show us what was absent in the advisory methods of my case studies' advisers?

As indicated earlier, policy advisers in Australia can be reluctant to discuss their work, particularly if they continue to hold official government positions. Speaking even without attribution can lead to speculation or discovery and, when the policy environment is as risk averse as my findings suggest, this is a reasonable concern, particularly in cases of perceived failure. But this becomes less of a concern when discussion centres on past policies viewed as successes. As we saw earlier, policy officials in various countries are generally more open to discussion with researchers, perhaps especially in the Netherlands, where there is 'a strong willingness to connect knowledge and policymaking' (Van Nispen and Scholten 2015: 2) owing to 'a high density of institutes specialised in policy analysis and a strongly institutionalised role of policy analysis in policymaking' (p. 4).

To help understand how the social realities of policy advisers might bear on how their advice is communicated and received, let us spend the remainder of this chapter listening to a handful of officials from two jurisdictions reflect on their work. From the Netherlands, three policy actors will discuss providing input into policies to address prison overcrowding; from Australia, advice on introducing the goods and services tax (GST) will be discussed by two officials who were closely involved in its implementation. It should be noted that, while the policies themselves form part of the overall background for these interviews, the way policy actors recount communicating their work to decision-makers is of key interest here. Given the greater willingness in Australia to speak on the record about past success, both policy samples depict a language of the unrebuffed. More broadly, we will see how a small sample of highly placed policy actors think about influence. I should add that all five agreed to be identified.

In May 2019, I spent three weeks in The Hague to talk to officials who had been involved in formulating and implementing alternative sanctions in the Netherlands throughout the 2000s and much of the 2010s— that is, they worked on how to address prison overcrowding by keeping people out of the prison system altogether or rehabilitating them in other settings. While Dutch postwar penal policy has ebbed and flowed between tolerance and punitivism (Campbell et al. 2017; Downes and van Swaaningen 2007), the Netherlands has been familiar with alternative forms of sanctions since the end of World War II. Although the reforms to incarceration under consideration here do not necessarily represent an unprecedented change to the status quo, they nonetheless occurred in a period of 'exacerbated public fears' and 'informal support for punitive policy' (Campbell et al. 2017: 548). My interview questions broadly asked how a potentially unpopular reform gained traction and how interviewed officials saw their role in the decision-making process.

My first interviewee, Michèle Blom, previously worked at the Ministry of Justice, where she was responsible for the development and implementation of prison reforms. When we spoke, she was director-general at the Netherlands Ministry of Infrastructure and Water Management. Blom acknowledged the hurdles to advising on unpopular policies:

> [O]f course, it's not popular to say prisons don't work; it's more popular that they work, and that people are behind bars for ages. So, we had this case as well in the 1990s and 2010s. In the 2000s, mainly because of the huge lack of capacity and lack of money. And in the 2010s, we again had politicians saying they [offenders] should be put behind bars for ages. (Blom 2019)

Her approach to overcoming these obstacles included consistent delivery of what she and her colleagues knew: '[W]hat we could do, because of all the studies, we could put all the figures upfront. We could say these are the facts. And, in my second period, we tried to put the topic again on the agenda' (Blom 2019).

But these facts were not simply handed by advisers to their ministers:

> What we did was not to start with the politicians here in The Hague at the state level, but we started with the politicians on the local level. In the Netherlands, the mayor of the city, they are responsible for social safety in their communities. And they were having a lot of problems with the people coming out of prison … At the same time, the state government had decentralised,

for example, youth work, which was at the higher level and it was decentralised to the local level. The mayors were getting responsibility for youth work … and saw that the people they were responsible for were the people leaving prison. They suddenly had a stake in the prison system.

What we did, when I was director-general, we started a process of telling those mayors, those people at the local level, that the people they were getting at their desks were receiving their help on welfare. We were telling them, actually, you have to deal with them, you have to help them. You have to get better agreements with us at the state level on people who are getting into the prison system. If we start at re-educating or resocialising them in prison, when they leave prison, half of the work is done and then you can do the rest of the work out of your own responsibility on welfare. Just by analysing who would have a stake, we were able to get, from the local level, on to the state level again the discussion of more money and more capacity not of prisons but of sanctions … I wasn't telling the minister what to do but the mayors were telling them they had a problem. They wanted to negotiate with him the state policy on prisons. (Blom 2019)

To help steer this multiplayer policy issue into the public arena, Blom described the mobilisation of a network of expertise:

My opinion of the civil servant is that he or she has to deliver the facts. There are different schemes for how to get to the solution but what we did, it wasn't just us who were giving the facts. It was also the mayors who were giving the facts to the minister, the people who work in this business, they gave the facts. There was actually a huge amount [sic] of stakeholders who were telling the same story. Not because we wanted them to tell the same story but because we organised it through the same process in which we invited all kinds of people and asked: Can you help us define the problem? What is the problem? Can you help define solutions as well? So, we were merely facilitating the process, then defining, as a civil servant, what the facts were. The outcome was the outcome of several stakeholders. Not the civil servants. That helped …

[T]he Dutch, they like facts. Maybe not the politicians, but the others, they like facts. Over the last years, you see an upcoming populism here as well, which we are very worried about because populism isn't based on facts, only on propaganda. So, as civil servants, we try to get those facts on the table all the time, again and again … [t]hrough these advisory boards, through getting all the stakeholders putting them on the table, by doing it ourselves. Actually, getting everybody in the policy arena to give the facts … on the table. (Blom 2019)

Blom's comments show civil servants steering a policy process in a particular way, not exactly as advocacy but rather by identifying interested stakeholders who could themselves carry their message, amplified by academics and advisory boards. A variety of groups repeating a unified message based on agreed facts made it easier for politicians to take policy action because it aligned with a group of informed exponents' preferred outcome.

Another perspective comes from Peter Hennephof, previously of the Custodial Institutions Agency at the Ministry of Justice, who went on to become the general secretary of the City of The Hague. In our discussion, he described a situation in which budget cuts had triggered a reconsideration of prison overcrowding. One of the solutions proposed was the use of anklets. This, however, raised the question of which crimes and sentences could be managed with anklets. Like Blom, Hennephof took a tactical approach when presenting this issue to his minister:

[W]e made up a list of the crimes and categories and took it to the minister. He looked at it and said, oh, no, no, no. No, this is politically impossible. But what we did, we had the numbers, but we had given him the list without the numbers. So, on our list we had a reduction of the number of cells of 1,800. By the time he was finished checking the list, he said, good plan, that's what we're going to do. Yes, but now there are only 324 left. 'Well, bad plan!'

… [W]hat we did, every time, was to make lists of possible scenarios. We started with about 30 or 35 locations. 'Oh, we have to close some' … But if you say, yes, we have this district and, dear minister, you still want a court and a police force and a prison in this district? 'Yes, yes, yes!' Okay. Well, then, this one we can't close because this is the only one in that district. So, we tried to, every time, we reflected on the effect of doing A or B. And sometimes we said no … you can't close the high-security prison because it is the only one we have. It is not possible. Unless you want the terrorists in the low-security prison. 'No, no, no!' The most difficult thing for us was, every time, to reflect on the political issues which were sometimes important … That was difficult, because the motivation of my own people, you have to be very keen on what's happening because, still, it's a prison with

> people who want different things, to keep them motivated, and
> on the other side, to confront the politicians with the possibilities
> and the impossibilities and the consequences. (Hennephof 2019)

Hennephof seemed doubtful of the power or efficacy of facts, expressing
a pragmatic attitude that expected to see real change only when scarce
resources prompted innovation:

> There was a point where we stopped thinking, our imagination
> stopped looking for more possibilities to reduce budgets. I learned
> something very important. In every mentionable book you can
> read, listen to the people who do the work … We decided [to] give
> the governors in the prisons the space to talk with their people …
> Then they started, I call them a student house. Now there are two
> or three blocks who are working on this principle. It reduces the
> number of people to run that block incredibly. Because the block
> itself, the prisoners, are responsible for running it … what you can
> save when you are changing the mindset … these kinds of things,
> more responsibility, that's why I say, give them the responsibility
> to run their own block. It's cheaper and more effective than many
> other programs … If you can't prove that it's worth it to invest in
> prisons and the whole chain, to rehabilitate people, it's worth it
> for society, if you can't prove that, I can understand that public
> opinion or the politicians say I am going to make an issue out of
> this. We have to invest in our prison system, in our rehabilitation.
> Okay, but why? … To be honest, we do measure. But open
> the black box—what happened? I think we are not that good.
> (Hennephof 2019)

This pragmatism and empathy with a sceptical public and political class,
however, did not replace attempts to be convincing and to effect policy
action; rather, they complemented them.

Finally, we will hear from an evidence producer. Frans Leeuw, a professor
of law, public policy and social science research at the University of
Maastricht, was the director of the International Institute of Justice and
Security Research (or WODC), which provides much of the scientific basis
for law-and-order policy for the Ministry of Justice. When I mentioned
the possibility of silence regarding disagreeable facts, Leeuw pointed out
he had himself been subject to an investigation that had tried to uncover
the same thing:

That is interesting that you say that, also on the basis of the investigations that have been taking place since last year by several committees, when I was accused in one of the reports— the weed [marijuana] credit card—of contextualising the results ... A committee looked into the more than 10,000 studies we had done—and published—over the last 15 years. Those were exactly my 15 years as director of the institute, and they found four studies where at least some people had said maybe something has been left out. Now, the point is why are issues left out? That point was not, or inadequately, addressed by that report. It can be that the program theory was only partially articulated, but it is also possible that a researcher is not focused on the specific problem and adds, so to say, anything and everything. The opposite is also possible: that researchers leave things out without a good, scientific reason. This is what happened, according to a second committee that looked very precisely into three drugs evaluation reports my institute had produced, and which concerned the accusation that I had 'contextualised' some things. That committee found that my involvement in that report had been to bring information back into the report, which was collected during the research but was left out by the researcher. I called that 'contextualisation'. According to the committee, this enhanced, instead of jeopardised, the quality of that evaluation. Moreover, all our reports are published on the website free as PDFs, so [they are] available to everybody. (Leeuw 2019)

The WODC is thus said to be comprehensive and open about its research, making all its reports public and even pushing back in the event of political pressure:

Many years ago, there was a situation where the Netherlands got a new Cabinet and one of the issues was to have minimum penalties. The question was if we could, with our prediction models, find out how many people would be in prison and what that would cost society ... We developed four scenarios and one of the senior researchers presented the scenarios in a meeting without documents and only a PowerPoint. I remember the then minister came up to me saying that he would appreciate to have a letter from me that same day saying that scenario X is the 'best' scenario. I said, 'I cannot do that as I do not know what best is as we did not have the time to do a thorough *ex ante* evaluation.' Then he mumbled something like that he 'had no use of this institute' or something similar and walked away. So, indeed ... sometimes policymakers believe so strong[ly] in their program theory, in their theory of the change, that they can't accept that things are working different[ly]. So, you simply have to say, 'Sorry, but we have to agree to disagree. This is your program, this is not a scientific theory, you are developing it as a policymaker or politician.' And we have the evidence after the program is implemented, multi-method and over the years. (Leeuw 2019)

Despite some of their differences—likely due to their different roles and perspectives—each of these speakers shows an understanding of what their ministerial audiences can tolerate and pull off in terms of policy implementation. Further, each is clear that informed and open problem-framing, as well as the participation of relevant stakeholders, can have a positive bearing on the prospects of a credible policy and political response. This, one might propose, is what Harding (1992) had in mind when calling for the use of 'standpoint epistemologies' to achieve 'strong objectivity'.

My Australian interviews contemplate the introduction of a consumption tax in 1999. Australia's GST represents a kind of microcosm of policy failure and success, which dominated two elections. The first, in 1993, led to the election loss of opposition leader John Hewson, who had advocated for a consumption tax, and the re-election of Prime Minister Paul Keating, who had campaigned against it. The second, in 1998, saw John Howard winning re-election on a platform that included the introduction of the GST. Its history also includes some stunning U-turns: despite being a passionate proponent of a consumption tax during the 1980s, Keating triumphantly denounced it in 1993, while Howard, who championed it in 1998, had only three years earlier promised to 'never ever' introduce it (Megalogenis 2012: 288). Paul McCullough, until recently a senior official at the Treasury, worked on implementing the tax package that included the GST as part of Treasury's Tax Taskforce from 1997. I interviewed him in Canberra on two occasions in early 2019. Reflecting on how he and the taskforce worked through the tax package in a way that would lead to an agreed position, he singled out understanding the 'detail on the implementation':

We probably spent as much, probably more, time on the implementation as the design of the thing in the first place. That, I think, meant the difference ... Because of all our work on the implementation ... things turned out almost exactly as we'd predicted ... The benefit of having been seen to have a well-managed process, it gave everybody a bit of confidence.

No matter how well [the government had] done in the '98 election, if the actual implementation of this thing in 2000 had been crap, they wouldn't have got up in 2001, other political issues notwithstanding. It wouldn't have mattered what had happened with other things if the GST had been implemented poorly. I reckon they would have lost in 2001. My thesis is, if it had been a bad implementation, nothing would have saved them. (McCullough 2019b)

To succeed at implementation, the taskforce's work was

very much an iterative process … So, whenever [the treasurer] asked a question, it was a kind of management of that issue. Look, if he's got a question and we don't have a convincing answer, that's on us. So, we had to find a way to respond to his questions, by the second time round, if we're going to stick to our guns, and say 'yes, this is true', we had to be able to explain it. Sometimes, the questions would make us say, 'Well, actually, we're not so strong on that, we've got to modify that, the language, the expressions, the concepts have got to be married to something else' or whatever. By the time you get to the Treasurer, and maybe we do two passes with him on each particular issue, we were pretty robust. (McCullough 2019b)

'We ended up,' McCullough (2019a) observed, 'with them truly understanding, rather than us trying to manipulate them.' McCullough also described another policy process, the Review of Self-Assessment, or ROSA, which is reminiscent of Blom's outreach:

In 2003–04, when it came to the Review of Self-Assessment, because it was so much to do with complaints from stakeholders … from people involved in the industry, the clear message was 'go out and involve them, make sure that they were happy with the answers'—doesn't matter what the answers are objectively, they've got to be good answers and answers that these people want. So, it was one of the first times Treasury started consulting. We did some wonderful things, we held kind of town forums, we went out to, I remember going to Wollongong and somewhere in regional Victoria, maybe somewhere in South Australia as well, where we invited a random sample of tax agents. We got 50 or 100 turning up, we gave a little spiel about what we were on about, what the government wanted to do and that we wanted to genuinely get their advice and their suggestions. We had a list of things for them to comment on … the success of ROSA—and it was regarded a success at the time—was just fundamentally about the change around the method of engagement, issuing a draft report and getting people to comment on the draft. That hadn't been done before, not since the old days of green papers and white papers. But for the 10 or 15 years in between, people had just gone straight to the white paper and it looked like government had ... [a] fait accompli. (McCullough 2019a)

Implementation and engagement were crucial to success, McCullough commented, and the difference between successful and unsuccessful processes

depends on whether you're prepared to listen. Only hearing and not saying ... collaboration is a concept that I think is tremendously important. If we are collaborating, I've got to accept that even if your views are different from mine, I can't just make a call ... That's the difference between good reports and bad reports. I think [A New Tax System, which included the GST] and ROSA, and a few of the other ones that might have been successful, genuinely say: here are these two conflicting views, and none of them can be successful without excluding the other. But here is a way of coming up with ... not a compromise, but a creative alternative that gives the best of both of these and the best of both of those. That, by the way, both of these interested parties say goes a long way to meeting a lot of their problems. (McCullough 2019a)

McCullough said he observed these kinds of strategies towards compromise or 'creative alternatives' less frequently now. Yet, even despite examples of effective policy processes, he seemed ultimately doubtful of policy advisers' influence. Asked whether policy advisers should ever pitch ideas to governments, McCullough responded:

I would have thought so ... I don't know whether we're stopp[ed] from pitching ideas, it's the influence with which we pitch ... I don't think we've ever really had it. I don't think we really ever had a clarity of ideas. We sort of got by asserting generalisations ... sometimes we haven't really understood the direction properly, sometimes we've argued amongst ourselves, but we've never effectively convinced them to go in a particular direction. That's the challenge that we're coming up to now ... I think the way you convince people is you bring the argument down to the practical level. You solve the implementation problems, you solve the communication problems ... if we are incapable of explaining it to the politicians in ways they can understand, well, no wonder everybody gets it wrong. (McCullough 2019b)

Even without influence, however, it still seemed possible to contribute to policy success in cases where the government had a clear policy direction:

> Distilled to its essence … the government had a particular intent [on tax reforms]. It was embodied in the collective choices of the Treasurer and the Prime Minister. Treasury's role was as the voice of experience, saying, 'Hey, you can do this' or 'Hey, you should modify that'. We used an active design process that took the gaps between those two things and tried to—that was the whole goal—try and get something we could both live with. If we could get that sort of process again, we could do anything … It does rely on the powerful element—the voice of intent, typically—agreeing to play. If they don't want to play, if they don't want to go through that design process, then, no, you can't. That's the only way you can ever do it, I think. If they just want to make their own choices—'you give us advice and we'll decide how to use it'—that's … a valid enough thing, they're the elected people, but it's a completely different process to the design process that actually has 'this is the goal I want to achieve, now let us work through, together, the best way for us to achieve that goal'. (McCullough 2019a)

While it was possible to simply be implementers of government preferences, it seems McCullough's philosophy was that a partnership between public servants and the government would make for truly effective policy outcomes. Intriguingly, here, as in the advice that provided the Australian Government's legal basis for invading Iraq in 2003, policy and politics can be viewed as mutually reinforcing. Unlike the Iraq example, however, which presented as a single requested piece of advice, McCullough's example displays an ongoing affiliation between policy and politics.

This sense of success through partnership is echoed by Ken Henry, who was secretary of the Treasury between 2001 and 2011. I interviewed Henry twice in Canberra in late 2017. Henry, who headed the Tax Taskforce, reflected that helping the government introduce the GST was

> probably the best policy process I'd ever been involved in … There have been more … exciting policy projects I've been involved in, but less satisfying in the sense of an appropriate partnering—I think partnership is the right word, an appropriate partnering—of the technical expertise and the policy messaging. Policy messaging is obviously principally the job of the politicians; it is their job to take ownership of the policy messaging; it is their policy, after all.

> But it's not something that public service advisers should … well,
> I guess they can divorce themselves from it, but I don't think they
> should divorce themselves from it. (Henry 2017b)

Yet, he questioned whether it was still possible to partner in this way
to 'deliver genuinely world's-best policy', not because policy advisers no
longer had the capacity, but because

> there's no political appetite … It's easy enough to understand why
> the politicians might be nervous about doing really challenging
> things, obviously, but there was a time in the 1980s and 1990s
> when politicians felt that they had no choice. John Howard did not
> announce this extraordinary review of Australia's taxation system
> because he thought it'd be a nice, fun thing to do. He genuinely
> thought he had no option. (Henry 2017b)

When asked whether there was a role for the APS to stimulate politicians
to do challenging things, Henry observed:

> It has to be the case that the public service cannot discharge its
> obligation to the executive government without having a very
> clear view itself on what might promote the welfare of the citizens.
> I took the view that it wasn't enough as a policy adviser or as a
> policy-advising department like the Treasury—it wasn't enough to
> have a view on what enhances the welfare of the citizens and then
> to develop policy proposals that you thought would do so and
> then to present them to the government and then leave it to the
> government. My view was if you did all of that, and the government
> still said 'not interested', then you should accept that you failed …
> That means you cannot take any comfort in the fact of providing
> outstanding technical advice that goes nowhere, well, that goes to
> government and then doesn't go anywhere; that doesn't translate
> into change, into something which does improve the lives of
> people, the wellbeing of the Australian people; then you've got to
> take some responsibility for that. Now, what does it imply about
> how you should do your job—well, I think it does mean you've
> got to be capable of preparing policy advice in a manner which is
> sufficiently compelling to motivate government action. I think it
> does mean that. The really tricky thing for a policy person is that,
> because you're part of the executive government, it's difficult for
> you to go out publicly and agitate. Public agitation always runs the
> risk of embarrassing the government—that's obviously inimical.
> That cannot possibly help you in achieving your mission. But it's
> also possible, I still think it is possible, for senior public servants
> anyway, to play a role—a public role—talking directly to the

public in a way which actually makes it easier for government to accept your advice, your policy advice, on ways to improve the wellbeing of the Australian people. (Henry 2017c)

Henry here goes further than Blom in setting out a public role for senior public servants, where public dialogue of some sort complements the production of persuasive policy advice. It is the responsibility of public servants, Henry seems to be saying, to communicate their expertise broadly. One way of making that possible, he argued, was to

> motivate either a public call for action or even just a preparedness on the part of the public to hear from government about particular initiatives, to deal with those emerging challenges. It might be something the government is not necessarily interested in, but … if there's growing public interest in the issues then government may be interested … I am convinced that the Hawke government and Keating government—they might not see it this way—but I reckon they were assisted mightily by the fact that a generation of mainly academics had agitated for very broad, sweeping reforms before they were elected to government. Some senior public servants, too, had contributed to the public debate in a way that ultimately proved helpful to the Hawke/Keating reforms. And also to Howard … when he decided that he was going to embrace a GST reform, in 1997, having ruled it out in the election campaign in 1996, he could not have done that, he could not have seen that as being a sensible thing to do politically, had it not been for decades of agitation from academics and from some leading public servants who had set up the case publicly. That ultimately proved helpful. Anyway, the optimistic side of me thinks that there is still a role for the public service to play … Maybe we need some institutional arrangements, I don't know, some tinkering or maybe even major changes to the arrangements. I don't think it's an inappropriate role for a public service to play because it is a role which I consider to be helpful to executive government even if it may not always be helpful to the government of the day. (Henry 2017c)

Henry's final words here remind us of Mulgan's (2008) thoughts on democratic integrity—that is, of a public service reasoning not on behalf of a transient political context but more durably and in the public interest. More broadly, there are some compelling similarities among these interviews, despite their differences in social, cultural and political contexts. One theme that emerged strongly is that of advisers encouraging others to be stakeholders and then facilitating their being heard (Blom, McCullough and Henry), thus making it politically possible for potentially unpopular policy change to occur. This strategy was also apparent in Chapter 2 when I briefly discussed tax reform in New Zealand. Constructing a public case for governments was evident not just in relationship-building, but also through policy–political partnerships (Blom, Henry, McCullough); understanding political limitations (Leeuw, Henry); openness to other ways of doing business (Hennephof, McCullough); comprehensiveness through multiplayer problem definition and fact negotiation (Blom, Leeuw, McCullough); the ability to vouch for the 'facts' to enable political players to understand and own the issues (Blom, Leeuw, McCullough); making those issues practical (Hennephof, McCullough); and tenacity and consistency (all of them). Based on their statements, it is easy to imagine each of my interviewees engaging comfortably with some of the hallmarks of a professional civil service, which, according to Paul du Gay, include 'the possession of enough skill, status and independence to offer frank and fearless advice about the formulation and implementation of distinctive public purposes and to try to achieve purposes impartially, responsibly and with energy if not enthusiasm' (2000: 146).

Indeed, they all indicated an openness to adaptation, a culture of curiosity and comfort with uncertainty, which Luetjens and 't Hart (2019: 28) named as the characteristics of successful policy advisers in their submission to Australia's most recent public service review. It is interesting to note the Netherlands and Australia here seemed far more alike than they did in my renewable energy case study.

Comparing these interviews with my rebuffed examples may seem like comparing apples with oranges. For example, interviews are substantially different accounts to FOI-released emails, the former being retrospective and potentially subjective while the latter were organisationally dependent and formulated in real time. Further, the case studies were part of ongoing policy processes while the interviews detailed policy reform outcomes. But I did not set out to achieve a neat comparison between two methodologies. Instead, I sought to cast my net wider to see whether something was missing from my findings that constrained policy advice appears to be common across both rebuffed and unrebuffed tropes, while robust, comprehensive advice seems rare. Giving policy advisers an opportunity to reflect on their practices revealed what was missing from my case studies: the ability to adapt and reason in the public interest, even in tricky circumstances. My interviews showed this to be the case in a contemporary setting in the Netherlands, as well as in Australia in the late 1990s. Although this clearly broadens and enriches my original findings, it does not stretch them out of shape. Indeed, it gives them greater emphasis in the sense that it is difficult to imagine the themes and behaviours observed in my policy advisers' firsthand reflections were present in my case studies.

We have now observed policy advisers who argue robustly in the public interest, and those who do not—the latter perhaps due to the absence of what McCullough called a political voice of intent. How and whether civil services should work in the public interest are as contested as the meaning of the phrase itself (Mulgan 2000a, 2000b; Raman et al. 2018). Yet, the public interest has been the underlying concern of this book as it sought to interrogate whether the language of policy advisers enables unfounded or arbitrary political manoeuvres. It will guide my conclusion as this discussion draws to a close.

6

Conclusion

I have critically analysed three case studies drawn from different streams of knowledge production across the Australian Public Service: the economy, energy and the environment, and national security. Each was chosen due to its originally confidential nature but eventual public availability by means of two FOI requests and a parliamentary review process. Viewing the written advice associated with these case studies through my framework made it possible to examine, as closely as publicly possible, the ways in which the written communications of policy advisers were overlooked or reinterpreted by their government audiences. I then unravelled the specific features of how those policy communications came to be rebuffed with the help of that framework, which is reproduced here both for ease of reference and to identify how it enabled my conclusions.

Table 6.1 Complete rebuffed framework

	Focus	Question
1.	*Kairos*	What effect does time have on the advice?
2.	Context	How does context potentially affect language — and does language affect context?
3.	Awareness of self and audience	How is the advice conceived of, how is it framed and what does its audience do with it?
4.	Response	What is the political reaction to the advice and how is it formed?
5.	Expectations	What are the expectations — legislated and/or institutional — of the adviser?
6.	Culture	Does culture influence the language of the policy adviser?
7.	Effect on knowledge	How might this bear on how policy expertise is constructed and communicated?

	Focus	Question
8.	Engagement with objectivity and evidence	Is the spectre of 'objectivity' present in policy advice? How does the advice engage with or construe the notion of evidence?
9.	International comparisons and contexts	What do international comparisons tell us about Australia's rebuffed advice? Are contexts and circumstances similar or is Australia unique?
10.	Language of contemporaneous unrebuffed advice	Can some conclusions be reached about rebuffed advice by viewing it alongside advice sourced from around the same time that was accepted?

The framework essentially grouped questions into three layers: words (which encompassed time, context, framing and response), institution (which included expectations, culture and the construction of policy expertise) and world (which considered how the requirement for objectivity influenced the construction of evidence, including internationally and against unrebuffed counterparts). By carefully locating how and when advice was constructed, the first grouping revealed a language that visibly avoided the political context even while being almost entirely propelled by it. My analysis of the organisational conditions under which advisers construct their expertise in the second grouping uncovered their struggle with uncertainty to produce advice that could represent responsiveness and evidence. By panning out to take in how objectivity is assembled when it rubs up against official interpretations of reality, the third grouping showed advisers providing expert validation for governments' preferred world view. Viewed separately, each grouping identified some key, largely hidden dimensions of official advice. Viewed as a whole, my framework uncovered the entrenched ways in which policy advisers stand in the way of facilitating public accountability.

This hindrance expressed itself in three broad types of articulating advice that seemed designed to fit almost any interpretation, each giving its ultimate communicator/s much rhetorical leverage:

1. Advice focused extensively on one strand of inquiry while sidestepping the wider context, making it possible for the government to claim, at various moments, that advice was both contrary to and consistent with its position.

2. Advice expunged complexity, thereby giving the appearance of certainty and solid evidence, enabling the government to maintain the threat of renewables to energy security.

3. Advice routinely raised the presence of inconclusiveness, leaving it unusable as evidence while handing the government its rationale for invading Iraq.

Each of these three types struggled to accommodate its legislated obligations to be objective and frank while also being responsive to the government of the day. This book, through its framework, witnessed the emergence of a policy rhetoric that appeared as a contorted language of myopic expertise, which, at least superficially, ensured the concurrence of objectivity and responsiveness. The first type, observed in Treasury's advice on negative gearing, addressed the treasurer's question but bypassed crucial context. The second (advice about South Australia's blackout) frequently responded with status updates but little else. The third (intelligence assessments on Iraq's WMD) weakened its impact by responding with an 'excess of objectivity' (Sarewitz 2004: 388), enabling the influence of those with a simpler, more conclusive story to tell. While they appear to have been constructed in ways that adhered to their obligations, this may be precisely why each type also proved problematic as means with which to account for political decisions. This left policy advice incapable of serving as a tool to govern democracy.

A brief review of my case studies will extract their key moves. My introductory case study on negative-gearing advice by Australia's Treasury was used to construct a three-tier framework comprising text, micro-context and macro-context, each of which revealed an aspect of the language of the rebuffed. By closely analysing the text of Treasury's briefing and emails, one saw how text connected to timing, context, framing and even self-perception. Featuring a policy-advising frame of 'pure information' that seemed to exist in a temporal vacuum, this policy advice allowed detail to dominate context, making it easy to invite multiple interpretations and doubts. Even when a further FOI request in 2018 revealed Treasury attempting greater clarity in some follow-up advice, the government was able to argue that its position was not inconsistent with Treasury's advice.[1] As we know, the way experts frame issues can shape perceptions of their credibility (Lachapelle et al. 2014), but the framing by Treasury experts here made it possible for government ministers to undermine Treasury's credibility while resurrecting it when needed. Even while some argued that Treasury's advice contradicted the

---

1   At the time, the acting treasurer noted that Treasury's advice 'confirms what we have been saying all along' (Karp 2018a).

government (Conifer and McKinnon 2019), the subsequently released FOI text revealed Treasury accommodating the government's position by helpfully suggesting its advice had not been 'inconsistent with what the Government has been saying' (see The Treasury 2019a).

The micro-context focused on the institutional effects on advisers' language. Here, one could observe a culture potentially overly reliant on its reputation. Treasury argued against making public its briefings on negative gearing for two years, claiming disclosure would prejudice its ability 'to provide candid and confidential advice to ministers'. When made public, the briefings revealed very little of its legislated requirement to be frank, nor did they display any degree of the forthrightness the APS frequently claims will be forgone with uncompromising FOI laws. The macro-context linked to trust in objectivity and evidence, both in Australia and internationally. As suggested earlier, an important characteristic of credibility is being seen to be objective (Porter 1995). Becoming credible by means of objectivity can require 'strategies of impersonality' (Porter 1995: 229). While those strategies can be used within civil services as a protective measure to defend against criticism, they also exert an inhibiting influence on how policy advisers articulate and argue. In the case of negative gearing, advising in this way was unmasked as inadequate; it was easy to rebuff and reinterpret advice when it became politically necessary. When objectivity is no longer enough to be credible and convincing, authority is increasingly attributed to those who convey judgement, practice and experience (Jasanoff 2005). Treasury conveyed none of these, maintaining its singular gaze on technicalities instead of providing a clear account of its knowledge so that policy rationales could be meaningfully appraised by interested others.

Chapter 3 chronicled FOI-released advice by the departments of the Prime Minister and Cabinet and Environment and Energy following South Australia's statewide blackout. To accommodate government rhetoric about renewable energy as the cause of the blackout, policy advice was careful not to contradict that rhetoric by excluding anything that might have challenged the government's narrative. This was achieved largely by issuing frequent factual updates, which gave the advice the appearance of being objective and responsive—as well as a variety of other behaviours, such as advisers' anticipatory compliance, their transactionality as vendors of rudimentary information, ambiguity, one-dimensionality and unknowingness. I also offered some insights into FOI itself and how officials often react to it. Others have discussed FOI as allowing those in authority to engage in 'feigned ignorance' (McGoey 2007: 217) to fly under the radar, and this can undoubtedly be the case. But communicating ignorance is a more pervasive institutional response that cannot be explained solely by way of FOI, because not knowing can hold broader political capital, which offers both a 'reprieve from having to answer for the consequences of one's knowledge' and 'protection from blame' (McGoey 2007: 230). This means ignorance can act to counter the challenge of being held accountable for unfortunate outcomes (Best 2012) and serve as a social glue for maintaining working relationships between officials and ministers. Yet, when not knowing or not advising becomes an institutional, cultural response, it is also part of bureaucratic identity and can lead to acceptance or standardisation of failure.

Feigned ignorance has additional downsides. By excising facts about relevant matters, policy advice appeared consistent with government rhetoric and implied that rhetoric was supported by policy evidence. Although politically convenient, by abandoning candid argument in favour of myopia, advisers in this case study effectively undermined the independence of their expertise. This realisation led me to speculate how such behaviours, frequently driven by the requirement for responsiveness, can impede the conditions for accountability in a democracy. It is understood that 'the completely neutral bureaucracy is a myth rather than an empirical reality' and 'all democracies have to balance demands for both neutral expertise and political responsiveness' (Hustedt and Salomonsen 2014: 746). It is also understood that 'the policies that can produce the greatest amount of political support are often not the policies that are most beneficial to citizens' (Holcombe 2016: 9). Yet, being responsive goes beyond acting in accordance with the wishes of one's political masters. It is also about telling governments what they need to know if they want to meet their chosen objectives, which is a duty that serves the public interest: it cuts across responsiveness and stems from independent considerations of democratic integrity (Mulgan 2008). The deliberate silence and ambiguity observed in this case study did not simply avoid criticism or preserve relevance; they overlooked the legislated obligation to help governments deliver on their promised commitments and compromised the public's ability to hold government to account.

My third case study considered Australian intelligence assessments of Iraq's WMD between 2002 and 2003. The assessments by ONA and DIO were split between responsiveness and objectivity, respectively. For its part, DIO repeatedly acknowledged gaps in evidence and the related lack of consensus generated by those gaps, signifying a more concerted attempt to be comprehensive than any of the other organisations examined in this book. Prime Minister John Howard used this element of doubt to dismiss arguments that absolute proof was needed, thus effectively borrowing the inconclusiveness emanating from DIO's assessments as his strategy for action. We have seen acknowledgement of doubt, such as DIO's, utilised in other types of expert advice like science and economics, and that this language is easy for political actors to disrupt. ONA's assessments, on the other hand, gradually aligned with the dominant political discourse. Despite ONA's responsiveness and DIO's objectivity, neither was used by the government and both went on to eventually shoulder the blame for Iraq's nonexistent WMD.

Even while reviews of intelligence in Australia have been cognisant of the difficulty of being both connected to political decision-making and sufficiently detached from it, and understand that it cannot always be accurate, expectations of intelligence still assume it can provide 'hard evidence about the often harsh realities of how the world works' (PM&C 2017a: 32). Yet, what my examination revealed was a culture mostly characterised by a reticence to exercise judgement and an eagerness to be responsive; an acceptance of its own world view as an undisputed marker of reality; indistinctiveness in 'the analytical and interpretative processes' (Eriksson 2016: 204); and, given its practice of executive filtering, an ingrained administrative milieu accustomed to limiting knowing in some directions (Vaughan 1999) similar to the previous case study. Despite or perhaps because at least parts of this culture were liable to soft politicisation (Rovner 2013), it was easily scapegoated for failure (Flood 2004; Chilcot 2016). Each of these alone, not to mention in combination, made it possible for political actors to credibly blame knowledge producers for failure. Indeed, advice became the backbone for the construal of failure. That is, even though subsequent review processes across each of the major players' jurisdictions made a show of holding their various governments to account, it was the language of advisers that ultimately bore the brunt of political failure. Certainly, some of that language may not have been as judicious as it could have been, particularly in the UK and US contexts. But in Australia's case, the language of intelligence advice made it possible for Howard to remain untouched by accountability mechanisms in the sense that he could truthfully claim to have been aware of all the evidence, whether certain or uncertain, and that he reflected those views publicly. With the implication that he followed intelligence in good faith, this gave his own claims of intelligence failure a canny ring of truth.

My penultimate chapter examined what appeared to be unrebuffed policy advice: amendments to Australian citizenship, marriage equality and the legal basis for military action in Iraq. Drawn from similar time frames to my case studies, these examples were examined to gauge whether their ostensibly successful outcomes could be attributed to a less-conflicted policy language and whether that looked different to the language of the rebuffed. Only the legal advice on invading Iraq could be said to have spoken that language, albeit with strong qualifications. That is, requested by and tailored precisely to the government, this advice could be forcefully argued because its drafters knew it would be accepted. In this circumstance, it seemed possible to argue frankly and fearlessly—perhaps because there was nothing to fear. Examples on citizenship and marriage equality were shown to feature characteristics related to my rebuffed examples in that each involved elements of constraint: policy advisers either constrained themselves or constrained the input of evidence destined for political decision-makers. Even when observing 'unrebuffed' types of advice-giving, this book was unable to find frankly argued advice that resisted accommodating political circumstances. This seemed to indicate that we had discovered a practice of avoiding making difficult judgements, making it difficult for citizens to trace and scrutinise policy rationales.

Although this confirmed my hypothesis that some policy advice is constructed in ways that render meaning malleable, enable arbitrary or unfounded political manoeuvres and thus obfuscate public accountability, it was still an alarming discovery. I therefore tested my findings by switching methodology. I speculated whether examining language and culture at arm's length—even while performed in almost forensic detail—may have held some limitations. To that end, I turned to interviews as providing a potentially more grounded appreciation of the social realities of advice-giving. We heard from two long-serving Australian policy officials about the introduction of a consumption tax and three Dutch policy officials, who discussed reforms to address prison overcrowding. There were some compelling similarities across these interviews, despite their small number and different contexts. These included advisers encouraging stakeholder participation, which helped facilitate politically uncomfortable policy change; a partnership between policy and politics; appreciation for political limitations; adaptability; and negotiated problem-solving by way of openness. All my interviewees, we might say, worked with the grain (Palmer et al. 2019). I also found my interviewees displayed many of the traits usually associated with successful policy advisers, such as 'status and independence' (du Gay 2000: 146), as well as 'space for doubt, [comfort] with uncertainty, well aware of limitations, and [seeking] errors and failures as data points rather than as sources of professional embarrassment and political risk' (Luetjens and 't Hart 2019: 28).

By hearing from just a handful of policy advisers, one was able to see a contrast with the constrained, almost timid communications of my case studies. This contrast thickened our understanding of policy advisers. Ultimately, however, we simply saw a gulf between empowered policy actors who use their judgement in the public interest and those who avoid it. Much in the same way as evaluation forms 'a legitimizing part of bureaucratic life' when it becomes captured and loses its '"instrumental function" of informing decisions and speaking truth to power' (Raimondo and Leeuw 2021: 145), the language of the rebuffed is not without advantage. All three of my main case studies indicated that advisers had assembled a way of reasoning that could both look truthful *and* be suited to whatever decision the government chose to adopt. This is different to Palmer et al.'s (2019) notion of working with the grain in the sense that, although it may look like a hybridisation of advice and politics on the surface, it is actually a withdrawal from actively engaging with either. In a counterfactual world where these three reasoned more strongly in the public interest, Treasury could have provided a more usable, contextually aware policy basis for the government to formulate a sustainable argument on negative gearing; advice on renewables could have more frequently articulated its awareness of inconclusive evidence and helped the government adapt to new information as it came to hand; and intelligence assessments could have explained the process by which their knowledge is constructed to qualify what their uncertainty meant. Even while these sorts of approaches may have made advice more robust and inclusive, it may still have been rebuffed; yet it would also have made it substantially easier for interested citizens to assess political actors' policy rationales.

It could be argued that the types of rebuffed policy language encountered in this book are essentially coping mechanisms for policy advisers in highly complex environments. Although pragmatic, coping in this way disregards the needs of those who wish to engage in the political decision-making process and follow the input that influences and guides those decisions. My introduction argued that this mode of operating renders meaning malleable and leaves political actors free to reinterpret the offerings of their policy advisers, contributing to the erosion of trust in democracy because *any* advice can thus conceivably give governments the rationale on which to make *any* decision. This malleability also effectively means there is no record properly available for scrutiny and, thus, no accountability for tracing how political decisions are made. Writing in the context of releasing government records, Goldfarb argues: 'If the public cannot scrutinize government policies by checking public records, democratic society is endangered' (2009: 57). The same is true of public records that camouflage or evade meaning.

Illustrated by three types, this book contends that the language of policy advice effectively excludes interested publics from gaining accurate impressions of the basis on which their elected representatives make decisions on their behalf and whether those decisions have been subject to robust reasoning in the public interest. Invoking the public interest is all very well; it alludes to a higher ground and suggests that serving it must be morally good. Surely this is what civil servants are working towards? But can it really be claimed that civil servants, such as those in the APS, are directly working in and for the public interest? There are two broad views on this in the Australian context.

One view proposes that 'the primary duty' of career public servants 'is to be true to their professional conscience as "statesmen in disguise"' by following a 'professional agenda of what they hold to be in the public interest' (Uhr 1999: 100). Here, public servants themselves interpret what is in the public interest. The other view sees that duty as being 'responsive to requests for assistance from the government of the day' by only providing 'advice that fits within the framework of the government's questioning' (Uhr 1999: 100). Although the latter may still include public servants' interpretation of the public interest, it can only guide their actions up to a certain point. That is, although 'public servants do have a role as guardians of the public interest in protecting constitutional processes', they have 'no right to impede or challenge a government decision' (Mulgan 2000b: 3). In the absence of 'explicit direction', such as exactly how a policy is to be achieved, a public servant 'will have to trust his or her own judgment about what the public interest demands', which can take the form of '"frank and fearless" advice'. However, such advice should only be given 'within the context of the government to reach its own goals and objectives', which precludes the 'right of the public servant to insist on his or her own view of the public interest' (Mulgan 2000a: 11). As such, there can potentially be two types of public interest: that of the public servant as a guardian whose responsibility is to what they deem to be in the public interest, and that of the public servant serving the government's construal of the public interest. My case studies leaned towards the latter and, as such, it seems severe to hold them responsible for inhibiting the public interest. But when public servants contribute to the inability of the governed to 'evaluate the knowledge claims that justify actions taken on [their] behalf' (Jasanoff 2006: 21), they stray dangerously close to serving only the interests of the government.

Locating the public interest—what it is and precisely whom it serves—is not easy. For instance, as Raman et al. show, when calling on the public to support scientific research, political discourse often tends to link science with the public interest, characterising it in terms of 'technological solutions to economic, health and environmental challenges' (2018: 232). This presumes a widely shared conception of scientific research as a public benefit. Yet, members of the public with divergent positions, such as those who engage in 'public protests against topics such as genetically modified (GM) crop trials or animal experiments' (Raman et al. 2018: 230), appeal and lay claim to the public interest as well. With more than one conception of it, it is harder for governments to maintain they are acting in the public interest. However, those with a different conception can periodically shift and renegotiate what is in the public interest (Raman et al. 2018: 230) when they insert themselves into wider debate: public support for scientific research can only be said to have been achieved when the public has had its say and been heard (p. 235). It is public engagement, in other words, that determines the public interest (Raman et al. 2018: 237). Under this reasoning, the public interest is only fully realised when the public itself is involved, not just the government or its civil service.

Most of the time, of course, this is not how public policy is made nor is it necessarily always practical. Indeed, the public's engagement is presumed through their participation in the election process. And, as Mulgan concludes, 'democratic principle dictates that elected politicians should generally have the right to decide the particular balance to be given to the various elements constituting the public interest' (2000a: 11). The overall impression is one of successive governments ascertaining what is in the public interest, and of their civil service policy advisers helping them work towards each government's conception of the public interest as their primary goal. When I claim that the language of the rebuffed does not serve the public interest, I am not disputing this arrangement.

Serving governments' constructions of the public interest is proper conduct for officials. Indeed, it is one of the most democratic functions of policy advisers.

The way in which officials carry out their advisory function here in Australia, however, neglects the public's ability to assess policy decisions made on its behalf. Further, serving successive governments' interpretation of the public interest does not preclude, nor should it stop, public policy officials from arguing and reasoning with a longer view towards accommodating the public's potential engagement with policy directions and decisions. This is not the same as impeding or challenging a government decision (Mulgan 2000b: 3). Rather, it facilitates a strengthening of such decisions in the sense that publics seeing and understanding policy rationales can enhance how effective those rationales are in their implementation or, alternatively, how they might usefully be shifted and renegotiated to become more effective. Policy advice thus argued is surely a key component in facilitating control of the government by the governed (Gruber 1987: 1).

In exactly this vein, Dewey has argued that 'discussion and publicity' can bring about 'some clarification' of what our common interests are (1946: 207). In Dewey's estimation, the public interest can be identified and developed by way of democratic discussion and deliberation, which include crafting policy advice in a way that does not hinder or obscure public assessment. There will be those who consider Dewey a somewhat outmoded preceptor for the issues outlined in this book. After all, why apply yesterday's solutions to tomorrow's problems? But with the seemingly inexorable executive concentration of governmental power and its concomitant squeezing out of public participation, one could do worse than look to Dewey as a proxy for supporting greater public assessment and, thus, accountability. When the public is not able to engage in 'discussion and publicity', he continues, there is 'no way of telling how apt for judgment and social policies the existing intelligence of the masses may be' (Dewey 1946: 209). Dewey instructs that what is needed in bringing about such meaningful deliberation is

> the improvement of the methods and conditions of debate, discussion and persuasion. That is *the* problem of the public. We have asserted that this improvement depends essentially upon freeing and perfecting the processes of inquiry and of dissemination of their conclusions. Inquiry, indeed, is a work which devolves upon experts. But their expertness is not shown in framing and

executing policies, but in discovering and making known the facts upon which the former depend. They are technical experts in the sense that scientific investigators and artists manifest *expertise*. It is not necessary that the many should have the knowledge and skill to carry on the needed investigations; what is required is that they have the ability to judge of the bearing the knowledge [sic] supplied by others upon common concerns. (1946: 208–9)

In this view, it is not enough simply to enact policies with rationales that are ostensibly based on malleable advice. What is needed is for policy advisers to clearly articulate relevant material so the public can track whether and how political decisions were made based on relevant knowledge. To fail to articulate policy expertise in this way is to deny the public the opportunity to judge whether their interests have been served. This was the inherent failure of my case studies.

Following Dewey, we can therefore posit that one key way of making democratic deliberation possible is making policy advice assessable by, and accountable to, the public. In turn, the public's ability to judge whether government decisions are in the public interest is at least partly facilitated by way of policy advisers' clear and comprehensive articulation of relevant material and argument. If it is difficult for the public to do so, the public interest cannot be established. But, more than this, Dewey also proposes that it is this type of exchange that creates a public. When he refers to the public and its problems, he singles out 'its most urgent problem: to find and identify itself' (Dewey 1946: 216). One way of bringing about this discovery is to become 'an articulate democratic public' (Dewey 1946: 217), which can only be generated by 'systematic and continuous inquiry' (p. 218) into 'the knowledge supplied by others upon common concerns' (p. 209), such as the facts on which policies depend (p. 208). Based on this view, I suggest that facilitating the public's ability to judge and assess policy rationales is not simply *in* the public interest; it *is* the public interest, because only in being able to scrutinise can the public build a picture of what is in its interest. The language of the rebuffed prevents this from happening.

I wrote these words almost at the same time as the final report of the government's latest review into the APS, as well as its response to the review's recommendations, were released. Refreshingly, the review recognised that major change was needed:

The APS is at a watershed. It is not broken but it faces a set of
current issues and future challenges that make transformation
essential. This report provides a strong, evidence-driven set of
recommendations to guide short-term change and long-term
reform. And, through extensive consultation and engagement,
the review has been part of an important conversation across and
outside the service about ensuring that an enduring institution
of Australia's democracy is fit for purpose. There is a mandate for
change. (PM&C 2019c: 31)

Armed with an arsenal of 755 public submissions and 814 online
comments (PM&C 2019b), these highly aspirational words are backed
by 40 recommendations, including three related to a cluster of work
labelled 'deep expertise, stronger advice' (PM&C 2019c: 220). While
not absolutely aligned, the focus of this cluster chimes with much of
what this book has observed. For instance, in highlighting the benefits of
performance evaluation, the review raises the importance of accounting
for how organisations arrive at their knowledge and finds that publishing
evaluation findings can embed greater transparency and rigour (PM&C
2019c: 221). 'The greater transparency of performance that will flow from
a new approach to evaluation,' the review suggests, 'must be welcomed,
not disparaged, by all affected parties' (PM&C 2019c: 222). Making
such assessments of performance widely available, anticipates a former
secretary quoted in the review, will enhance 'people's trust in government'
(PM&C 2019c: 222).

The review also finds that 'senior APS leaders continue to be risk averse
and reluctant to find new ways of working', which 'reflects a culture
that rejects experimentation, innovation and learning from successes
and failures' (PM&C 2019c: 224), singling out a departmental reflex
to 'pre-empt or divert criticism' (p. 225). Again, to embed change that
counters these behaviours, the review proposes greater transparency—
this time, through wider dissemination of evidence bases: 'Research is
of interest and value to the APS and governments, as well as the broader
public. Publishing research, and public debate on it, strengthens the
quality of work' (PM&C 2019c: 225).

This resonates strongly not only with the work practices and mindsets
encountered in this book, but also with my adaptation of Dewey's thoughts
on democratic deliberation. Such candidness is likely to generate anxiety
among governments and bureaucracies more commonly accustomed to
caution. To that end, the review puts forward a possible handling strategy:

> The panel recognises that, at times, the publication of research can be sensitive, and proposes that Secretaries Board [sic] agrees protocols with the minister responsible for the public service on timely publication of research, after an appropriate period for the Government's consideration. This must preserve the independence of the research itself. (PM&C 2019c: 225)

Finally, to rise to the challenges of a world that 'has become more interconnected, diverse, and complex in the face of advances in technology, and societal and geopolitical shifts', where 'the connections between Australia's social, economic and security interests are becoming more entwined', the review urges the APS to get better at providing robust advice that 'frames challenges, identifies ways to manage risks broadly, and balances these interests to provide truly integrated advice to ministers' (PM&C 2019c: 227). 'Given the entrenched ways of working within the APS', the review concludes, 'a structural solution is needed to stimulate a change in culture' (PM&C 2019c: 228). Readers may recall the more timid words of the review's interim report, partly reproduced in my introduction. Here, in the review's final recommendations, one finds a greater depth of self-analysis and appreciation for the limitations that can give rise to weak, ineffective advice. Even though, as the review notes, it is the eighteenth of its kind in just a decade (PM&C 2019c: 16), there is cause for optimism that a way can be found for the language of policy advice to become stronger: through transparency, a relative increase of independence, less risk aversion, as well as attention to multiple viewpoints and the public interest.

The then government's somewhat equivocal response to these recommendations, however, did not seem as promising. For instance, while its endorsement of 'appropriate publication of completed evaluations' (Australian Government 2019: 22) seemed auspicious, it rejected 'publication of research' and 'does not consider it necessary' to pursue mechanisms to bring about more robust advice through cultural change (p. 23). When one considers that the release of the review and the government's response to it were preceded by the then prime minister terminating the employment of five departmental secretaries and his announcement that good policy advice was simply the implementation of government instructions (Morrison 2019), it is difficult to foresee— even with a change of government—a cultural change that embraces risk, greater independence, multiple viewpoints or, indeed, the public interest as vital ingredients in the formulation of policy advice. Further, lacking official backing for evaluation is likely to maintain a status quo in which rebuffable language continues to be helpful to political actors.

I have revealed three types of ineffective rebuffed policy language. There may be many more. But if these past exemplars—spanning more than a decade in which the APS served both sides of government—are any indication, one may reasonably expect similar responses in the future. What, then, might the future hold? According to Dewey, there are two options. The first is oligarchy: 'No government by experts in which the masses do not have the chance to inform the experts as to their needs can be anything but an oligarchy managed in the interests of the few' (Dewey 1946: 208).

This option resonates with the timidly enabling advice on renewable energy, with its seeming disinclination for frankness.

The second is a situation where silence or withheld views and opinions— by either the public or advisers—are reduced to soliloquy: 'Ideas which are not communicated, shared, and reborn in expression are but soliloquy, and soliloquy is but broken and imperfect thought' (Dewey 1946: 218).

DIO's delicate neutrality in some ways resembled such soliloquy. But Dewey also sees a third option, where it is possible for policy advisers to maintain a line of sight towards the public, even in the environments this book has described: 'The enlightenment [of the public] must proceed in ways which force the administrative specialists to take account of [its] needs' (Dewey 1946: 208).

Advice destined for government decision-making processes must be forthright, complete and comprehensive. This should not exclude a focus on political relevance (Palmer et al. 2019), nor should it preclude embracing the notion of a strong objectivity that reaches outside the experience of the institutions (Harding 1992) producing that advice. Those institutions could also show greater awareness of their communicative milieu by understanding the effects their advice produces. Advice thus constructed would provide its ministerial audience with constructive information and constitute an important form of public account. This would not entail sacrificing its responsiveness to the needs of democratically elected governments, nor does it mean ignoring what governments determine to be in the public interest. But with press freedom, whistleblower protections and the public's right to know seemingly all up for grabs in Australia, such advice could become the public's only relevant impartial point of reference. As such, its responsiveness to governments must also encompass the needs and enlightenment of the public.

Bibliography

Abbott, Tony, 2013, '2013 Election Speech', Brisbane, 25 August, available from: electionspeeches.moadoph.gov.au/speeches/2013-tony-abbott.

Abbott, Tony, 2018a, 'Address to the Sydney Institute', Governor Phillip Tower, Sydney, 20 February, available from: tonyabbott.com.au/2018/02/address-sydney-institute-governor-phillip-tower-sydney/#.

Abbott, Tony, 2018b, 'How Cheap Shots Become Own Goals', *The Australian*, 23 February.

ABC News, 2016, 'Chilcot Report: John Howard Defends Decision to Send Australian Troops to Iraq', *ABC News*, 7 July, available from: www.abc.net.au/news/2016-07-07/chilcot-inquiry-john-howard-responds/7577306.

ABC TV News and Current Affairs, 2008, *The Howard Years*, [Documentary], Sydney: ABC.

Ackland, Richard, 2006, 'This Inquiry Is Only Half the Job', *Sydney Morning Herald*, 14 April, available from: www.smh.com.au/national/this-inquiry-is-only-half-the-job-20060414-gdnd36.html.

Adams, David, 2004, 'Usable Knowledge in Public Policy', *Australian Journal of Public Administration*, vol. 63, no. 1, pp. 29–42. doi.org/10.1111/j.1467-8500.2004.00357.x.

Albright, David, 2003, *Iraq's Aluminium Tubes: Separating Fact from Fiction*, 5 December, Washington, DC: Institute for Science and International Security, available from: www.isis-online.org/publications/iraq/IraqAluminum Tubes12-5-03.pdf.

Alvesson, Mats, 2003, 'Beyond Neopositivists, Romantics, and Localists: A Reflexive Approach to Interviews in Organizational Research', *Academy of Management Review*, vol. 28, no. 1, pp. 13–33. doi.org/10.2307/30040687.

Alvesson, Mats & Dan Kärreman, 2000, 'Taking the Linguistic Turn in Organizational Research: Challenges, Responses, Consequences', *The Journal of Applied Behavioral Science*, vol. 36, no. 2. doi.org/10.1177/00218863 00362002.

Attorney-General's Department, n.d., 'Solicitor-General', Canberra: Australian Government, available from: www.ag.gov.au/About/Pages/SolicitorGeneral. aspx.

Attorney-General's Department, 2018, 'PSPF Policy 8: Sensitive and Classified Information', *Protective Security Policy Framework*, v.2018.6, Canberra: Australian Government, available from: www.protectivesecurity.gov.au/ information/sensitive-classified-information/Pages/default.aspx.

Australian Bureau of Statistics (ABS), 2018, *Report on the Conduct of the Australian Marriage Law Postal Survey 2017*, Canberra: ABS, available from: www. abs.gov.au/ausstats/abs@.nsf/6630eff525d4cdc1ca25763e0075754f/7cbde 85f96095fa4ca25822400162fc2/$FILE/700652_ABS_AMLPS_A4_Report_ Conduct_0118_FA4.002.pdf/700652_ABS_AMLPS_A4_Report_Conduct_ 0118_FA4.pdf.

Australian Council of Social Service (ACOSS), 2015, *Fuel on the Fire: Negative Gearing, Capital Gains Tax & Housing Affordability*, Tax Talks 2, Sydney: ACOSS, available from: www.acoss.org.au/images/uploads/Fuel_on_the_ fire.pdf.

Australian Energy Market Operator (AEMO), 2016a, 'Media Statement—South Australia—Wednesday 28 September 2016, 5.32 pm', Melbourne: AEMO, available from: www.aemo.com.au/Media-Centre/Media-Statement---South-Australia---Wednesday-28-September-2016 [page discontinued].

Australian Energy Market Operator (AEMO), 2016b, 'Media Statement—South Australia—Update as at 2200 AEST', 28 September, Melbourne: AEMO, available from: www.aemo.com.au/Media-Centre/Media-Statement---South-Australia-Update [page discontinued].

Australian Energy Market Operator (AEMO), 2016c, 'Media Statement—South Australia—Update 10.30 am', 29 September, Melbourne: AEMO, available from: www.aemo.com.au/Media-Centre/Media-Statement-3---South-Australia-Update [page discontinued].

Australian Energy Market Operator (AEMO), 2016d, 'Preliminary Report—Black System Event in South Australia on 28 September 2016, Information as at 9.00 am, Monday 3 October 2016, Published 5 October 2016', Melbourne: AEMO, available from: file:///C:/Users/u9113681/Downloads/AEMO-SA-PRELIMINARY-REPORT-at-900am-3-October.pdf [page discontinued].

Australian Energy Market Operator (AEMO), 2017a, *AEMO Annual Report 2017*, Melbourne: AEMO, available from: www.aemo.com.au/-/media/Files/About_AEMO/Annual-Report/AEMO-Annual-Report-2017.pdf.

Australian Energy Market Operator (AEMO), 2017b, *Black System South Australia 28 September 2016*, March, Melbourne: AEMO, available from: www.aemo.com.au/-/media/Files/Electricity/NEM/Market_Notices_and_Events/Power_System_Incident_Reports/2017/Integrated-Final-Report-SA-Black-System-28-September-2016.pdf.

Australian Government, 2019, *Delivering for Australians. A World-Class Australian Public Service: The Government's APS Reform Agenda*, Canberra: Australian Government, available from: www.pmc.gov.au/sites/default/files/publications/delivering-for-australians.pdf.

Australian Labor Party (ALP), 2016, *Positive Plan to Help Housing Affordability*, 5 March, Canberra: ALP, available from: apo.org.au/node/230866.

Australian Law Reform Commission (ALRC), 2010, 'The Defence and Defence Intelligence Agencies', [Online], 16 August, Brisbane: Australian Government, available from: www.alrc.gov.au/publications/34.%20Intelligence%20and%20Defence%20Intelligence%20Agencies/defence-and-defence-intelligence-age.

Australian National Audit Office (ANAO), 2001, *Developing Policy Advice*, The Auditor-General, Audit Report No. 21 2001–2002, Performance Audit, 20 November, Canberra: ANAO, available from: www.anao.gov.au/sites/g/files/net4181/f/anao_report_2001-2002_21.pdf.

Australian National Audit Office (ANAO), 2016, *Machinery of Government Changes*, Auditor-General Report No. 3 of 2016–17, Performance Audit Report, 31 August, Canberra: ANAO, available from: www.anao.gov.au/work/performance-audit/management-machinery-government-changes.

Australian National Audit Office (ANAO), 2020, *Award of Funding under the Community Sport Infrastructure Program*, Auditor-General Report No. 23 of 2019–20, Performance Audit Report, 15 January, Canberra: ANAO, available from: www.anao.gov.au/work/performance-audit/award-funding-under-the-community-sport-infrastructure-program.

Australian Public Service Commission (APSC), n.d., 'Overview', [Online], Canberra: APSC, available from: www.apsc.gov.au/overview-5 [page discontinued].

Australian Public Service Commission (APSC), 2012a, *Capability Review: Department of the Prime Minister and Cabinet*, August, Canberra: APSC, available from: www.apsc.gov.au/sites/default/files/2021-06/PMC%20Capability%20review.pdf.

Australian Public Service Commission (APSC), 2012b, *Integrated Leadership System (ILS)*, 15 March, Canberra: APSC, available from: view.officeapps.live.com/op/view.aspx?src=https%3A%2F%2Fwww.apsc.gov.au%2Fsites%2Fdefault%2Ffiles%2F2021-06%2Fils-aps-guide.doc&wdOrigin=BROWSELINK.

Australian Public Service Commission (APSC), 2013a, *Capability Review: The Department of Resources, Energy and Tourism*, September, Canberra: APSC, available from: www.apsc.gov.au/sites/default/files/2021-06/DRET%20Capability-review.pdf.

Australian Public Service Commission (APSC), 2013b, *Capability Review: The Treasury*, September, Canberra: APSC, available from: www.apsc.gov.au/sites/default/files/2021-06/Treasury%20Capability-review.pdf.

Australian Public Service Commission (APSC), 2017, *State of the Service Report 2016–17*, 30 November, Canberra: APSC, available from: www.apsc.gov.au/initiatives-and-programs/workforce-information/research-analysis-and-publications/state-service/state-service-report-2016-17.

Australian Public Service Commission (APSC), 2018a, *APS Values and Code of Conduct in Practice: A Guide to Official Conduct for APS Employees and Agency Heads*, March, Canberra: APSC, available from: view.officeapps.live.com/op/view.aspx?src=https%3A%2F%2Fwww.apsc.gov.au%2Fsites%2Fdefault%2Ffiles%2F2021-03%2FIn-practiceweb.docx&wdOrigin=BROWSELINK.

Australian Public Service Commission (APSC), 2018b, 'Commissioner's Foreword', *Challenges of Evidence-Based Policy-Making*, Canberra: APSC, available from: legacy.apsc.gov.au/challenges-evidence-based-policy-making [page discontinued].

Australian Public Service Commission (APSC), 2018c, *Integrated Leadership System (ILS) EL–SES Comparative*, Canberra: APSC, available from: www.apsc.gov.au/working-aps/aps-employees-and-managers/classifications/integrated-leadership-system-ils/ils-resources-profiles-comparatives-and-self-assessment/integrated-leadership-system-ils-el-ses-comparative.

Australian Public Service Commission (APSC), 2018d, *State of the Service Report 2017–18*, 26 November, Canberra: APSC, available from: www.apsc.gov.au/state-service/state-service-report-2017-18.

Australian Public Service Commission (APSC), 2019a, *Machinery of Government (MoG) Changes: What Is a MoG Change?*, Canberra: APSC, available from: www.apsc.gov.au/working-aps/information-aps-employment/machinery-government-mog.

Australian Public Service Commission (APSC), 2019b, 'Mobility and Tenure', [Online], Canberra: APSC, available from: legacy.apsc.gov.au/mobility-and-tenure [page discontinued].

Australian Public Service Commission (APSC), 2019c, *State of the Service Report 2018–19*, 26 November, Canberra: APSC, available from: www.apsc.gov.au/state-service/state-service-report-2018-19.

Australian Public Service Commission (APSC), 2020, *APS Values*, 11 December, Canberra: APSC, available from: www.apsc.gov.au/working-in-the-aps/your-rights-and-responsibilities-as-an-aps-employee/aps-values.

Australian Public Service Commission (APSC), 2021a, *Capability Review Program*, 3 June, Canberra: APSC, available from: www.apsc.gov.au/initiatives-and-programs/workforce-information/research-analysis-and-publications/capability-review-program.

Australian Public Service Commission (APSC), 2021b, *Working with Ministers: Strengthening Partnerships*, 16 November, Canberra: APSC, available from: www.apsc.gov.au/publication/working-ministers.

Banks, Gary, 2009, *Evidence-Based Policy Making: What Is It? How Do We Get It?*, ANU Public Lecture Series, presented by ANZSOG, Canberra, February 2009, Canberra: Productivity Commission, available from: www.pc.gov.au/news-media/speeches/cs20090204/20090204-evidence-based-policy.pdf. doi.org/10.22459/CRAPP.05.2009.10.

Barker, Geoffrey, 2003, *Sexing It Up: Iraq, Intelligence and Australia*, Sydney: UNSW Press.

Barratt, Paul, 2016, 'Attorney-General's Move to Control Access to Solicitor-General', *Pearls and Irritations: John Menadue's Public Policy Journal*, [Online], 1 July, available from: johnmenadue.com/paul-barratt-attorney-generals-move-to-control-access-to-solicitor-general/.

Barstow, David, 2004, 'The Nuclear Card: The Aluminium Tube Story—A Special Report; How White House Embraced Suspect Iraq Arms Intelligence', *The New York Times*, 3 October, available from: www.nytimes.com/2004/10/03/washington/us/the-nuclear-card-the-aluminum-tube-story-a-special-report-how.html.

Baxendale, Rachel, 2018, 'Housing Industry Backs Morrison Line', *The Australian*, 22 February.

Beatty, John, 2006, 'Masking Disagreement among Experts', *Episteme*, vol. 3, no. 1–2. doi.org/10.1353/epi.0.0001.

Belot, Henry, 2016, 'Australia's Top Public Servants Call for FOI Reform to Hide Advice from Public', *The Canberra Times*, 11 April, available from: www.canberratimes.com.au/national/public-service/australias-top-public-servants-call-for-foi-reform-to-hide-advice-from-public-20160411-go3gxt.html.

Bennett, Scott, 2000, *Four-Year Terms for the House of Representatives*, Research Paper 4 2000–01, 29 August, Canberra: Parliamentary Library, available from: www.aph.gov.au/About_Parliament/Parliamentary_Departments/Parliamentary_Library/pubs/rp/rp0001/01RP04.

Benson, Simon, 2018a, 'Plan Now or Quality of City Life Will Fall', *The Australian*, 23 February.

Benson, Simon, 2018b, 'Ken Henry Calls Out a Decade of "Failure" to Implement Reform', *The Australian*, 2 March.

Bertelsmann Stiftung, 2016, *Policy Performance and Governance Capabilities in the OECD and EU: Sustainable Governance Indicators 2016*, Gütersloh, Germany: Bertelsmann Stiftung, available from: www.bertelsmann-stiftung.de/fileadmin/files/BSt/Publikationen/GrauePublikationen/Studie_NW_Policy_Performance_and_Governance_Capacities_in_the_OECD_and_EU_2016.pdf.

Bertelsmann Stiftung, 2021, 'About the SGI: Methodology', *Sustainable Governance Indicators*, Gütersloh, Germany: SGI Network, available from: www.sgi-network.org/2017/Methodology.

Best, Jacqueline, 2012, 'Bureaucratic Ambiguity', *Economy and Society*, vol. 41, no. 1, pp. 84–106. doi.org/10.1080/03085147.2011.637333.

Bitzer, Lloyd F., 1968, 'The Rhetorical Situation', *Philosophy & Rhetoric*, vol. 1, no. 1, pp. 1–14.

Blackwell, Eoin, 2016, '"There Was No Lie": John Howard Says Iraq War Was "Justified at the Time"', *HuffPost Australia*, 7 July, [updated 14 July 2016], available from: www.huffingtonpost.com.au/2016/07/06/australia-needs-its-own-chilcot-report-mp_a_21425448/.

Blavatnik School of Government, 2017, *International Civil Service Effectiveness (InCiSE) Index: Technical Report*, Oxford, UK: University of Oxford, available from: www.bsg.ox.ac.uk/sites/default/files/2019-01/International%20Civil%20Service%20Effectiveness%20%28InCiSE%29%202017%20technical%20report.PDF.

Blavatnik School of Government, 2019, *International Civil Service Effectiveness (InCiSE) Index: Technical Report 2019*, Oxford, UK: University of Oxford, available from: www.bsg.ox.ac.uk/sites/default/files/2019-04/InCiSE%202019%20Technical%20Report.pdf.

Blix, Hans, 2004, *Disarming Iraq: The Search for Weapons of Mass Destruction*, London: Bloomsbury.

Blom, Michèle, 2019, Interview with the Author, 7 May.

Blunden, Hazel, 2016, 'Discourses around Negative Gearing of Investment Properties in Australia', *Housing Studies*, vol. 31, no. 3, pp. 340–357. doi.org/10.1080/02673037.2015.1080820.

Bolsen, Toby, James N. Druckman & Fay Lomax Cook, 2014, 'How Frames Can Undermine Support for Scientific Adaptations: Politicization and the Status-Quo Bias', *Public Opinion Quarterly*, vol. 78, no. 1, pp. 1–26. doi.org/10.1093/poq/nft044.

Bongiorno, Frank, 2018, 'Moment after Moment of Madness: Liberals Manage the Ugliest, Messiest Leadership Challenge in History', *The Conversation*, 24 August, available from: theconversation.com/moment-after-moment-of-madness-liberals-manage-the-ugliest-messiest-leadership-challenge-in-history-102035.

Borys, Stephanie & Louise Yaxley, 2018, 'Islamic State Involvement Sees Five Australian Terrorists Stripped of Citizenship', *ABC News*, 9 August, available from: www.abc.net.au/news/2018-08-09/islamic-state-terrorists-lose-australian-citizenship/10092678.

Boswell, Christina, 2009, *The Political Uses of Expert Knowledge: Immigration Policy and Social Research*, Cambridge, UK: Cambridge University Press. doi.org/10.1017/CBO9780511581120.

Boswell, John, 2018, 'How Do You Go from Demonising Adversaries to Deliberating with Them?', in R.A.W. Rhodes (ed.), *Narrative Policy Analysis: Cases in Decentred Policy*, New York, NY: Springer International Publishing AG. doi.org/10.1007/978-3-319-76635-5_6.

Boswell, John & Jack Corbett, 2015, 'Stoic Democrats? Anti-Politics, Élite Cynicism and the Policy Process', *Journal of European Public Policy*, vol. 22, no. 10, pp. 1388–1405. doi.org/10.1080/13501763.2015.1010561.

Bowman, Scott, 2015, 'We Must Overcome Our Leadership Change Addiction', *The Drum*, [ABC TV], 30 January, available from: www.abc.net.au/news/2015-01-30/bowman-we-must-overcome-our-leadership-change-addiction/6054586.

Bradford, Gillian, 2006, 'PM Says Cable Proves Govt Didn't Know of AWB Kickbacks', *PM*, [ABC Radio], 22 February, available from: www.abc.net.au/pm/content/2006/s1576190.htm.

Brown, Andrew, 2017, '"Our Fears Have Been Realised": Plebiscite Sees Spike in Calls to Counsellors', *The Canberra Times*, 26 August, [updated 24 April 2018], available from: www.canberratimes.com.au/national/act/our-fears-have-been-realised-plebiscite-sees-spike-in-calls-to-counsellors-20170824-gy377x.html.

Bryant, Nick, 2015, 'Australia: Coup Capital of the Democratic World', *BBC News*, 14 September, available from: www.bbc.com/news/world-australia-34249214.

Burke, Liz, 2016, 'Politicians Blame Renewable Energy for South Australia's Freak Blackout', *News.com.au*, 29 September, available from: www.news.com.au/technology/environment/politicians-blame-renewable-energy-for-south-australias-freak-blackout/news-story/e60198eb2325fca65cf11ee0a8cab80d/.

Bush, George W., 2002a, 'President's Remarks at the United Nations General Assembly', New York, NY, 12 September, available from: georgewbush-whitehouse.archives.gov/news/releases/2002/09/20020912-1.html.

Bush, George W., 2002b, 'President Bush Outlines Iraqi Threat', Remarks by the President on Iraq, Cincinnati Museum Center–Cincinnati Union Terminal, Cincinnati, OH, 7 October, available from: georgewbush-whitehouse.archives.gov/news/releases/2002/10/20021007-8.html.

Bush, George W., 2003, 'President Delivers "State of the Union"', The US Capitol, Washington, DC, 28 January, available from: georgewbush-whitehouse.archives.gov/news/releases/2003/01/20030128-19.html.

Business Council of Australia (BCA), 2018, 'Business and Industry United in Calling for an End to Energy Uncertainty', Media Release, 6 August, BCA, Melbourne, available from: www.bca.com.au/business_and_industry_united_in_calling_for_an_end_to_energy_uncertainty.

Butler, Josh, 2017, 'Scott Morrison Brought a Lump of Coal and Waved It Around in Parliament', *HuffPost Australia*, 8 February, available from: www.huffingtonpost.com.au/2017/02/08/scott-morrison-brought-a-lump-of-coal-and-waved-it-around-in-par_a_21710206/.

Butler, Richard, 1999, *Report: Disarmament*, Report No. S/1999/94, 25 January, Geneva: United Nations Special Commission, available from: www.un.org/Depts/unscom/s99-94.htm.

Butler, Rt. Hon. Lord (Frederick Edward) Robin of Brockwell, 2004, *Review of Intelligence on Weapons of Mass Destruction: Report of a Committee of Privy Councillors to the House of Commons*, 14 July, London: The Stationery Office, available from: news.bbc.co.uk/nol/shared/bsp/hi/pdfs/14_07_04_butler.pdf.

Button, James, 2013, *Speechless: A Year in My Father's Business*, rev. edn, Melbourne: Melbourne University Press.

Buzan, Barry, Ole Waever & Jaap de Wilde, 1998, *Security: A New Framework for Analysis*, Boulder, CO: Lynne Rienner Publishers.

Cairney, Paul & Kathryn Oliver, 2017, 'Evidence-Based Policymaking Is Not Like Evidence-Based Medicine, So How Far Should You Go to Bridge the Divide between Evidence and Policy?', *Health Research Policy and Systems*, vol. 15, no. 35. doi.org/10.1186/s12961-017-0192-x.

Campbell, Christopher M., David A. Makin & Sanne A.M. Rijkhoff, 2017, 'A Rhetorical Balancing Act: Popular Punitivism in the Netherlands', *Punishment & Society*, vol. 19, no. 5. doi.org/10.1177/1462474516672882.

Chang, Charis, 2018, 'What the Leadership Challenge Is Really All About', *News.com.au*, 22 August, available from: www.news.com.au/national/politics/what-the-leadership-challenge-is-really-about/news-story/3b2ccabd337b4fd5a6bc06bd67f24b76.

Charteris-Black, Jonathan, 2011, *Politicians and Rhetoric: The Persuasive Power of Metaphor*, 2nd edn, Basingstoke, UK: Palgrave Macmillan. doi.org/10.1057/9780230319899.

Cheney, Dick, 2002, 'Vice President Speaks at VFW 103rd National Convention', Remarks by the Vice President to the Veterans of Foreign Wars 103rd National Convention, Nashville, 26 August, available from: georgewbush-whitehouse.archives.gov/news/releases/2002/08/20020826.html.

Chilcot, John, 2016, 'Sir John Chilcot's Public Statement', 6 July, *The Iraq Inquiry*, London: House of Commons, available from: webarchive.national archives.gov.uk/20171123124608/www.iraqinquiry.org.uk/the-inquiry/sir-john-chilcots-public-statement/.

Christensen, Johan, 2013, 'Bureaucracies, Neoliberal Ideas, and Tax Reform in New Zealand and Ireland', *Governance: An International Journal of Policy, Administration, and Institutions*, vol. 26, no. 4, pp. 563–584. doi.org/10.1111/gove.12009.

Clean Energy Finance Corporation (CEFC), 2016, 'CEFC Board Commences Search for New CEO', Media Release, 19 October, CEFC, Sydney, available from: www.cefc.com.au/media/files/cefc-board-commences-search-for-new-ceo.aspx.

Cohen, David K. & Charles E. Lindblom, 1980, 'Solving Problems of Bureaucracy', in Carol H. Weiss & Allen H. Barton (eds), *Making Bureaucracies Work*, Thousand Oaks, CA: Sage Publications.

Colby, Itkowitz, 2018, 'The Health 202: Trump Officials Ignored HHS Advice on Two Big Issues', *The Washington Post*, 1 August.

Committee of Privy Counsellors, 2016, *The Report of the Iraq Inquiry*, 6 July, London: House of Commons, available from: webarchive.nationalarchives. gov.uk/20171123122743/www.iraqinquiry.org.uk/the-report/.

Commonwealth of Australia, 2003, House of Representatives, Official Hansard, No. 4, 2003, Tuesday, 18 March, Fortieth Parliament First Session—Fourth Period, *Parliamentary Debates*, available from: www.aph.gov.au/binaries/ hansard/reps/dailys/dr180303.pdf.

Commonwealth Consolidated Acts, 1982, *Freedom of Information Act 1982*, available from: www8.austlii.edu.au/cgi-bin/viewdoc/au/legis/cth/consol_act/ foia1982222.

Conifer, Dan, 2018, 'Scott Morrison Explains Why He Snubbed Treasury's Advice on Negative Gearing, Says He Drew on His Own Experience', *ABC News*, 6 February, available from: www.abc.net.au/news/2018-02-06/ morrison-explains-snubbing-treasurys-negative-gearing-advice/9399622.

Conifer, Dan & Michael McKinnon, 2019, 'Federal Treasury Scolds Coalition for Exaggerating Impact of Labor's Proposed Negative Gearing Overhaul', *ABC News*, 6 March, available from: www.abc.net.au/news/2019-03-06/ federal-treasury-scolds-coalition-labor-negative-gearing-changes/10873514.

Constitutional Education Fund (CEFA), 2015, *Are the New Citizenship Laws Unconstitutional?*, 4 December, Sydney: CEFA, available from: www.cefa.org. au/ccf/are-new-citizenship-laws-unconstitutional.

Cook, Henrietta, 2017, 'Schools Put on Standby for Distressed Students Ahead of Gay Marriage Vote', *The Age*, [Melbourne], 25 August, available from: www.theage.com.au/national/victoria/schools-put-on-standby-for-distressed-students-ahead-of-gay-marriage-vote-20170825-gy437h.html.

Coombs, Herbert Cole, 1976, *Royal Commission on Australian Government Administration: Report*, Canberra: Government Printer, available from: apo. org.au/sites/default/files/resource-files/1976-08/apo-nid34221.pdf.

Cooper, Hayden, 2016, 'Josh Frydenberg on South Australia's Power Outage', *7.30*, [ABC TV], 28 September, available from: www.abc.net.au/7.30/josh-frydenberg-on-south-australias-power-outage/7886646.

Coorey, Phillip, 2018, 'Liberal Leadership Crisis: Australian Politics Is Sick and Broken', *Australian Financial Review*, 23 August, available from: www.afr. com/opinion/columnists/liberal-party-has-too-many-faceless-men-to-serve-the-national-interest-20180821-h14ao9.

Cubby, Ben, 2012, 'Science on Wind Turbine Illness Dubious, Say Experts', *Sydney Morning Herald*, 24 January, available from: www.smh.com.au/environment/sustainability/science-on-wind-turbine-illness-dubious-say-experts-20120123-1qe98.html.

Daley, John & Danielle Wood, 2016, *Hot Property: Negative Gearing and Capital Gains Tax Reform*, Grattan Institute Report No. 2016-8, Melbourne: Grattan Institute, available from: grattan.edu.au/wp-content/uploads/2016/04/872-Hot-Property.pdf.

Daley, Paul, 2018, 'Turnbull's Rise Was Inevitable. But a Devil's Deal Meant So Too Was His Fall', *The Guardian*, [Australia], 24 August, available from: www.theguardian.com/australia-news/2018/aug/24/turnbulls-rise-was-inevitable-but-a-devils-deal-meant-so-too-was-his-fall.

Daston, Lorraine & Peter Galison, 1992, 'The Image of Objectivity', *Representations*, no. 40 [SI]. doi.org/10.2307/2928741.

Department of Defence, n.d., 'Defence Intelligence Organisation: About Us', [Online], Canberra: Australian Government, available from: www.defence.gov.au/dio/about-us.shtml.

Department of the Environment, 2015, 'The Role of Science in Australia's Environmental Policy: A Presentation from Professor Ian Chubb, Chief Scientist of Australia, and Dr Gordon de Brouwer, Secretary, Department of the Environment', Australian Academy of Science, Canberra, 12 June, available from: www.youtube.com/watch?v=Qa83pw67UFs.

Department of the Environment and Energy (DEE), n.d., *Freedom of Information Disclosure Log*, Canberra: Australian Government, available from: www.environment.gov.au/about-us/freedom-information/foi-disclosure-log.

Department of Finance, 2015, *Efficiency through Contestability Programme*, Canberra: Australian Government, available from: www.finance.gov.au/resource-management/governance/contestability/ [page discontinued].

Department of the Prime Minister and Cabinet (DPMC), 2017, *Policy Quality Framework*, Wellington: New Zealand Government, available from: www.dpmc.govt.nz/sites/default/files/2017-05/policy-quality-framework-development-insights-and-applications.pdf [page discontinued].

Department of the Prime Minister and Cabinet (DPMC), 2022, *Policy Quality*, Wellington: New Zealand Government, available from: dpmc.govt.nz/our-programmes/policy-project/policy-improvement-frameworks/policy-quality.

Department of the Prime Minister and Cabinet (PM&C), n.d., *Departmental FOI Disclosure Logs*, Canberra: Australian Government, available from: www.pmc.gov.au/government/departmental-foi-disclosure-logs.

Department of the Prime Minister and Cabinet (PM&C), 2017a, *2017 Independent Intelligence Review*, June, Canberra: Australian Government, available from: www.pmc.gov.au/sites/default/files/publications/2017-Independent-Intelligence-Review.pdf.

Department of the Prime Minister and Cabinet (PM&C), 2019a, 'About: Terms of Reference', *Independent Review of the APS*, Canberra: Australian Government, available from: www.apsreview.gov.au/about.

Department of the Prime Minister and Cabinet (PM&C), 2019b, *Independent Review of the APS*, [Home page], Canberra: Australian Government, available from: www.apsreview.gov.au/.

Department of the Prime Minister and Cabinet (PM&C), 2019c, *Our Public Service, Our Future: Independent Review of the Australian Public Service*, Canberra: Australian Government, available from: www.pmc.gov.au/resource-centre/government/independent-review-australian-public-service.

Department of the Senate, n.d., *About the Senate*, Canberra: Parliament of Australia, available from: www.aph.gov.au/About_Parliament/Senate/About_the_Senate.

de Vries, Annick, Willem Halffman & Rob Hoppe, 2010, 'Policy Workers Tinkering with Uncertainty: Dutch Econometric Policy Advice in Action', in Hal K. Colebatch, Robert Hoppe & Mirko Noordegraaf (eds), *Working for Policy*, Amsterdam: Amsterdam University Press. doi.org/10.1515/97890485 13086-008.

Dewey, John, 1946, *The Public and Its Problems*, Chicago, IL: Gateway Books.

Dharmawan, Budi, Michael Böcher & Max Krott, 2017, 'Endangered Mangroves in Segara Anakan, Indonesia: Effective and Failed Problem-Solving Policy Advice', *Environmental Management*, vol. 60, pp. 409–421. doi.org/10.1007/s00267-017-0868-6.

Dickinson, Helen, Helen Sullivan & Graeme Head, 2015, 'The Future of the Public Service Workforce: A Dialogue', *Australian Journal of Public Administration*, vol. 74, no. 1, pp. 23–32. doi.org/10.1111/1467-8500.12143.

Di Francesco, Michael, 2000, 'An Evaluation Crucible: Evaluating Policy Advice in Australian Central Agencies', *Australian Journal of Public Administration*, vol. 59, no. 1, pp. 36–48. doi.org/10.1111/1467-8500.00138.

Downer, Alexander, 2002, 'House of Representatives, Ministerial Statements, Foreign Affairs: Iraq', Speech, Tuesday, 17 September, *Parliamentary Debates*, available from: parlinfo.aph.gov.au/parlInfo/genpdf/chamber/hansardr/2002-09-17/0035/hansard_frag.pdf;fileType=application%2Fpdf.

Downes, David & René van Swaaningen, 2007, 'The Road to Dystopia? Changes in the Penal Climate of the Netherlands', *Crime and Justice*, vol. 35, pp. 31–71. doi.org/10.1086/650186.

Druckman, James N., 2001, 'The Implication of Framing Effects for Citizen Competence', *Political Behavior*, vol. 23, pp. 225–256. doi.org/10.1023/A:1015006907312.

Dryzek, John S., 1993, 'Policy Analysis and Planning: From Science to Argument', in Frank Fischer & John Forester (eds), *The Argumentative Turn in Policy Analysis and Planning*, Durham, NC: Duke University Press. doi.org/10.1215/9780822381815-010.

du Gay, Paul, 2000, *In Praise of Bureaucracy: Weber, Organization, Ethics*, Thousand Oaks, CA: Sage Publications. doi.org/10.4135/9781446217580.

Dunlop, Claire A., 2010, 'The Temporal Dimension of Knowledge and the Limits of Policy Appraisal: Biofuels Policy in the UK', *Policy Sciences*, vol. 43, no. 4, pp. 343–363. doi.org/10.1007/s11077-009-9101-7.

Dunton, Jim, 2019, 'UK Civil Service Tops Global League Table', *Civil Service World*, 25 April, available from: www.civilserviceworld.com/articles/news/uk-civil-service-tops-global-league-table.

Dutton, Peter, 2018, 'Interview with Chris Kenny, Radio 2GB, Sydney', 3 January, available from: minister.homeaffairs.gov.au/peterdutton/Pages/Interview-with-Chris-Kenny.aspx.

Eccleston, Richard, 2007, *Taxing Reforms: The Politics of the Consumption Tax in Japan, the United States, Canada and Australia*, Cheltenham, UK: Edward Elgar.

Edelman, 2019, *2019 Edelman Trust Barometer: Global Report*, Chicago, IL: Edelman, available from: www.edelman.com/sites/g/files/aatuss191/files/2019-03/2019_Edelman_Trust_Barometer_Global_Report.pdf?utm_source=web site&utm_medium=global_report&utm_campaign=downloads.

Edelman, Murray, 1977, *Political Language: Words That Succeed and Policies That Fail*, London: Academic Press.

Edelman, Murray, 1988, *Constructing the Political Spectacle*, Chicago, IL: University of Chicago Press.

Egeberg, Morten, 1999, 'The Impact of Bureaucratic Structure on Policy Making', *Public Administration*, vol. 77, no. 1, pp. 155–170. doi.org/10.1111/1467-9299.00148.

Eichbaum, Chris & Richard Shaw, 2008, 'Revisiting Politicization: Political Advisers and Public Servants in Westminster Systems', *Governance: An International Journal of Policy, Administration, and Institutions*, vol. 21, no. 3, pp. 337–363. doi.org/10.1111/j.1468-0491.2008.00403.x.

Eriksson, Gunilla, 2016, *Swedish Military Intelligence: Producing Knowledge*, Edinburgh: Edinburgh University Press. doi.org/10.1515/9781474413459.

Ervik, Rune & Tord Skogedal Lindén, 2015, 'The Shark Jaw and the Elevator: Arguing the Case for the Necessity, Harmlessness and Fairness of the Norwegian Pension Reform', *Scandinavian Political Studies*, vol. 38, no. 4, pp. 386–409. doi.org/10.1111/1467-9477.12049.

Farmer, David John, 1995, *The Language of Public Administration: Bureaucracy, Modernity, and Postmodernity*, Tuscaloosa, AL: University of Alabama Press.

Farrell, Don, 2022, *Ministerial Staff Code of Conduct, Canberra: Special Minister of State*, available from: www.smos.gov.au/ministerial-staff-code-conduct.

Federal Register of Legislation, 1977, *Office of National Assessments Act 1977*, Act No. 107 of 1977 as amended, Canberra: Australian Government, available from: www.legislation.gov.au/Details/C2005C00687.

Federal Register of Legislation, 1999, *Public Service Act 1999*, No. 147, 1999, Compilation No. 19, Canberra: Australian Government, available from: www.legislation.gov.au/Details/C2017C00270.

Federal Register of Legislation, 2001, *Corporations Act 2001*, No. 50, 2001, Compilation No. 82, Canberra: Australian Government, available from: www.legislation.gov.au/Details/C2018C00031.

Fernando, Gavin & Stephanie Bedo, 2018, 'Scott Morrison Has Been Sworn in as Australia's 30th Prime Minister', *News.com.au*, 25 August, available from: www.news.com.au/national/politics/the-race-is-on-bishop-to-run-turnbull-out-as-showdown-nears/news-story/5b48d2f4fa017cc30c93a301746f469d.

Finkel, Alan, 2017, *Independent Review into the Future Security of the National Electricity Market: Blueprint for the Future*, June, Canberra: Commonwealth of Australia, available from: www.energy.gov.au/sites/default/files/independent-review-future-nem-blueprint-for-the-future-2017.pdf.

FINSIA Staff, 2017, 'Why Treasury's Forecasting Is Broken', *InFinance*, 8 June, available from: finsia.com/insights/news/news-article/2017/06/08/why-treasury-s-forecasting-is-broken [page discontinued].

Fischer, Frank, 1990, *Technocracy and the Politics of Expertise*, Thousand Oaks, CA: Sage Publications.

Fischer, Frank, 2003, *Reframing Public Policy: Discursive Politics and Deliberative Practices*, Oxford, UK: Oxford University Press.

Fischer, Frank & John Forester (eds), 1993, *The Argumentative Turn in Policy Analysis and Planning*, Durham, NC: Duke University Press. doi.org/10.1215/9780822381815.

Fischer, Frank & Herbert Gottweis (eds), 2012, *The Argumentative Turn Revisited: Public Policy as Communicative Practice*, Durham, NC: Duke University Press. doi.org/10.1515/9780822395362.

Fischer, Frank & Herbert Gottweis, 2013, 'The Argumentative Turn in Public Policy Revisited: Twenty Years Later', *Critical Policy Studies*, vol. 7, no. 4, pp. 425–433. doi.org/10.1080/19460171.2013.851164.

Flood, Philip, 2004, *Report of the Inquiry into Australian Intelligence Agencies*, July, Canberra: Commonwealth of Australia, available from: fas.org/irp/world/australia/flood.pdf.

Foreign and Commonwealth Office (FCO), 2002, *Iraq's Weapons of Mass Destruction: The Assessment of the British Government*, 24 September, London: The Stationery Office, available from: web.archive.org/web/20100130144134/www.fco.gov.uk/resources/en/pdf/pdf3/fco_iraqdossier.

Forester, John, 2012, 'On the Theory and Practice of Critical Pragmatism: Deliberative Practice and Creative Negotiations', *Planning Theory*, vol. 12, no. 1. doi.org/10.1177/1473095212448750.

Foster, Michelle, Jane McAdam & Davina Wadley, 2016, 'Part Two: The Prevention and Reduction of Statelessness in Australia—An Ongoing Challenge', *Melbourne University Law Review*, vol. 40, no. 2. doi.org/10.2139/ssrn.3367970.

Foucault, Michel, 1991, 'Questions of Method', in Graham Burchell, Colin Gordon & Peter M. Miller (eds), *The Foucault Effect*, London: Harvester Wheatsheaf.

Garrett, Peter, 2014, 'Witness Statement: Peter Robert Garrett', Royal Commission into the Home Insulation Program, Brisbane, 8 May, available from: www.homeinsulationroyalcommission.gov.au/Hearings/Documents/Evidence13May2014/STA-001-069-0001.pdf [page discontinued].

Geuijen, Karin, Paul 't Hart, Sebastiaan Princen & Kutsal Yesilkagit, 2008, *The New Eurocrats: National Civil Servants in EU Policymaking*, Amsterdam: Amsterdam University Press. doi.org/10.5117/9789053567975.

Gillard, Julia, 2010, 'Edited Transcript of Julia Gillard's Acceptance Speech', *The Australian*, 24 June, available from: www.theaustralian.com.au/news/ edited-transcript-of-julia-gillards-acceptance-speech/news-story/5cc8e65950 b9e0d407ffe397dc96a010.

Gittins, Ross, 2015, *Gittins: A Life among Budgets, Bulldust and Bastardry*, Sydney: Allen & Unwin.

Glees, Anthony & Philip H.J. Davies, 2006, 'Intelligence, Iraq and the Limits of Legislative Accountability during Political Crisis', *Intelligence and National Security*, vol. 21, no. 5, pp. 848–883. doi.org/10.1080/02684520600957787.

Gleeson, Kathleen, 2014, *Australia's 'War on Terror' Discourse*, Aldershot, UK: Ashgate.

Goldfarb, Ronald, 2009, *In Confidence: When to Protect Secrecy and When to Require Disclosure*, New Haven, CT: Yale University Press.

Gottweis, Herbert, 2006, 'Argumentative Policy Analysis', in P. Guy Peters & Jon Pierre (eds), *Handbook of Public Policy*, Thousand Oaks, CA: Sage Publications. doi.org/10.4135/9781848608054.n28.

Grattan, Michelle, 2015, 'Cabinet Ministers Brawl Over Same-Sex Marriage Popular Vote', *The Conversation*, 13 August, available from: theconversation. com/cabinet-ministers-brawl-over-same-sex-marriage-popular-vote-46086.

Greenhalgh, Trish & Jill Russell, 2006, 'Reframing Evidence Synthesis as Rhetorical Action in the Policy Making Drama', *Healthcare Policy*, vol. 1, no. 2, pp. 34–42. doi.org/10.12927/hcpol.2006.17873.

Grube, Dennis, 2013, *Prime Ministers and Rhetorical Governance*, Basingstoke, UK: Palgrave Macmillan. doi.org/10.1057/9781137318367.

Grube, Dennis, 2014a, 'Administrative Learning or Political Blaming? Public Servants, Parliamentary Committees and the Drama of Public Accountability', *Australian Journal of Political Science*, vol. 49, no. 2, pp. 223–236. doi.org/ 10.1080/10361146.2014.880402.

Grube, Dennis, 2014b, 'The Gilded Cage: Rhetorical Path Dependency in Australian Politics', in John Uhr & Ryan Walter (eds), *Studies in Australian Political Rhetoric*, Canberra: ANU Press. doi.org/10.22459/SAPR.09.2014.05.

Grube, Dennis, 2015, 'Responsibility to Be Enthusiastic? Public Servants and the Public Face of "Promiscuous Partisanship"', *Governance: An International Journal of Policy, Administration, and Institutions*, vol. 28, no. 3, pp. 305–320. doi.org/10.1111/gove.12088.

Gruber, Judith E., 1987, *Controlling Bureaucracies: Dilemmas in Democratic Governance*, Berkeley, CA: University of California Press. doi.org/10.1525/9780520330351.

Gyngell, Allan, 2017, 'The Australian Intelligence Tradition', *The Interpreter*, 24 July, Sydney: Lowy Institute, available from: www.lowyinstitute.org/the-interpreter/australian-intelligence-tradition.

Hage, Volker, 2004, 'Die Macht der geheimen Dienste [The Power of the Secret Services]', *Der Spiegel*, [Hamburg, Germany], 1 October, available from: www.spiegel.de/spiegel/print/d-53135621.html.

Hajer, Maarten, 1993, 'Discourse Coalitions and the Institutionalization of Practice: The Case of Acid Rain in Great Britain', in Frank Fischer & John Forester (eds), *The Argumentative Turn in Policy Analysis and Planning*, Durham, NC: Duke University Press. doi.org/10.1215/9780822381815-003.

Hajer, Maarten & David Laws, 2006, 'Ordering through Discourse', in Michael Moran, Martin Rein & Robert E. Goodin (eds), *The Oxford Handbook of Public Policy*, Oxford, UK: Oxford University Press.

Hanger, Ian, 2014, *Report of the Royal Commission into the Home Insulation Program*, Canberra: Commonwealth of Australia.

Harding, Sandra, 1992, 'After the Neutrality Ideal: Science, Politics, and "Strong Objectivity"', *Science and Politics*, vol. 59, no. 3, pp. 567–587.

Hartcher, Peter, 2015, 'Tony Abbott Rolled by His Own Ministers over Stripping Terrorists of Citizenship', *Sydney Morning Herald*, 28 May, [updated 29 May], available from: www.smh.com.au/opinion/tony-abbott-rolled-by-his-own-ministers-over-stripping-terrorists-of-citizenship-20150529-ghcuxf.html.

Hartcher, Peter, 2018, 'Malcolm Turnbull Made a Deal with the Devil. Now the Devil Has Called Time', *Sydney Morning Herald*, 23 August, available from: www.smh.com.au/politics/federal/malcolm-turnbull-made-a-deal-with-the-devil-now-the-devil-has-called-time-20180823-p4zzfc.html.

Hartelius, Elin Johanna, 2008, The Rhetoric of Expertise, PhD thesis, The University of Texas at Austin.

Hartnett, Stephen J. & Laura A. Stengrim, 2004, '"The Whole Operation of Deception": Reconstructing President Bush's Rhetoric of Weapons of Mass Destruction', *Cultural Studies ↔ Critical Methodologies*, vol. 4, no. 2. doi.org/10.1177/1532708603262787.

Head, Brian, 2013, 'Evidence-Based Policymaking—Speaking Truth to Power?', *Australian Journal of Public Administration*, vol. 72, no. 4, pp. 397–403. doi.org/10.1111/1467-8500.12037.

Head, Brian & Michael Di Francesco, 2019, 'Using Evidence in Australia and New Zealand', in Annette Boaz, Huw Davies, Alec Fraser & Sandra Nutley (eds), *What Works Now? Evidence-Informed Policy and Practice*, Bristol, UK: Policy Press.

Heclo, Hugh & Aaron Wildavsky, 1974, *The Private Government of Public Money*, London: Macmillan Press.

Henderson, Anna & Malcolm Sutton, 2016, 'South Australian Blackout: Unclear Whether Wind Power Played a Role in Outage, Report Says', *ABC News*, 5 October, available from: www.abc.net.au/news/2016-10-05/south-australian-blackout-wind-power-role-unclear-report-finds/7904282.

Hennephof, Peter, 2019, Interview with the Author, 9 May.

Henry, Ken, 2009, *Australia's Future Tax System: Report to the Treasurer*, December, Canberra: The Treasury, available from: treasury.gov.au/sites/default/files/2019-10/afts_final_report_part_1_consolidated.pdf.

Henry, Ken, 2017a, 'Challenges Confronting Economic Policy Advisers', anzsog. edu.au/research-insights-and-resources/research/challenges-confronting-economic-policy-advisers/.

Henry, Ken, 2017b, Interview with the Author, 20 October.

Henry, Ken, 2017c, Interview with the Author, 5 December.

Hersh, Seymour M., 2003, 'Selective Intelligence', *The New Yorker*, 12 May.

Heydt, Stephen, 2017, 'Same Sex Marriage Debate Leads to Psychological Distress', *Sydney Morning Herald*, 14 September, available from: www.smh.com.au/opinion/psychological-distress-20170912-gyfjif.html.

Hodgson, Helen, 2015, 'The Tax White Paper—Only Good for Fish and Chips Now?', *The Conversation*, 15 April, available from: theconversation.com/the-tax-white-paper-only-good-for-fish-and-chips-now-40069.

Holcombe, Randall G., 2016, *Advanced Introduction to Public Choice*, Cheltenham, UK: Edward Elgar Publishing.

Hood, Christopher & Martin Lodge, 2004, 'Competency, Bureaucracy and Public Management Reform: A Comparative Analysis', *Governance: An International Journal of Policy, Administration, and Institutions*, vol. 17, no. 3, pp. 313–333. doi.org/10.1111/j.0952-1895.2004.00248.x.

Hoppe, Robert & Margarita Jeliazkova, 2006, 'How Policymakers Define their Jobs: A Netherlands Case Study', in H.K. Colebatch (ed.), *The Work of Policy: An International Survey*, Lanham, MD: Lexington Books.

Horn, Eva, 2003, 'Knowing the Enemy: The Epistemology of Secret Intelligence', *Grey Room*, no. 11, Spring, pp. 58–85. doi.org/10.1162/15263810360661435.

Horn, Eva, 2010, 'Experts or Impostors? Blindness and Insight in Secret Intelligence', in Martin Kohlrausch, Katrin Steffen & Stefan Wiederkehr (eds), *Expert Cultures in Central Eastern Europe: The Internationalization of Knowledge and the Transformation of Nation States since World War I*, Osnabrück, Germany: Fibre Verlag.

Horn, Eva, 2013, *The Secret War: Treason, Espionage, and Modern Fiction*, Evanston, IL: Northwestern University Press.

House of Commons, 2009, *Bad Language: The Use and Abuse of Official Language*, First Report of Session 2009–10, 30 November, London: The Stationery Office, available from: publications.parliament.uk/pa/cm200910/cmselect/cmpubadm/17/17.pdf.

Howard, John, 2002a, 'Transcript of the Prime Minister the Hon John Howard MP Doorstop Interview—United Nations, New York', 30 January, available from: pmtranscripts.pmc.gov.au/release/transcript-12685.

Howard, John, 2002b, 'Radio Interview with Alan Jones, Radio 2GB', [Transcript], 10 September, available from: pmtranscripts.pmc.gov.au/release/transcript-12465.

Howard, John, 2002c, 'Radio Interview with Jon Faine, 3LO', [Transcript], 13 September, available from: pmtranscripts.pmc.gov.au/release/transcript-12497.

Howard, John, 2003a, 'House of Representatives, Ministerial Statements: Iraq', Speech, Tuesday, 4 February, *Parliamentary Debates*, available from: parlinfo.aph.gov.au/parlInfo/genpdf/chamber/hansardr/2003-02-04/0015/hansard_frag.pdf;fileType=application%2Fpdf.

Howard, John, 2003b, 'Transcript of the Prime Minister the Hon John Howard MP Address to the National Press Club, The Great Hall, Parliament House', Canberra, 13 March, available from: parlinfo.aph.gov.au/parlInfo/search/display/display.w3p;query=Id%3A%22media%2Fpressrel%2FPDS86%22.

Howard, John, 2003c, 'Transcript of the Prime Minister the Hon John Howard MP Address to the Nation', Canberra, 20 March, available from: parlinfo.aph.gov.au/parlInfo/search/display/display.w3p;query=Id%3A%22media%2Fpressrel%2FRZU86%22.

Howard, John, 2013a, 'Iraq 2003: A Retrospective', Speech to the Lowy Institute, Sydney, 9 April, available from: www.lowyinstitute.org/publications/iraq-2003-retrospective.

Howard, John, 2013b, *Lazarus Rising: A Personal and Political Autobiography*, rev. edn, Sydney: HarperCollins.

Howlett, Michael, 2009, 'Policy Analytical Capacity and Evidence-Based Policy-Making: Lessons from Canada', *Canadian Public Administration*, vol. 52, no. 2, pp. 153–175. doi.org/10.1111/j.1754-7121.2009.00070_1.x.

Howlett, Michael & Adam M. Wellstead, 2011, 'Policy Analysts in the Bureaucracy Revisited: The Nature of Professional Policy Work in Contemporary Government', *Politics and Policy*, vol. 49, no. 4, pp. 613–633. doi.org/10.1111/j.1747-1346.2011.00306.x.

Hughes, William & Jonathan Lavery, 2008, *Critical Thinking: An Introduction to the Basic Skills*, Peterborough, Ontario: Broadview Press.

Hunter, Fergus, 2018, 'Ministers Line Up to Criticise Abbott's "Absurd" Immigration Comments', *Sydney Morning Herald*, 22 February, available from: www.smh.com.au/politics/federal/ministers-line-up-to-criticise-abbott-s-absurd-immigration-comments-20180222-p4z184.html.

Hustedt, Thurid & Heidi Houlberg Salomonsen, 2014, 'Ensuring Political Responsiveness: Politicization Mechanisms in Ministerial Bureaucracies', *International Review of Administrative Sciences*, vol. 80, no. 4. doi.org/10.1177/0020852314533449.

Hutchens, Gareth, 2017, 'Turnbull Ignored Advice That Renewable Energy Not to Blame for SA Blackout', *The Guardian*, [Australia], 13 February, available from: www.theguardian.com/australia-news/2017/feb/13/turnbull-ignored-advice-that-renewable-energy-not-to-blame-for-sa-blackouts?CMP=share_btn_link.

Hutton, Lord, 2004, *Report of the Inquiry into the Circumstances Surrounding the Death of Dr David Kelly, C.M.G.*, 28 January, London: The Stationery Office, available from: fas.org/irp/world/uk/huttonreport.pdf.

Intergovernmental Panel on Climate Change (IPCC), 2007, *IPCC Fourth Assessment Report: Climate Change 2007*, Geneva: IPCC, available from: www.ipcc.ch/assessment-report/ar4/.

International Monetary Fund (IMF), 2018, *World Economic Outlook, April 2018: Cyclical Upswing, Structural Change*, Washington, DC: IMF, available from: www.imf.org/en/Publications/WEO/Issues/2018/03/20/world-economic-outlook-april-2018.

Irving, Helen, 2015, 'Bill Relies on Legal Fiction of Self-Executing Law to Revoke Citizenship', *The Conversation*, 17 August, available from: theconversation.com/bill-relies-on-legal-fiction-of-self-executing-law-to-revoke-citizenship-46017.

Jackson, Liz, 2003, 'Spinning the Tubes', *Four Corners*, [ABC TV], 27 October, available from: www.abc.net.au/4corners/spinning-the-tubes---2003/2844956.

Jacobs, Keith, 2015, 'The "Politics" of Australian Housing: The Role of Lobbyists and their Influence in Shaping Policy', *Housing Studies*, vol. 30, no. 5, pp. 694–710. doi.org/10.1080/02673037.2014.1000833.

Jasanoff, Sheila, 1997, 'Civilization and Madness: The Great BSE Scare of 1996', *Public Understanding of Science*, vol. 6. doi.org/10.1088/0963-6625/6/3/002.

Jasanoff, Sheila, 2005, 'Judgment under Siege: The Three-Body Problem of Expert Legitimacy', in Sabine Maasen & Peter Weingart (eds), *Democratization of Expertise? Exploring Novel Forms of Scientific Advice in Political Decision-Making*, Dordrecht, Netherlands: Springer.

Jasanoff, Sheila, 2006, 'Transparency in Public Science: Purposes, Reasons, Limits', *Law and Contemporary Problems*, vol. 69, no. 3, pp. 21–46.

Jasanoff, Sheila, 2007, *Designs on Nature: Science and Democracy in Europe and the United States*, Princeton, NJ: Princeton University Press.

Jasanoff, Sheila, 2009, 'Lessons for Science Envoys', *Seed*, 17 September.

Jasanoff, Sheila & Hilton Simmet, 2017, 'No Funeral Bells: Public Reason in a "Post-Truth" Age', *Social Studies of Science*, vol. 47, no. 5. doi.org/10.1177/0306312717731936.

Jericho, Greg, 2014, 'Hawke–Keating Reforms Were a Slow and Difficult Process', *The Guardian*, 1 January, available from: www.theguardian.com/world/2014/jan/01/hawke-keating-reforms-were-a-slow-and-difficult-process?CMP=share_btn_link.

Jervis, Robert, 2006, 'Reports, Politics, and Intelligence Failures: The Case of Iraq', *Journal of Strategic Studies*, vol. 29, no. 1, pp. 3–52. doi.org/10.1080/01402390600566282.

Jervis, Robert, 2017, 'The Mother of All Post-Mortems', *Journal of Strategic Studies*, vol. 40, nos 1–2, pp. 287–294. doi.org/10.1080/01402390.2017.1286077.

Joint Standing Committee on Foreign Affairs, Defence and Trade (JFADT), 1997, 'Appendix B—The ANZUS Treaty', *Australia's Defence Relations with the United States*, Issues Paper, Canberra: AGPS, available from: www.aph.gov.au/Parliamentary_Business/Committees/Joint/Completed_Inquiries/jfadt/usrelations/appendixb.

Karp, Paul, 2018a, 'Labor Says Treasury Document Shows Negative Gearing Claims "Outright Lies"', *The Guardian*, [Australia], 8 January.

Karp, Paul, 2018b, 'Coalition Backbenchers Unite to Lobby for Coal under Banner of Monash Forum', *The Guardian*, [Australia], 3 April, available from: www.theguardian.com/australia-news/2018/apr/03/monash-forum-coalition-backbenchers-lobby-coal.

Karp, Paul, 2022, 'Australian government to restore powers to strip citizenship from terrorism suspects', *The Guardian*, 24 October, available from: www.the guardian.com/australia-news/2022/oct/24/australian-government-to-restore-powers-to-strip-citizenship-from-terrorism-suspects.

Kelly, Paul, 2010, *The March of the Patriots: The Struggle for Modern Australia*, Melbourne: Melbourne University Press.

Kelly, Paul, 2018, 'Turnbull Liberals Doomed while Conservatism in Crisis', *The Australian*, 9 March, available from: www.theaustralian.com.au/news/inquirer/turnbull-liberals-doomed-while-conservatism-in-crisis/news-story/6 8cbd0e9603b745b9b36486ef645ba74.

Kerr, John R. & Marc Stewart Wilson, 2018, 'Changes in Perceived Scientific Consensus Shift Beliefs about Climate Change and GM Food Safety', *PLoS One*, vol. 13, no. 7. doi.org/10.1371/journal.pone.0200295.

Khodr, Hiba & Katarina Uherova Hasbani, 2013, 'The Dynamics of Energy Policy in Lebanon when Research, Politics and Policy Fail to Intersect', *Energy Policy*, vol. 60, pp. 629–642. doi.org/10.1016/j.enpol.2013.05.080.

Knorr Cetina, Karin, 2007, 'Culture in Global Knowledge Societies: Knowledge Cultures and Epistemic Cultures', *Interdisciplinary Science Reviews*, vol. 32, no. 4, pp. 361–375. doi.org/10.1179/030801807X163571.

KPMG, 2009, *Benchmarking Australian Government Administration Performance*, November, Sydney: KPMG, available from: web.archive.org/web/201304300 13239/www.dpmc.gov.au/consultation/aga_reform/docs/benchmarking_australian_government_KPMG.pdf.

Kueffer, Christoph & Brendon M.H. Larson, 2014, 'Responsible Use of Language in Scientific Writing and Science Communication', *BioScience*, vol. 64, no. 8, pp. 719–724. doi.org/10.1093/biosci/biu084.

Kuhn, Thomas, 1962, *The Structure of Scientific Revolutions*, Chicago, IL: University of Chicago Press.

Lachapelle, Erick, Éric Montpetit & Jean-Phillipe Gauvin, 2014, 'Public Perceptions of Expert Credibility on Policy Issues: The Role of Expert Framing and Political Worldviews', *Policy Studies Journal*, vol. 42, no. 4, pp. 674–697. doi.org/10.1111/psj.12073.

Latour, Bruno & Steve Woolgar, 1979, *Laboratory Life: The Social Construction of Scientific Facts*, Thousand Oaks, CA: Sage Publications.

Leach, Joan, 2000, 'Rhetorical Analysis', in Martin W. Bauer & George Gaskell (eds), *Qualitative Researching with Text, Image and Sound*, Thousand Oaks, CA: Sage Publications. doi.org/10.4135/9781849209731.n12.

Leeuw, Frans, 2019, Interview with the Author, 9 May.

Lefsrud, Lianne M. & Renate E. Meyer, 2012, 'Science or Science Fiction? Professionals' Discursive Construction of Climate Change', *Organization Studies*, vol. 33, no. 11. doi.org/10.1177/0170840612463317.

Levey, Matt, 2014, 'Statement of Matt Levey', Royal Commission into the Home Insulation Program, 18 March, available from: www.homeinsulationroyal commission.gov.au/hearings/Documents/Evidence21March2014/STA.001. 003.0001.pdf [page discontinued].

Lewis, Peter, 2016, 'Turnbull's Popularity Plunge Has Redefined the Election', *The Drum*, [ABC TV], 16 March, available from: www.abc.net.au/news/ 2016-03-16/lewis-turnbulls-popularity-plunge-has-redefined-the-election/ 7248686.

Lewis, Rosie, 2015, 'Prince Philip Knighthood: Tony Abbott Defends Decision', *The Australian*, 26 January, available from: www.theaustralian.com.au/news/ prince-philip-knighthood-tony-abbott-defends-decision/news-story/1465d0 aea652e67f9698248e9f190b19.

Littlefield, Scott R., 2013, 'Security, Independence, and Sustainability: Imprecise Language and the Manipulation of Energy Policy in the United States', *Energy Policy*, vol. 52, pp. 779–788. doi.org/10.1016/j.enpol.2012.10.040.

Luetjens, Jo & Paul 't Hart, 2019, *Appendix C. Governing by Looking Back: Learning from Successes and Failures*, An ANZSOG Research Paper for the Australian Public Service Review Panel, March 2019, Melbourne: Australia and New Zealand School of Government, available from: www.apsreview. gov.au/sites/default/files/resources/appendix-c-governing-looking-back.pdf.

Mackie, Kathleen, 2015, 'Success and Failure in Environment Policy: The Role of Policy Officials', *Australian Journal of Public Administration*, vol. 75, no. 3, pp. 291–304. doi.org/10.1111/1467-8500.12170.

Majone, Giandomenico, 1989, *Evidence, Argument, and Persuasion in the Policy Process*, New Haven, CT: Yale University Press.

Manne, Robert, 2003, 'Explaining the Invasion', in Raimond Gaita (ed.), *Why the War Was Wrong*, Melbourne: Text Publishing.

Marando, Dylan & Jonathan Craft, 2017, 'Digital Era Policy Advising: Clouding Ministerial Perspectives?', *Canadian Public Administration*, vol. 60, no. 4, pp. 498–516. doi.org/10.1111/capa.12242.

Martin, Chris, Kath Hulse & Hal Pawson, 2017, *The Changing Institutions of Private Rental Housing: An International Review*, AHURI Final Report No. 292, Melbourne: Australian Housing and Urban Research Institute Limited, available from: www.ahuri.edu.au/research/final-reports/292. doi.org/10.18408/ahuri-7112201.

Martin, Peter, 2018, 'Why Treasury Thought Turnbull Was Wrong on Negative Gearing', *Sydney Morning Herald*, 8 January, available from: www.smh.com.au/politics/federal/why-treasury-thought-turnbull-was-wrong-on-negative-gearing-20180108-h0f481.html.

Martin, Sarah, 2015, 'Abbott v Turnbull: How the Liberal Party Room Voted', *The Australian*, 15 October, available from: www.theaustralian.com.au/national-affairs/abbott-v-turnbull-how-the-liberal-party-room-voted/news-story/5f2ef2b4340a9f72140e806a837cc09e.

Massola, James, Peter Ker & Lisa Cox, 2014, 'Coal Is "Good for Humanity", Says Tony Abbott at Mine Opening', *Sydney Morning Herald*, 13 October, available from: www.smh.com.au/politics/federal/coal-is-good-for-humanity-says-tony-abbott-at-mine-opening-20141013-115bgs.html.

Masters, Adam B. & John Uhr, 2017, *Leadership Performance and Rhetoric*, Cham, Switzerland: Palgrave Macmillan. doi.org/10.1007/978-3-319-58774-5.

Mathiesen, Thomas, 2004, *Silently Silenced: Essays on the Creation of Acquiescence in Modern Society*, Hook, UK: Waterside Press.

Maynard, Phil & Agencies, 2016, '"It Isn't about a Lie": Tony Blair on Iraq from 2001 to 2016—Video', *The Guardian*, 7 July, available from: www.theguardian.com/politics/video/2016/jul/06/it-isnt-about-a-lie-tony-blair-on-iraq-from-2001-to-2016-video.

McCloskey, Deirdre, 1994, *Knowledge and Persuasion in Economics*, Cambridge, UK: Cambridge University Press. doi.org/10.1017/CBO9780511599347.

McConnell, Allan, Anika Gauja & Linda Courtenay Botterill, 2008, 'Policy Fiascos, Blame Management and AWB Limited: The Howard Government's Escape from the Iraq Wheat Scandal', *Australian Journal of Political Science*, vol. 43, no. 4, pp. 599–616. doi.org/10.1080/10361140802429239.

McCullough, Paul, 2019a, Interview with the Author, 22 January.

McCullough, Paul, 2019b, Interview with the Author, 31 January.

McDermott, Kathy, 2008, *Whatever Happened to Frank and Fearless? The Impact of New Public Management on the Australian Public Service*, Canberra: ANU E Press. doi.org/10.22459/WHFF.07.2008.

McDonald, Matt & Matt Merefield, 2010, 'How Was Howard's War Possible? Winning the War of Position over Iraq', *Australian Journal of International Affairs*, vol. 64, no. 2, pp. 186–204. doi.org/10.1080/10357710903544346.

McGhee, Ashlynne & Michael McKinnon, 2018, 'The Cabinet Files', *ABC News*, 31 January, [updated 10 February], available from: www.abc.net.au/news/2018-01-31/cabinet-files-reveal-inner-government-decisions/9168442.

McGoey, Linsey, 2007, 'On the Will to Ignorance in Bureaucracy', *Economy and Society*, vol. 36, no. 2, pp. 212–235. doi.org/10.1080/03085140701254282.

McKeown, Deirdre, 2018, *Chronology of Same-Sex Marriage Bills Introduced into the Federal Parliament: A Quick Guide*, Research Paper Series, 2018–19, 15 February, Canberra: Parliamentary Library, available from: www.aph.gov.au/About_Parliament/Parliamentary_Departments/Parliamentary_Library/pubs/rp/rp1718/Quick_Guides/SSMarriageBills.

McKinnon, Michael & Dan Conifer, 2018, 'Treasury Public Servants Wanted Negative Gearing Documents Kept Secret from ABC', *ABC News*, 8 January, available from: www.abc.net.au/news/2018-01-08/bureaucrats-threatened-to-stop-giving-honest-advice-to-treasury/9309708.

McQuade, Brendan, 2016, 'The Puzzle of Intelligence Expertise: Spaces of Intelligence Analysis and the Production of "Political" Knowledge', *Qualitative Sociology*, vol. 39, pp. 247–265. doi.org/10.1007/s11133-016-9335-6.

Mearsheimer, John J. & Stephen M. Walt, 2009, 'An Unnecessary War', *Foreign Policy*, 3 November, available from: foreignpolicy.com/2009/11/03/an-unnecessary-war-2/.

Megalogenis, George, 2012, *The Australian Moment: How We Were Made for These Times*, Melbourne: Penguin.

Michaels, David, 2008, *Doubt Is Their Product: How Industry's Assault on Science Threatens Your Health*, Oxford, UK: Oxford University Press.

Middleton, Karen, 2019, 'Morrison Ignored Boat Security Advice', *The Saturday Paper*, no. 241, 23 February – 1 March, available from: www.thesaturday paper.com.au/news/politics/2019/02/23/morrison-ignored-boat-security-advice/15508404007499.

Millstone, Erik & Patrick van Zwanenberg, 2001, 'Politics of Expert Advice: Lessons from the Early History of the BSE Saga', *Science and Public Policy*, vol. 28, no. 2. doi.org/10.3152/147154301781781543.

Minns, Bob, 2004, *A History in Three Acts: Evolution of the Public Service Act 1999*, APSC Occasional Paper No. 3, Canberra: Australian Public Service Commission, available from: www.apsc.gov.au/publications-and-media/archive/publications-archive/history-in-3-acts [page discontinued].

Minteer, Ben A., 2005, 'Environmental Philosophy and the Public Interest: A Pragmatic Reconciliation', *Environmental Values*, vol. 14, no. 1, pp. 37–60. doi.org/10.3197/0963271053306104.

Monbiot, George, 2016, 'Chilcot's Judgment Is Utterly Damning—But It's Still Not Justice', *The Guardian*, 6 July, available from: www.theguardian.com/commentisfree/2016/jul/06/chilcot-judgment-damning-not-justice-tony-blair-crime-aggression.

Moore, Alfred, 2017, *Critical Elitism: Deliberation, Democracy, and the Problem of Expertise*, Cambridge, UK: Cambridge University Press. doi.org/10.1017/9781108159906.

Moran, Terry, 2010, *Ahead of the Game: Blueprint for the Reform of Australian Government Administration*, March, Advisory Group on Reform of Australian Government Administration, Canberra: Commonwealth of Australia, available from: www.apsreview.gov.au/sites/default/files/files/Ahead%20of%20the%20Game%20-%20Blueprint%20for%20the%20Reform%20of%20Australian%20Government.pdf.

Moran, Terry, 2019, 'The Accountability Roundtable: An Oration in Honour of Jim Carlton AO: The Next Long Wave of Reform—Where Will the Ideas Come From?', University of Melbourne, 25 March, available from: cpd. org.au/wp-content/uploads/2019/06/Accountability-Roundtable——-Terry-Moran-AC.pdf.

Morris, Mark, 2014, 'Guest Post: Clarity Is King—The Evidence That Reveals the Desperate Need to Re-Think the Way We Write', *Government Digital Service*, [GOV.UK Blog], 17 February, available from: gds.blog.gov.uk/2014/02/17/guest-post-clarity-is-king-the-evidence-that-reveals-the-desperate-need-to-re-think-the-way-we-write/.

Morrison, Scott, 2015, Joint Doorstop Interview, Helloworld Ashburton, Melbourne, 21 February, available from: sjm.ministers.treasury.gov.au/transcript/016-2018/ [page discontinued].

Morrison, Scott, 2016, 'Scott Morrison: 'Labor's Higher Taxes Are Not about Delivering Tax Relief for Australians', *The Sunday Telegraph*, [Sydney], 14 February, available from: ministers.treasury.gov.au/ministers/scott-morrison-2015/media-releases/opinion-piece-sunday-telegraph.

Morrison, Scott, 2019, 'Transcript', Press Conference, Canberra, 25 July, available from: www.pm.gov.au/media/press-conference.

Mulgan, Richard, 2000a, 'Perspectives on the "Public Interest"', *Canberra Bulletin of Public Administration*, no. 95.

Mulgan, Richard, 2000b, 'Public Servants and the Public Interest', *Canberra Bulletin on Public Administration*, no. 97.

Mulgan, Richard, 2007, 'Truth in Government and the Politicization of Public Service Advice', *Public Administration*, vol. 85, no. 3, pp. 569–586. doi.org/10.1111/j.1467-9299.2007.00663.x.

Mulgan, Richard, 2008, 'How Much Responsiveness Is Too Much or Too Little?', *Australian Journal of Public Administration*, vol. 67, no. 3 pp. 345–356. doi.org/10.1111/j.1467-8500.2008.00592.x.

Murphy, Katharine, 2018, 'Coalition Signs Off on Neg but Tony Abbott Continues Internal Dissent', *The Guardian*, [Australia], 14 August, available from: www.theguardian.com/australia-news/2018/aug/14/coalition-signs-off-on-neg-but-tony-abbott-continues-internal-dissent.

Nair, Sreeja & Michael Howlett, 2017, 'Policy Myopia as a Source of Policy Failure: Adaptation and Policy Learning under Deep Uncertainty', *Policy & Politics*, vol. 45, no. 1, pp. 103–118. doi.org/10.1332/030557316X14788776017743.

Naquin, Charles E. & Terri R. Kurtzberg, 2004, 'Human Reactions to Technological Failure: How Accidents Rooted in Technology vs. Human Error Influence Judgments of Organizational Accountability', *Organizational Behavior and Human Decision Processes*, vol. 93, no. 2, pp. 129–141. doi.org/10.1016/j.obhdp.2003.12.001.

National Energy Resources Australia (NERA), 2017, 'Energy Policy Certainty Key to Australia's Economic Future', Media Release, 9 June, NERA, Perth, available from: www.nera.org.au/MediaReleases/EnergyPolicyCertainty.

Neilsen, Mary Anne, 2016, 'Same-Sex Marriage', *Parliamentary Library Briefing Book: Key Issues for the 45th Parliament*, July, Canberra: Parliament of Australia, available from: parlinfo.aph.gov.au/parlInfo/search/display/display.w3p;query=Id:%22library/prspub/4789188%22.

New Zealand Institute for Economic Research (NZIER), 2013, *Policy Advice Quality Review 2013; NZIER Report to Ministry of Women's Affairs*, August, Wellington: NZIER, available from: www.parliament.nz/resource/en-nz/50SCGA_EVI_00DBSCH_FIN_12706_1_A372431/e526ca859540fea572b4869430d6cde8244853ed.

Ng, Yee-Fui, 2017, 'Between Law and Convention: Ministerial Advisers in the Australian System of Responsible Government', Senate Occasional Lecture Series No. 68, Parliament House, Canberra, 21 July, available from: www.aph.gov.au/About_Parliament/Senate/Powers_practice_n_procedures/pops.

Nichols, Tom, 2017, *The Death of Expertise: The Campaign against Established Knowledge and Why it Matters*, Oxford, UK: Oxford University Press.

Nyman, Jonna, 2018, 'Rethinking Energy, Climate and Security: A Critical Analysis of Energy Security in the US', *Journal of International Relations and Development*, vol. 1, no. 1, pp. 118–145, available from: eprints.whiterose.ac.uk/105608. doi.org/10.1057/jird.2015.26.

Oakes, Laurie, 2010, 'Rudd Was Blind', *Herald Sun*, [Melbourne], 29 October.

Office of the Australian Information Commissioner (OAIC), 2016, 'Part 6—Conditional Exemptions', *FOI Guidelines*, Sections 6.79–6.85, Version 1.3, 19 December, Sydney: OAIC, available from: www.oaic.gov.au/freedom-of-information/foi-guidelines/part-6-conditional-exemptions.

Office of the Australian Information Commissioner (OAIC), 2019, *Annual Report 2018–19*, Sydney: OAIC, available from: www.oaic.gov.au/about-us/our-corporate-information/annual-reports/oaic-annual-reports/annual-report-2018-19.

Office of National Assessments (ONA), n.d.(a), *About ONA: Director-General's Message*, Canberra: Australian Government, available from: www.ona.gov.au/about-ona/overview/director-generals-message [page discontinued].

Office of National Assessments (ONA), n.d.(b), *A Short History of the Office of National Assessments*, Canberra: Australian Government, available from: www.ona.gov.au/about-ona/overview/history-ona [page discontinued].

Office of National Assessments (ONA), n.d.(c), 'Overview', [Online], Canberra: Australian Government, available from: www.ona.gov.au/about-ona/overview [page discontinued].

Owens, Jared, 2016, 'South Australia Blackout: Jay Weatherill Resists Calls for Inquiry', *The Australian*, 29 September, available from: www.theaustralian.com.au/national-affairs/barnaby-joyce-ignorant-for-blaming-blackout-on-wind-energy/news-story/8846b63ad10c7f3c4ed2bdfa43624ceb.

Padula, Marinella, 2017, *The Best Laid Plans: Australia's Home Insulation Program*, Part (A) 2017-190.1, Part (B) 2017-190.2 and (Epilogue) 2017-190.3, Melbourne: John L. Alford Case Library, Australia and New Zealand School of Government, available from: anzsog.edu.au/research-insights-and-resources/research/best-laid-plans-australias-home-insulation-program-a-2017-190-1/.

Pallett, Helen, 2015, 'Public Participation Organizations and Open Policy: A Constitutional Moment for British Democracy', *Science Communication*, vol. 37, no. 6. doi.org/10.1177/1075547015612787.

Palmer, James, Susan Owens & Robert Doubleday, 2019, 'Perfecting the "Elevator Pitch"? Expert Advice as Locally-Situated Boundary Work', *Science and Public Policy*, vol. 46, no. 2, pp. 244–253. doi.org/10.1093/scipol/scy054.

Parkinson, Giles, 2017, 'AEMO Says Wind Farm Changes Mean SA Blackout Won't Be Repeated', *Renew Economy*, 6 February, available from: reneweconomy.com. au/aemo-says-wind-farm-changes-mean-sa-blackout-wont-repeated-43631/.

Parkinson, Martin, 2016, 'Closing Remarks at the Launch of Peter Shergold's Report', Institute of Public Administration, Canberra, 11 April, available from: www.pmc.gov.au/news-centre/pmc/closing-remarks-launch-peter-shergold's-report.

Parliament of Australia, n.d.(a), 'Hon Scott Morrison MP', *Senators and Members*, Canberra: Parliament of Australia, available from: www.aph.gov.au/Senators_and_Members/Parliamentarian?MPID=E3L.

Parliament of Australia, n.d.(b), 'Senate Estimates', *Parliamentary Business*, Canberra: Parliament of Australia, available from: www.aph.gov.au/Parliamentary_Business/Senate_Estimates.

Parliament of Australia, 2015, House of Representatives, Questions without Notice, Marriage, Question, Wednesday, 12 August, *Parliamentary Debates*, available from: parlinfo.aph.gov.au/parlInfo/genpdf/chamber/hansardr/a42cf478-4ae3-41a7-a650-a236ec98ee4c/0088/hansard_frag.pdf;fileType=application%2Fpdf.

Parliament of Australia, 2016a, House of Representatives, Official Hansard, No. 1, 2016, Tuesday, 30 August, *Parliamentary Debates*, available from: parlinfo.aph.gov.au/parlInfo/download/chamber/hansardr/1133bdef-2731-42fb-a226-6522e1a8fec5/toc_pdf/House%20of%20Representatives_2016_08_30_4429_Official.pdf;fileType=application/pdf.

Parliament of Australia, 2016b, House of Representatives, Official Hansard, No. 3, 2016, Monday, 10 October, *Parliamentary Debates*, available from: parlinfo.aph.gov.au/parlInfo/download/chamber/hansardr/53c9fd8e-e207-4e59-aa4a-a1953f715e20/toc_pdf/House%20of%20Representatives_2016_10_10_4462_Official.pdf;fileType=application%2Fpdf#search=%22chamber/hansardr/53c9fd8e-e207-4e59-aa4a-a1953f715e20/0000%22.

Parliament of Australia, 2016c, House of Representatives, Official Hansard, No. 3, 2016, Wednesday, 12 October, *Parliamentary Debates*, available from: parlinfo.aph.gov.au/parlInfo/download/chamber/hansardr/3bef5bfd-10a1-42ac-8cdf-41e8b9c0f758/toc_pdf/House%20of%20Representatives_2016_10_12_4468_Official.pdf;fileType=application%2Fpdf#search=%22chamber/hansardr/3bef5bfd-10a1-42ac-8cdf-41e8b9c0f758/0000%22.

Parliament of Australia, 2017, *The Opening of Parliament*, Senate Brief No. 2, July, Canberra: Parliament of Australia, available from: www.aph.gov.au/About_Parliament/Senate/Powers_practice_n_procedures/Senate_Briefs/Brief02.

Parliamentary Joint Committee on ASIO, ASIS and DSD (PJCAAD), 2003, *Intelligence on Iraq's Weapons of Mass Destruction*, December, Canberra: Parliament of Australia, available from: www.aph.gov.au/Parliamentary_Business/Committees/House_of_Representatives_committees?url=pjcaad/wmd/report.htm.

Parliamentary Joint Committee on Intelligence and Security (PJCIS), 2016, *Criminal Code Amendment (High Risk Terrorist Offenders) Bill 2016*, Canberra: Parliament of Australia, available from: www.aph.gov.au/Parliamentary_Business/Committees/Joint/Intelligence_and_Security/HRTOBill.

Patrick, Aaron, 2018, 'Malcolm Turnbull and the Great Paradox of Australian Politics', *Australian Financial Review*, 22 March, available from: www.afr.com/news/politics/national/malcolm-turnbull-and-the-great-paradox-of-australian-politics-20180308-h0x6t6.

Pawson, Isla, 2018, 'Reframing Australia's Housing Affordability Problem: The Politics and Economics of Negative Gearing', *Journal of Australian Political Economy*, no. 81, pp. 121–143.

Peatling, Stephanie, 2016, 'Politics Live: February 24, 2016', *Sydney Morning Herald*, available from: www.smh.com.au/federal-politics/the-pulse-live/politics-live-february-24-2016-20160223-gn1w1b.html.

Perrigo, Billy, 2018, 'Why Does Australia Keep Getting Rid of Its Prime Ministers?', *TIME*, 24 August, available from: time.com/5377190/why-australia-changes-prime-ministers/.

Peter, B. Guy, 2004, 'Review of "Reframing Public Policy: Discursive Politics and Deliberative Practices"', *Political Science Quarterly*, vol. 119, no. 3, pp. 566–567. doi.org/10.2307/20202425.

Phythian, Mark, 2006, 'The Perfect Intelligence Failure? U.S. Pre-War Intelligence on Iraqi Weapons of Mass Destruction', *Politics & Policy*, vol. 34, no. 2. doi.org/10.1111/j.1747-1346.2006.00019.x.

Pillai, Sangeetha, 2015a, 'Committee Recommendations Improve Citizenship Bill, but Fundamental Flaws Remain', *The Conversation*, 7 September, available from: theconversation.com/committee-recommendations-improve-citizenship-bill-but-fundamental-flaws-remain-45720.

Pillai, Sangeetha, 2015b, 'Improved Citizenship Bill Still Invites Criticism and High Court Challenges', *The Conversation*, 12 November, available from: theconversation.com/improved-citizenship-bill-still-invites-criticism-and-high-court-challenges-47153.

Podger, Andrew, 2007, 'What Really Happens: Department Secretary Appointments, Contracts and Performance Pay in the Australian Public Service', *Australian Journal of Public Administration*, vol. 66, no. 2, pp. 131–147. doi.org/10.1111/j.1467-8500.2007.00524.x.

Poenaru, Florin, 2017, 'The Knowledge of the Securitate: Secret Agents as Anthropologists', *Studia UBB Sociologica*, vol. 62, no. 1, pp. 105–125. doi.org/10.1515/subbs-2017-0007.

Porter, Theodore M., 1995, *Trust in Numbers: The Pursuit of Objectivity and Science and Public Life*, Princeton, NJ: Princeton University Press. doi.org/10.1515/9780691210544.

Potter, Ben, 2017, 'It's Time to Strip Treasury of Forecasting: Bob Gregory', *Australian Financial Review*, 29 May, [updated 30 May], available from: www.afr.com/news/its-time-to-strip-treasury-of-forecasting-bob-gregory-20170529-gwfv8z.

Potter, Ben, Angela Macdonald Smith & Mark Ludlow, 2018, 'Explained: How to Understand Australia's New Energy Mess', *Australian Financial Review*, 7 October, available from: www.afr.com/news/special-reports/afr-focus-energy/australias-energy-policy-is-shipwrecked-on-the-same-reef-again-20181001-h163p5.

Powell, Colin L., 2003, 'Remarks to the United Nations Security Council: Secretary Colin L. Powell', New York City, NY, 5 February, available from: 2001-2009.2001-2009.state.gov/secretary/former/powell/remarks/2003/17300.htm.

Radin, Beryl, 2013, *Beyond Machiavelli: Policy Analysis Reaches Midlife*, 2nd edn, Washington, DC: Georgetown University Press.

Raimondo, Estelle & Frans L. Leeuw, 2021, 'Evaluation Systems and Bureaucratic Capture: Locked in the System and Potential Avenues for Change', in Burt Perrin & Tony Tyrell (eds), *Changing Bureaucracies: Adapting to Uncertainty, and How Evaluation Can Help*, New York, NY: Routledge. doi.org/10.4324/9781003100584-12.

Raman, Sujatha, Pru Hobson-West, Mimi E. Lam & Kate Millar, 2018, '"Science Matters" and the Public Interest: The Role of Minority Engagement', in Brigitte Nerlich, Sarah Hartley, Sujatha Raman & Alexander Smith (eds), *Science and the Politics of Openness*, Manchester, UK: Manchester University Press.

Rappert, Brian, 2012a, *How to Look Good in a War: Justifying and Challenging State Violence*, London: Pluto Press.

Rappert, Brian, 2012b, 'States of Ignorance: The Unmaking and Remaking of Death Tolls', *Economy and Society*, vol. 41, no. 1, pp. 42–63. doi.org/10.1080/03085147.2011.637334.

Rappert, Brian, 2015, 'Sensing Absence: How to See What Isn't There in the Study of Science and Security', in Brian Rappert & Brian Balmer (eds), *Absence in Science, Security and Policy: From Research Agendas to Global Strategy*, London: Palgrave Macmillan. doi.org/10.1057/9781137592613.

Rayner, Steve, 2012, 'Uncomfortable Knowledge: The Social Construction of Ignorance in Science and Environmental Policy Discourses', *Economy and Society*, vol. 41, no. 1, pp. 107–125. doi.org/10.1080/03085147.2011.637335.

Rein, Martin, 2006, 'Reframing Problematic Policies', in Michael Moran, Martin Rein & Robert E. Goodin (eds), *The Oxford Handbook of Public Policy*, Oxford, UK: Oxford University Press.

Remeikis, Amy & Katharine Murphy, 2018, 'Turnbull Sets Out Power Price Fix to Stay Ahead of Coalition Rebellion', *The Guardian*, [Australia], 19 August, available from: www.theguardian.com/australia-news/2018/aug/19/turnbull-sets-out-power-price-fix-to-stay-ahead-of-coalition-rebellion.

Reuters, 2016, 'Tony Blair: I Accept Full Responsibility for Iraq War Decision—Video', *The Guardian*, 7 July, available from: www.theguardian.com/uk-news/video/2016/jul/06/tony-blair-chilcot-iraq-war-decision-video.

Rhodes, R.A.W., 2005, 'Everyday Life in a Ministry: Public Administration as Anthropology', *American Review of Public Administration*, vol. 35, no. 1. doi.org/10.1177/0275074004271716.

Rhodes, R.A.W., 2018, *Narrative Policy Analysis: Cases in Decentred Policy*, New York, NY: Springer International Publishing AG. doi.org/10.1007/978-3-319-76635-5.

Rovner, Joshua, 2011, 'Fixing the Facts or Missing the Mark? Intelligence, Policy, and the War in Iraq', *Foreign Policy Research Institute E-Notes*, October, Philadelphia, PA: Foreign Policy Research Institute. doi.org/10.7591/cornell/9780801448294.003.0007.

Rovner, Joshua, 2013, 'Is Politicization Ever a Good Thing?', *Intelligence and National Security*, vol. 28, no. 1, pp. 55–67. doi.org/10.1080/02684527.2012. 749065.

Rudd, Kevin, 2007, '2007 Election Speech', Brisbane, 14 November, available from: electionspeeches.moadoph.gov.au/speeches/2007-kevin-rudd.

Rudd, Kevin, 2008, 'Address to Heads of Agencies and Members of Senior Executive Service, Great Hall, Parliament House, Canberra', 30 April, available from: pmtranscripts.pmc.gov.au/release/transcript-15893.

Rudd, Kevin, 2014, 'Witness Statement: The Hon Kevin Michael Rudd', Royal Commission into the Home Insulation Program, Brisbane, 14 May, available from: www.abc.net.au/news/2014-05-15/royal-commission-home-insulation---witness-statement---kevin-ru/5454890?nw=0.

Rumsfeld, Donald, 2002, 'Press Conference by US Secretary of Defence, Donald Rumsfeld', 6 June, NATO, Brussels, available from: www.nato.int/docu/speech/2002/s020606g.htm.

Salminen, Ari & Venla Mäntysalo, 2013, 'Exploring the Public Service Ethos', *Public Integrity*, vol. 15, no. 2, pp. 167–186. doi.org/10.2753/PIN1099-9922150204.

Sanderson, Ian, 2009, 'Intelligent Policy Making for a Complex World: Pragmatism, Evidence and Learning', *Political Studies*, vol. 57, no. 4. doi.org/10.1111/j.1467-9248.2009.00791.x.

Sarewitz, Daniel, 2004, 'How Science Makes Environmental Controversies Worse', *Environmental Science & Policy*, vol. 7, no. 5, pp. 385–403. doi.org/10.1016/j.envsci.2004.06.001.

SBS News, 2018, 'Julie Bishop: Australia Referred to as "Coup Capital of the World"', *SBS News*, 24 September, available from: www.sbs.com.au/news/julie-bishop-australia-referred-to-as-coup-capital-of-the-world.

SBS News, 2022, 'Dual National Whose Citizenship Was Cancelled by Australian Government Wins Landmark High Court Case', *SBS News*, 8 June, available from: www.sbs.com.au/news/article/dual-national-whose-citizenship-was-cancelled-by-australian-government-wins-landmark-high-court-case/u4bjz90f1.

Schmidt, Vivien A., 2008, 'Discursive Institutionalism: The Explanatory Power of Ideas and Discourse', *Annual Review of Political Science*, vol. 11, pp. 303–326. doi.org/10.1146/annurev.polisci.11.060606.135342.

Seligmann, Linda J. & Brian P. Estes, 2020, 'Innovations in Ethnographic Methods', *American Behavioral Scientist*, vol. 64, no. 2. doi.org/10.1177/0002764219859640.

Senate Environment and Communications Legislation Committee, 2016, Estimates, 17 October, *Official Committee Hansard*, Canberra: Parliament of Australia, available from: parlinfo.aph.gov.au/parlInfo/download/committees/estimate/7af87243-819e-4a43-aa2b-d32530bd97c4/toc_pdf/Environment%20and%20Communications%20Legislation%20Committee_2016_10_17_4508_Official.pdf;fileType=application%2Fpdf#search=%22committees/estimate/7af87243-819e-4a43-aa2b-d32530bd97c4/0000%22.

Senate Legal and Constitutional Affairs References Committee, 2016a, 'Consultations Prior to the Making of Directions Concerning Opinions of the Solicitor-General', 14 October, *Official Committee Hansard*, Canberra: Parliament of Australia, available from: parlinfo.aph.gov.au/parlInfo/download/committees/commsen/65445157-84a3-4618-ac9f-718be462646f/toc_pdf/Legal%20and%20Constitutional%20Affairs%20References%20Committee_2016_10_14_4498_Official.pdf;fileType=application%2Fpdf#search=%22gleeson%20brandis%20october%202016%20committees%22.

Senate Legal and Constitutional Affairs References Committee, 2016b, *Nature and Scope of the Consultations Prior to the Making of the Legal Services Amendment (Solicitor-General Opinions) Direction 2016*, Submission 3, Solicitor-General of the Commonwealth of Australia, 8 November, Canberra: Parliament of Australia, available from: www.aph.gov.au/Parliamentary_Business/Committees/Senate/Legal_and_Constitutional_Affairs/SolicitorGeneralOpinion/Submissions.

Senate Select Committee on Intelligence (SSCI), 2004, *Report of the Select Committee on Intelligence on the U.S. Intelligence Community's Prewar Intelligence Assessments on Iraq, Together with Additional Views*, Senate Report 108-301, 7 July, Washington, DC: United States Senate, available from: nsarchive2.gwu.edu/NSAEBB/NSAEBB254/doc12.pdf.

Senate Select Committee on Intelligence (SSCI), 2008, 'Senate Intelligence Committee Unveils Final Phase II Reports on Prewar Iraq Intelligence', Press Release of Intelligence Committee, United States Senate, Washington, DC, 5 June, available from: www.intelligence.senate.gov/press/senate-intelligence-committee-unveils-final-phase-ii-reports-prewar-iraq-intelligence.

Senate Standing Committee on Environment and Communications, 2016, 'Question No. 258. 5.1: Energy', Questions on Notice Index, *Supplementary Budget Estimates 2016–17 (October 2016): Environment Portfolio*, Canberra: Parliament of Australia, available from: www.aph.gov.au/Parliamentary_Business/Senate_Estimates/ecctte/estimates/supp1617/environment%20and%20energy/index.

Senate Standing Committee on Finance and Public Administration (SSCFPA), 2018, *Report: Arrangements for the Postal Survey*, 13 February, Canberra: Parliament of Australia, available from: www.aph.gov.au/Parliamentary_ Business/Committees/Senate/Finance_and_Public_Administration/postal survey/Report.

Shapiro, Michael J., 1981, *Language and Political Understanding: The Politics of Discursive Practices*, New Haven, CT: Yale University Press.

Shergold, Peter, 2015, *Learning from Failure: Why Large Government Policy Initiatives Have Gone So Badly Wrong in the Past and How the Chances of Success in the Future Can Be Improved*, Canberra: Commonwealth of Australia, available from: www.apsc.gov.au/publication/learning-from-failure.

Shuchart, Scott, 2018, 'Civil Servants Said Separating Families Was Illegal. The Administration Ignored Us', *The Washington Post*, 25 October.

Smith, John E., 1969, 'Time, Times and the "Right Time"; *Chronos* and *Kairos*', *The Monist*, vol. 53, no. 1, pp. 1–13. doi.org/10.5840/monist196953115.

Smith, John E., 2002, 'Time and Qualitative Time', in Phillip Sipiora & James S. Baumlin (eds), *Rhetoric and Kairos: Essays in History, Theory, and Praxis*, Albany: SUNY Press.

Spillius, Alex, 2008, 'George W Bush Says Iraq Intelligence Failure Is His Biggest Regret', *The Telegraph*, [London], 1 December, available from: www. telegraph.co.uk/news/worldnews/northamerica/usa/3540733/George-W-Bush-says-Iraq-intelligence-failure-is-his-biggest-regret.html.

Srivastava, Sameer B. & Amir Goldberg, 2017, 'Language as a Window into Culture', *California Management Review*, vol. 60, no. 1. doi.org/10.1177/ 0008125617731781.

Stevens, Alex, 2011, 'Telling Policy Stories: An Ethnographic Study of the Use of Evidence in Policy-Making in the UK', *Journal of Social Policy*, vol. 40, no. 2. doi.org/10.1017/S0047279410000723.

Stirling, Andy, 2014, 'Transforming Power: Social Science and the Politics of Energy Choices', *Energy Research & Social Science*, vol. 1. doi.org/10.2139/ ssrn.2742109.

Stone, Deborah, 1997, *Policy Paradox: The Art of Political Decision Making*, New York, NY: W.W. Norton & Company.

Strassheim, Holger & Pekka Kettunen, 2014, 'When Does Evidence-Based Policy Turn into Policy-Based Evidence? Configurations, Contexts and Mechanisms', *Evidence & Policy*, vol. 10, no. 2, pp. 259–277. doi.org/10.1332/174426514X13990433991320.

Strutt, Jessica, 2018, 'Scott Morrison Strives for "Man of the People" Image on First WA Visit, in Contrast to Malcolm Turnbull', *ABC News*, 7 October, available from: www.abc.net.au/news/2018-10-06/scott-morrisons-first-visit-to-perth-as-prime-minister/10339380.

Sullivan, Helen, 2011, '"Truth" Junkies: Using Evaluation in UK Public Policy', *Policy & Politics*, vol. 39, no. 4, pp. 499–512. doi.org/10.1332/030557311X574216.

Sullivan, Patrick, 2008, 'Bureaucratic Process as Morris Dance: An Ethnographic Approach to the Culture of Bureaucracy in Australian Aboriginal Affairs Administration', *Critical Perspectives on International Business*, vol. 4, nos 2–3. doi.org/10.1108/17422040810869981.

Sunshine Coast Daily, 2016, 'John Howard Replies to Chilcot Inquiry', *Sunshine Coast Daily*, [Maroochydore, Qld], 7 July.

Sydney Morning Herald (SMH), 2003, 'The Government's Legal Advice on Using Force', *Sydney Morning Herald*, 19 March, available from: www.smh.com.au/world/middle-east/the-governments-legal-advice-on-using-force-20030319-gdggf5.html.

Taussig, Michael, 1999, *Defacement: Public Secrecy and the Labor of the Negative*, Stanford, CA: Stanford University Press. doi.org/10.1515/9781503617131.

Tease, Warren, 2016, 'Forecasting in Treasury: Address to CEDA's Economic and Political Overview Conference Warren Tease, Principal Adviser, Macroeconomic Conditions Division, Treasury', Melbourne, 18 February, available from: treasury.gov.au/speech/forecasting-in-treasury/.

The Age, 2003, 'Troops to Leave for Middle East Tomorrow', *The Age*, [Melbourne], 22 January, available from: www.theage.com.au/articles/2003/01/22/1042911424779.html.

The Treasury, n.d., 'About Treasury', [Online], Canberra: Australian Government, available from: treasury.gov.au/the-department/about-treasury/.

The Treasury, 2008–10, *The Australia's Future Tax System Review*, Canberra: Australian Government, available from: treasury.gov.au/review/the-australias-future-tax-system-review.

The Treasury, 2011, *Strategic Review of the Treasury*, December, Canberra: Australian Government, available from: treasury.gov.au/sites/default/files/2019-03/A9RC613.pdf.

The Treasury, 2018, 'Tax—Negative Gearing/Capital Gains Tax', FOI 1876, *FOI Disclosure Log*, 5 January, Canberra: Australian Government, available from: static.treasury.gov.au/uploads/sites/1/2018/01/FOI_1876_Documents_for_release.pdf.

The Treasury, 2019a, 'Tax—Negative Gearing/Capital Gains Tax', FOI 2397 Document 1, *FOI Disclosure Log*, 1 March, available from: treasury.gov.au/sites/default/files/2019-03/foi-2397-document-set-final-redacted.pdf.

The Treasury, 2019b, *Treasury Annual Report 2018–19*, Canberra: Australian Government, available from: treasury.gov.au/sites/default/files/2019-10/p2019-25128-tsyar-2018-19_0.pdf.

The Treasury, 2019c, *Treasury Corporate Plan 2019–20*, Canberra: Australian Government, available from: treasury.gov.au/media/28931.

The White House, 2002, *The National Security Strategy of the United States of America*, September, Washington, DC: The White House, available from: georgewbush-whitehouse.archives.gov/nsc/nss/2002/.

Thodey, David, 2019, *Independent Review of the APS: Priorities for Change*, 19 March, Canberra: Commonwealth of Australia, available from: www.apsreview.gov.au/sites/default/files/resources/aps-review-priorities-change.pdf.

Thomas, Nina K., 2016, 'We Didn't Know: Silence and Silencing in Organizations', *International Journal of Group Psychotherapy*, vol. 66, no. 4, pp. 492–505. doi.org/10.1080/00207284.2016.1176489.

Thompson, Mark, 2016, *Enough Said: What's Gone Wrong with the Language of Politics?*, New York, NY: St Martin's Press.

Throgmorton, J.A., 1991, 'The Rhetorics of Policy Analysis', *Policy Sciences*, vol. 24, pp. 153–179. doi.org/10.1007/BF00138058.

Thwaites, Rayner, 2015, 'New Laws Make Loss of Citizenship a Counter-Terrorism Tool', *The Conversation*, 11 December, available from: theconversation.com/new-laws-make-loss-of-citizenship-a-counter-terrorism-tool-51725.

Tingle, Laura, 2015, 'Political Amnesia: How We Forgot to Govern', *Quarterly Essay*, no. 60.

Tingle, Laura, 2016, 'George Brandis in Bitter Legal Fight Goes to Rule of Law', *Australian Financial Review*, 16 June, [updated 17 June], available from: www.afr.com/news/politics/george-brandis-in-bitter-legal-fight-goes-to-rule-of-law-20160616-gpkvyv.

Toulmin, Stephen, 1983, 'The Construal of Reality: Criticism in Modern and Postmodern Science', in W.J.T. Mitchell (ed.), *The Politics of Interpretation*, Chicago, IL: University of Chicago Press.

Towell, Noel, 2015, 'More Job Losses as Tax Office Cuts Senior Communications Staff', *Sydney Morning Herald*, 5 April, available from: www.smh.com.au/public-service/more-job-losses-as-tax-office-cuts-senior-communications-staff-20150402-1mdirx.html.

Towell, Noel, 2016, 'APS Bosses "Self Serving" in Calls for Greater Secrecy over FoI Laws', *The Canberra Times*, 14 April, [updated 24 April], available from: www.canberratimes.com.au/national/public-service/aps-bosses-self-serving-in-calls-for-greater-secrecy-over-foi-laws-20160414-go6aps.html.

Turnbull, Malcolm, 2009, 'Abbott's Climate Change Policy Is Bullshit', *Sydney Morning Herald*, 7 December, available from: www.smh.com.au/politics/federal/abbotts-climate-change-policy-is-bullshit-20091207-kdmb.html.

Turnbull, Malcolm, 2015, 'Malcolm Turnbull's Speech in Full: "We Need a New Style of Leadership"', *The Guardian*, [Australia], 14 September, available from: www.theguardian.com/australia-news/2015/sep/14/malcolm-turnbulls-speech-in-full-we-need-a-new-style-of-leadership.

Turnbull, Malcolm, 2016a, '2016 Election Speech', Sydney, 26 June, available from: electionspeeches.moadoph.gov.au/speeches/2016-malcolm-turnbull.

Turnbull, Malcolm, 2016b, 'Doorstop—Launceston City Deal MOU Signing, University of Tasmania', [Transcript], Launceston, Tas., 29 September, available from: www.malcolmturnbull.com.au/media/doorstop-launceston-city-deal-mou-signing-university-of-tasmania1.

Turnbull, Malcolm, 2016c, 'Doorstop—Launching "Making Headlines" by Chris Mitchell', [Transcript], 30 September, available from: pmtranscripts.pmc.gov.au/release/transcript-40480.

Turnbull, Malcolm, 2016d, 'Interview with Neil Mitchell, 3AW', [Transcript], 30 September, available from: pmtranscripts.pmc.gov.au/release/transcript-40478.

Turnbull, Malcolm, 2016e, 'Interview on FiveAA Breakfast', 7 October, available from: www.malcolmturnbull.com.au/media/interview-on-fiveaa-breakfast.

Turnbull, Malcolm, 2016f, 'Address to the Australian Minerals Industry Parliamentary Dinner', [Transcript], Parliament House, Canberra, 12 October, available from: pmtranscripts.pmc.gov.au/release/transcript-40501.

Turnbull, Malcolm, 2017, 'Address to the National Press Club', Canberra, 1 February, available from: pmtranscripts.pmc.gov.au/release/transcript-40718.

Uba, Katrin, 2010, 'Who Formulates Renewable-Energy Policy? A Swedish Example', *Energy Policy*, vol. 38, no. 11, pp. 6674–6683. doi.org/10.1016/j.enpol.2010.06.037.

Uhr, John, 1999, 'Three Accountability Anxieties: A Conclusion to the Symposium', *Australian Journal of Public Administration*, vol. 58, no. 11, pp. 98–101. doi.org/10.1111/1467-8500.00079.

Uhr, John, 2015, *Prudential Public Leadership: Promoting Ethics in Public Policy and Administration*, New York, NY: Palgrave Macmillan. doi.org/10.1057/9781137506498.

Uhr, John & Keith Mackay (eds), 1996, *Evaluating Policy Advice: Learning from Commonwealth Experience*, Canberra: Federalism Research Centre, The Australian National University & Commonwealth Department of Finance.

Van Dyne, Linn, Soon Ang & Isabel C. Botero, 2003, 'Conceptualizing Employee Silence and Employee Voice as Multidimensional Constructs', *Journal of Management Studies*, vol. 40, no. 6, pp. 1359–1392. doi.org/10.1111/1467-6486.00384.

Van Nispen, Frans & Peter Scholten (eds), 2015, *Policy Analysis in the Netherlands*, Bristol, UK: Bristol University Press. doi.org/10.1332/policypress/9781447313335.001.0001.

van Rooijen, Sascha N.M. & Mark T. van Wees, 2006, 'Green Electricity Policies in The Netherlands: An Analysis of Policy Decisions', *Energy Policy*, vol. 34, no. 1, pp. 60–71. doi.org/10.1016/j.enpol.2004.06.002.

Vaughan, Diane, 1996, *The Challenger Launch Decision: Risky Technology, Culture, and Deviance at NASA*, Chicago, IL: University of Chicago Press. doi.org/10.7208/chicago/9780226346960.001.0001.

Vaughan, Diane, 1999, 'The Role of the Organization in the Production of Techno-Scientific Knowledge', *Social Studies of Science*, vol. 29, no. 6. doi.org/10.1177/030631299029006005.

Vines, Tim, 2015, 'The "Allegiance to Australia" Bill: Arguably Unconstitutional, Definitely Questionable', *The Guardian*, 24 June, available from: www. theguardian.com/commentisfree/2015/jun/24/the-allegiance-to-australia-bill-arguably-unconstitutional-definitely-questionable.

Wagenaar, Hendrik, 2004, '"Knowing the Rules": Administrative Work as Practice', *Public Administration Review*, vol. 64, no. 6, pp. 643–656. doi.org/10.1111/ j.1540-6210.2004.00412.x.

Walby, Kevin & Mike Larsen, 2011, 'Access to Information and Freedom of Information Requests: Neglected Means of Data Production in the Social Sciences', *Qualitative Inquiry*, vol. 18, no. 1. doi.org/10.1177/1077800411 427844.

Wardekker, J. Arjan, Jeroen P. van der Sluijs, Peter H.M. Janssen, Penny Kloprogge & Arthur C. Petersen, 2008, 'Uncertainty Communication in Environmental Assessments: Views from the Dutch Science–Policy Interface', *Environmental Science & Policy*, vol. 11, no. 7, pp. 627–641. doi.org/10.1016/ j.envsci.2008.05.005.

Watson, Don, 2002, *Recollections of a Bleeding Heart: A Portrait of Paul Keating PM*, Sydney: Knopf.

Watson, James & Anne Hill, 2015, *Dictionary of Media and Communication Studies*, 9th edn, London: Bloomsbury Academic. doi.org/10.5040/9781501304712.

Watson, Verity, 2018, 'Policy Certainty Needed to Deliver a More Connected Energy Future', *Energy Insider*, 19 July, Melbourne: Energy Networks Australia, available from: www.energynetworks.com.au/news/energy-insider/ policy-certainty-needed-deliver-more-connected-energy-future.

Watts, Rob, 2014, 'Truth and Politics: Thinking about Evidence-Based Policy in the Age of Spin', *Australian Journal of Public Administration*, vol. 73, no. 1, pp. 34–46. doi.org/10.1111/1467-8500.12061.

Weiss, Carol H., 1980, 'Efforts at Bureaucratic Reform: What Have We Learned?', in Carol H. Weiss & Allen H. Barton (eds), *Making Bureaucracies Work*, Thousand Oaks, CA: Sage Publications.

Whelan, James, 2011, *The State of the Australian Public Service: An Alternative Report*, August, Sydney: Centre for Policy Development.

Wikimedia Commons, 2015, 'Australian Election Polling: Two Party Preferred', 3 August, available from: commons.wikimedia.org/wiki/File:Australian_ election_polling_-_two_party_preferred.png.

Wildavsky, Aaron, 1979, *Speaking Truth to Power: The Art and Craft of Policy Analysis*, Boston, MA: Little, Brown & Company. doi.org/10.1007/978-1-349-04955-4.

Wilkie, Andrew, 2004, *Axis of Deceit*, Melbourne: Black Inc. Agenda.

Wilkinson, Katy, 2011, 'Organised Chaos: An Interpretive Approach to Evidence-Based Policy Making in Defra', *Political Studies*, vol. 59, no. 4. doi.org/10.1111/j.1467-9248.2010.00866.x.

Wilks, Stephen, 1987, 'Administrative Culture and Policy Making in the Department of the Environment', *Public Policy and Administration*, vol. 2, no. 1. doi.org/10.1177/095207678700200103.

Williams, Amanda, 2010, 'Is Evidence-Based Policy Making Really Possible? Reflections for Policymakers and Academics on Making Use of Research in the Work of Policy', in Hal K. Colebatch, Robert Hoppe & Mirko Noordegraaf (eds), *Working for Policy*, Amsterdam: Amsterdam University Press. doi.org/10.1515/9789048513086-016.

Wood, Danielle & John Daley, 2018, *A Crisis of Trust: The Rise of Protest Politics in Australia*, March, Melbourne: Grattan Institute.

Woolcott, Peter, 2018, 'Where To for the Australian Public Service, Keynote Address Delivered by Mr Peter Woolcott AO, Australian Public Service Commissioner', Canberra, 10 October, available from: www.apsc.gov.au/where-australian-public-service [page discontinued].

Wynne, Brian, 1989, 'Sheepfarming After Chernobyl: A Case Study in Communicating Scientific Information', *Environment*, vol. 31, no. 2, pp. 10–39. doi.org/10.1080/00139157.1989.9928930.

Wynne, Brian, 2010, 'When Doubt Becomes a Weapon', *Nature*, vol. 466, pp. 441–442. doi.org/10.1038/466441a.

Zaltman, Gerald, 1983, 'Knowledge Disavowal in Organizations', in R.H. Kilman, K.W. Thomas, D.P. Slevin, R. Nath & S.L. Jerell (eds), *Producing Useful Knowledge for Organizations*, Westport, CT: Praeger.

Zarefsky, David, 2007, 'Making the Case for War: Colin Powell at the United Nations', *Rhetoric & Public Affairs*, vol. 10, no. 2, pp. 275–302. doi.org/10.1353/rap.2007.0043.

Ziman, John, 1978, *An Exploration of the Grounds for Belief in Science*, Cambridge, UK: Cambridge University Press.

Index

A page number containing 'n.' indicates a reference appearing in a footnote on that page.

de Brouwer, Gordon 121
Defence Intelligence Organisation
(DIO) 8, 127–30, 132–4, 136–7,
140–1, 146, 152–60, 162, 163,
168, 169, 171, 174, 179, 190–1,
194–202, 233–4, 243
Department for Environment, Food
and Rural Affairs (Defra) (UK)
118, 119
Department of Energy (US) 130, 137
Department of Environment 97, 100,
101, 105
Department of Environment and
Energy (DEE) 58, 87–8, 95, 97,
103, 104, 117, 121
and freedom of information
(FOI) 8, 58–9, 104, 232
annual reports 97, 103
culture 106, 107, 108, 111, 117
'hiding' of information 58, 87–8,
106, 107, 108, 114, 209
response to SA blackout 58, 61,
63, 77, 82n.12, 83, 97, 103,
104, 106, 107
silencing 83, 107
Department of Finance 49
Department of Foreign Affairs 157,
173, 211
Department of Health and Human
Services (US) 1
Department of Immigration 207–8,
209
Department of Industry, Innovation
and Science 44n.5
Department of the Prime Minister
and Cabinet (PM&C) 39–40,
105, 117
and freedom of information
(FOI) 8, 58–59, 61–3, 232
annual reports 103
criticism of 97, 98, 105, 241
culture 97, 106, 107, 108, 111,
241

'hiding' of information 58, 86,
87–8, 107, 116, 209
response to SA blackout 58–59,
61–3, 68–71, 74–5, 77,
82n.12, 106, 107, 114
reviews 40, 97–8
silence 83, 107, 108, 114
skillset 98–9, 105
Department of Resources, Energy and
Tourism (RET) 97, 99–100, 105
Department of State (US) 130, 148,
211
Department of the Treasury 11n.1,
29n.2, 51, 52, 82, 223, 224
and freedom of information
(FOI) 7, 29, 30, 39, 43, 44,
231–2
and tax reform 220, 221, 223
criticism of 21, 22, 45, 98
expectations on 33, 224
negative-gearing advice 7, 28,
29–39, 43, 53–4, 75, 96, 103,
212, 231–2, 236
rejection of advice 7, 29, 32,
36–7, 71, 75
reputation 45, 46, 53, 231
reviews 45, 98
dissemination of information 79,
106, 180, 239, 241
Downer, Alexander 135, 137, 140,
145, 146, 151, 156, 164, 165,
196
Dreyfus, Mark 208
Dutch, see Netherlands
Dutton, Peter 54

ElBaradei, Mohamed 130, 152, 153,
200, 201
ethics 14, 33, 161
evidence 2, 3, 4, 12, 14, 49, 90, 99,
111, 156
ambiguous presentation of 3, 12,
77, 103, 104, 176